More Praise for

"Will America survive as a unified nation until its 300th birthday in 2076? In this urgent, timely, and passionate book, Major Garrett and David Becker persuasively argue that the answer will turn on what happens between now and its 250th in 2026. With razor-sharp argument and encyclopedic command of the evidence, they dismantle Donald Trump's wild claims of 2020 fraud and document the full sweep of what they accurately call his 'attempted coup.'"

—RON BROWNSTEIN, senior political analyst at CNN and *New York Times* bestselling author of *Rock Me on the Water: 1974—The Year Los Angeles Transformed Music, Movies, Television and Politics*

"If American democracy has a modern mirror, Major Garrett and David Becker hold it up and brazenly stand behind it. From the very first page, the authors argue the fragility of the American experiment and the need to defend it, connecting the past to our turbulent present. From their posts in journalism and election law, Garrett and Becker narrate the facts of the 2020 election and call out the lies perpetrated by the craven grifters seeking to undermine our democracy."

—KYUNG LAH, senior national correspondent, CNN

"Concerned that the sanctity of the 2022 midterm elections is at stake, if not democracy itself, Major Garrett, CBS's chief Washington correspondent, and elections expert David Becker have written one of the definitive books on the subject. Vivid, doggedly researched, and deeply important, it is a crucial work at an important time. It will be of interest to citizens of all parties and political persuasions alike."

—JAY WINIK, historian and *New York Times* bestselling author of *April 1865: The Month That Saved America* and *1944: FDR and the Year That Changed History*

"*The Big Truth* shows how American democracy is threatened, even as everyone claims to be defending and protecting it. This book is a stark warning for every American who thinks that it can't happen here, that our nation cannot turn against itself. Major Garrett and David Becker show that our union is closer to dissolving than we might think and our democracy is very much at risk. The political project of our time is to rebuild national trust and defend democracy."

—JENNIFER MERCIECA, award-winning historian and author of *Demagogue for President: The Rhetorical Genius of Donald Trump*

the
big
truth

the big truth

Upholding Democracy in the Age of THE BIG LIE

MAJOR GARRETT
&
DAVID BECKER

DIVERSION
BOOKS

Diversion Books
A division of Diversion Publishing Corp.
www.diversionbooks.com

First Diversion Books edition, September 2022
Hardcover ISBN: 9781635767841
eBook ISBN: 9781635767865

Printed in The United States of America

10 9 8 7 6 5 4 3 2 1

Library of Congress cataloging-in-publication data is available on file

CONTENTS

INTRODUCTION

Americans talk a lot about civil war. Some say it is here. Some say it is coming. It's difficult for anyone to accurately predict because no one remembers how bloody, costly, and destructive our first and only civil war actually was.

Yes, we are discontented people frustrated by the convulsions of a digital economy, a global pandemic, and an anguished reassessment of our racial history. Surveys show, where politics is concerned, we are prepared to assume the worst about one another. Demographic data show we are becoming more isolated and homogenized in like-minded communities. These trends have made us less tolerant, more fearful that political differences are about something deeper—our own identity and place in the American story. But civil strife is not the same as civil war. We have not dissolved the bonds of our union—yet. That we toy with the idea and terminology may mean nothing or everything.

"We're so divided in our country, more than at any point since the Civil War," historian Doris Kearns Goodwin told us. Her fears were most pronounced about elections and faith in democracy. We talked to others who have felt these anxieties and antagonisms up close. Bob Harvie is a commissioner in Bucks County, Pennsylvania, a picturesque suburb northwest of Philadelphia. Among his many duties, Harvie oversees elections in Bucks County and has received numerous death threats since the 2020 election—as have dozens of his non-elected county employees. Harvie described his county's election experience in 2020 as "the most contentious in one hundred and fifty years."

Harvie is soft-spoken, well tailored, a Democrat, and a late-in-life convert to local government. "I have spent twenty-six years," he says, "more than half my life, teaching high school social studies, specifically American history. This is not something I've seen in the history of this country, except for before the Civil War. And it does scare me. I'm really worried we're approaching a precipice that's going to be impossible to come back from."

Kathy Bernier is a member of the Wisconsin legislature, a fierce Trump supporter, and among the most conservative voices in state politics. She's been working elections for nearly forty years, starting as a poll worker in the mid-1980s in Anson, a town of about 1,500 in Chippewa County. Bernier later became county clerk and then wrote election laws in the legislature while a member of the assembly and senate elections committees. Bernier knows election law and politics. In late 2021, she took heavy criticism for defending the 2020 election and calling for an end to ceaseless Republican-led investigations.

Bernier speaks bluntly and emphatically, her voice flat as an icy lake: "I care about the Republicans in this state, but we can't continue to beat a dead horse. We need to move on. Lies are destroying America."

Ricky Hatch lives in Weber County, Utah, and has been a Republican election official there since 2012. He has also testified before Congress on election security matters and served as an adviser on election security to the Department of Homeland Security. He lives and works in Ogden and in April 2022 still heard complaints about the 2020 election—even though Weber County, like the rest of Utah, saw no allegations of election fraud or contested results.

"It happens all the time, the emails and the phone calls, people telling me we have to go back to voting in person, having ID at the polls," Hatch told us. "They tell me we have to get rid of this voting by mail crap, that voting by mail is not secure, that its fraught with fraud and Democrats want to use it to take over the world."

Hatch offers tours of the county's vote counting machinery, walks the curious through the process of checking and double-checking results. He also reminds suspicious Republicans about a 2012 statewide push for voting by mail—led by the Utah Republican Party. For some, Hatch's explanations are persuasive. For others, no amount of information or transparency will suffice.

"They say 'I know your machines have been hacked by China.' I show them there is no means to hack the machines, that nothing is connected. They just say, 'They have been hacked. You just don't know it.' It's just crazy. I have answers. They won't believe me."

Hatch has also noticed a pattern among those he is able to persuade that Weber County's systems are verifiable and secure. Voters will say they now believe in the county's methods, but not in election results and the officials who produced them in Arizona, Michigan, Georgia, Wisconsin, or other states contested in 2020.

"They say 'I trust you.' And I tell them there are 9,000 other mes, people like me, around the country and they care as much as I do and they are just as competent as I am."

Hatch has commiserated with Republican election officials around the country who have encountered skepticism, hostility, threats, physical intimidation, and vandalism. His own car was vandalized twice—on election day and on the day Utah certified its electoral count. He attributes the volatile mindset to a cultish grip former president Trump wields over his supporters.

"I hate saying this, but he has the same characteristics as a cult leader. He pulls people into a belief system. I thought it would die down. It's getting stronger. People are more skeptical now than they were a year ago."

That election denialism has grown more potent in places like Utah, where election results were never questioned, looms darkly over the nation's political landscape.

"At end of the day, the character of the people we elect matters," said Rep. Liz Cheney, Wyoming Republican, and member of the January 6 Committee. "But if you have a president who's willing to go through all the guardrails of our democracy, the structure and the framework of our laws will prove insufficient. Ultimately, we had a president who for the first time in American history was not committed to ensuring the peaceful transfer of power and committed to supporting the Constitution in carrying out his duties and instead did everything possible to overturn the results of the election and to stay in power."

In the pages ahead, you will hear from these voices and from many others we interviewed—election professionals, poll workers, and secretaries of state—who live on the suddenly unsettled, sometimes dangerous front lines of American democracy.

Our conversations and deep experience with politics and election law have made us wonder if we are using the proper terminology to describe our current crisis. Are we divided or divisible? Divided to us sounds permanent. Divisible is voluntary and can certainly be temporary. Divisible is also an antonym of the word our Pledge of Allegiance (adopted after the Civil War) says we are—indivisible. It seems we are choosing to be more antagonistic to one another, as if divisibility is a game, a diversion, a self-erasing SnapChat.

We argue it is not. We fear America is heading heedlessly into dangerous psychological territory. Our aggressions, our divisions, and even our fears impel us to imagine the previously unimaginable. This, many have said, was the experience before and during "The Troubles" in Northern Ireland. As Finian O'Toole, a writer for the *Irish Times* who grew up in Dublin, wrote in *The Atlantic* in early 2022: "The belief there was going to be a civil war in Ireland made everything worse. Once that idea takes hold, it has a force of its own." When aggressions, divisions, and fears burrow deeply enough, they can become inevitable—to a person, a family, a clan, a county, a state and, yes, a nation. This psychic energy concerns us more than we have ever experienced. We remember what Margaret Atwood said about her 1985 novel, *The Handmaid's Tale*, a dystopian vision of America ruled by a totalitarian, patriarchal theocracy. "I didn't put in anything that we haven't already done, we're not already doing, we're seriously trying to do, coupled with trends that are already in progress." It's not that we fear America becoming Gilead of Atwood's speculative fiction. We fear casual talk of civil war and actions that suggest that it is, or could be, an acceptable alternative to current discontents. We fear dissolution of the union and all its ravages. Atwood described "trends that are already in progress." We detect frightful trends in our politics and discourse.

Balance must be struck between undue alarm and ignorant indifference. Alarmism can be dismissed as hysteria. Indifference is a license for inaction. We will initially view our current predicament through the lens of three Januarys. This will constitute the opening third of the book, the springboard for a deeper dive into Election 2020, the slanders against it, the conspiracies that grew out of it, and remedies for the future. But we begin by taking stock of the month of January in three recent years and describe what was, what could have been, what is, and what might be. We start with a possible January 2023, when pressures arising from midterm election furies could push America toward civil war. We follow that with an alternate January 2017, a month we all remember. We explain what happened and then present an alternative history—a lengthy, messy fight to block President Trump's ascendancy to the presidency. We conclude with January 2022, where we catalog real events implicating and imperiling democracy, where no imagination is required to perceive bleak horizons for life, liberty, and the pursuit of happiness. Each of these Januarys is really about the events precipitated by another January—January 2021.

Herewith a cautionary tale about a possible and avoidable American unraveling, fiction amplified and informed by available facts.

part
one

1

JANUARY 2023

AMERICA'S second civil war could start with a bang or with a whimper. It could begin with a skirmish or sneak up on us through a series of small compromises and acts of political cowardice. Civil war could announce itself loudly and bloodily, leaving no doubt as to its awful entrance. Or it could creep in through the back door, only to be recognized in hindsight as a series of seemingly disconnected events that could have and should have been stopped. We may be midstream in such a flow of events already. We now examine this possible future as if we have just emerged from its aftermath.

During the 2022 campaign, national Democrats were bracing for a tidal wave that might eject them from control of the U.S. House of Representatives and the U.S. Senate, crippling President Biden's agenda and possibly accelerating former president Trump's formal announcement (he toyed with it throughout 2021 and 2022) as a candidate for the presidency in 2024. Democrats had long since lost patience with Republican accusations about the "stolen" 2020 election, which they came to believe led to a flurry of unnecessary and regressive laws in states dominated by Republican legislators. In

Texas, a law passed that set new restrictions on mail-in ballot access, limited the use of drop boxes for early votes, and then went further by weaponizing and empowering hyper-partisan poll watchers to interfere with the voting process. This in a state where it was already harder to vote in than most other states. In states like Florida, Iowa, and Texas, professional election administrators found their efforts criminalized. In states like Arizona and Georgia, it appeared legislators were seizing control of elections by limiting the authority of election administrators at the state and county level, thereby creating the real possibility of partisan politicians rejecting the will of the voters. In several states—Arizona, Colorado, Georgia, Michigan, and Nevada—there were candidates running for secretary of state on a platform of denying elections and delivering outcomes for their preferred candidates. All of this was very much on the minds of national Democrats. Many were seething.

In such an environment, many were worried about armed poll watchers, inflamed passions, and even possible violence. In Texas, voters saw unusually long lines in voting precincts in urban areas like Houston, Austin, San Antonio, and Dallas, where recent legislation had resulted in concentrating more voting into a single day. The lines were longest in communities of color, thus confirming fears about the consequences of the new election law. Before the March 1, 2022, primary, voters in predominantly Democratic counties like Harris, Travis, and Bexar were seeing requests for mail-in ballots rejected at historically high rates, fifteen times higher than Texas had previously experienced in their most populous counties.

About this time, Democrats in Washington began wondering aloud if midterm election results could or should be believed. "I think there's a real possibility that we will see in the next two elections, get some results sent to us for ratification . . . that's not consistent or that we're gonna have to question," Texas Democratic representative Colin Allred said. "That's the reality of the situation. We can no longer pretend like these elections are just going to continue to proceed the way they have in the past." At a press conference marking his administration's one-year anniversary, President Biden amplified this sentiment. When asked if the midterm elections would be legitimate, Biden said: "Well, it all depends on whether we are able to make the case to the American people that some of this is being set up to try to alter the outcome of this election." Biden's statements weren't as toxic as Trump's, but it deepened confusion and consternation—setting the country up for months of midterm election fearmongering.

Imagine a polling station in Texas on Election Day 2022. The location doesn't matter. Neither does the underlying dispute. What matters is a person came to the polls, purportedly on the hunt for voter fraud. States like Texas had given poll watchers more latitude to move around polling places, question procedures, and exercise authority. This person, in accordance with Texas law, was armed with a semiautomatic pistol. A discussion escalated into a confrontation, perhaps about the proper place to stand inside the polling precinct in relation to others, or about how to properly mark the ballot and use the ballot scanning machine.

Tragically, things spun out of control. The person feared fraud was afoot, and meant to stop it, by any means necessary. It first came through a raised voice, then physical intervention, and ultimately through the brandished weapon. Tension and shouts ensued, followed by a scuffle. One shot rang out and a poll worker lay bleeding on the floor of the gymnasium—the polling place was a high school. As the blood pooled, the victim passed away. Simultaneously, a friend of the victim hit SEND on a video taken of the conflict and its horrible aftermath. The video, as these things do, flew faster than news coverage and became a national sensation. Raw emotions frayed further.

As Election Day played out in Texas, Democrats believed they were seeing some of their worst fears realized. The perception of long lines and disproportionate damage done to minority voters sparked genuine anguish and rage. Now a death—video confirmation of what Democrats came to see as senseless violence marring and jeopardizing democracy.

As for the polling place death, the causes and motives behind it were opaque. It might have been an unintentional escalation—not exactly an accident because there was a weapon and a confrontation, but certainly not premeditated. Every frame of the cell phone video was analyzed and then hyper-analyzed. It yielded no definitive answers to the discerning and just enough to those quick to judge and blame. What the video did capture quite clearly was the grisly, harrowing aftermath—a life taken by a single bullet fired in a single precinct in a single county within a vast country now unified by hatred, suspicion, and contempt. It seemed to be the only true unity this once great but now wayward nation appeared able to summon.

The death video, as they say, went viral, but not benignly so. Quite fortunately, it did not lead to more violence. But in the hours after it appeared, more people began taking weapons to polling places. There were standoffs. There were fistfights. Police and sheriff's departments nationwide were deployed in almost SWAT-like fashion to protect poll workers, repel weekend vigilantes, and generally keep the peace. It was scary as hell up close, on cable, on cell phones, on Facebook, and myriad other apps. But it worked. An uneasy peace was erected and brittlely maintained, though an atmosphere of foreboding and crisis pervaded.

Or perhaps no such incident occurred. Maybe none was necessary to push the nation to the edge. In the months leading up to the November election, Trump and the circle of grifters that surrounded him continued to push, and profit from, The Big Lie (Trump's multi-faceted yet groundless vilification of the 2020 election). Con artists continued to successfully push for incompetent investigations of the last election. Legislation based on the false pretext of election integrity—but which actually reduced it—was passed and voter confidence suffered. Election deniers running for governor, or secretary of state, or Congress, won their primaries and amplified their platforms, or almost as dangerously, lost their primaries and doubled down on their divisive and destructive disinformation. Leading up to the November 2022 election, concerns about voter suppression and voter fraud were so amped up that whether either actually existed didn't matter anymore. When reports of long lines at polling places in Texas, or Arizona, or wherever came up, that alone was enough to light the fire.

It could be a gunshot. It could be accumulated grievances. The combustibles are before us—voting, immigration, racism, abortion, crime. Things could move in dreadful directions, even if key players initially resist predictable grassroots pressure to lash out. We now describe events that could plausibly play out if either of the situations described above came to be.

Whether it's nationally broadcast election bloodshed or a slow-boil confrontation over voter suppression in a state like Texas, it is not hard to imagine House Speaker Nancy Pelosi facing hard questions from her leadership team about Texas's entire delegation and other close House races. Texas could trigger a startling conversation about countermeasures. Democrats had already sued there over redistricting, alleging Republicans diluted minority voters by dispersing them in ways assuring more House seats in 2022. These gains were coming to be and were also emblematic of noxious trends. Republicans were on pace to win at least twenty-five Texas seats—many tainted, in the view of national Democrats, by violence, suppression, or both. With Texas at the center of these midterm aggravations, Democrats could feel it necessary, maybe even imperative, to use Texas as a pretext to prevent certification and recognition of the entire thirty-eight-member state delegation. This wouldn't be easy. Each term of the House is limited to two years. A new House majority would swear in members and Republicans would hold sway. To cover their bets, House Democrats might also litigate all other close House races—generating lengthy delays and, possibly, widespread protests.

Texas, as it turned out, was the fulcrum in the House of Representatives. Republicans, when all voters were counted, won nearly twice as many seats there as Democrats. That advantage would loom large in control of the House. But so would other races that turned out to be surprisingly close in states with new and more restrictive voting laws and in districts where suburban voter attitudes shifted over abortion and privacy-related politics. These close races gave Democrats ground to challenge results, slowing certification and sowing confusion while generating new partisan hostility.

Under the Constitution, Congress is the judge of its own membership. There are limits, but Congress can, in theory and practice, refuse to seat or expel a member. As law professor Nicholas Stephanopoulos of Harvard University points out, the "choice to seat or oust is a nonjusticiable political question. No court can second-guess a chamber's judgment as to whether an election was free and fair or which candidate won a race." Congress has delayed or refused to seat a member whose victory has been certified. A dispute in 1984 over a House seat in Indiana initially won by a Republican but awarded to a Democrat convulsed the chamber for months. Slowing certification would gum up the process of creating a new House, even with an incoming GOP majority. An idea took hold: refuse to seat the full Texas delegation and hold off recognition of disputed races in other states.

This was not a novel idea, having been floated the previous year. Marc Elias, the prominent Democratic lawyer, had written in 2021 that as "Republican legislatures enact new voter suppression laws, Congress should reaffirm the House's promise in 1965 to refuse to seat, or to unseat, members who benefit from discriminatory voting laws. If there ever was a need for it to do so, it is now." Professor Stephanopoulos of Harvard similarly noted:

Given the history and law of the Judging Elections Clause, the most familiar way for a congressional chamber to enforce the provision would be by refusing to seat candidates-elect whose elections the chamber deems defective. . . . Imagine that, in the wake of the 2020 election, states under unified Republican control enact stringent new voting restrictions: photo-ID requirements, cutbacks to early and mail-in voting, voter roll purges, and so on. Also imagine that, in these states, several Republican candidates receive slightly more votes than their Democratic opponents in the 2022 election. Then, after that election, it would be a conventional application of the Judging Elections Clause for a chamber to decline to seat these Republican candidates-elect (and even to seat their rivals) because they owed their victories to voter suppression. This is exactly what the House and Senate have done many times before, especially in the decades after the Civil War.

Texas would be the symbol and the explanation—a rejection of Democratic and Republican members of Congress to contest deeper issues of access, suppression, and violence. Refusing to seat an entire state delegation would be novel, volatile, and unprecedented. It would not be undertaken lightly. But in pressurized times, lines can be crossed, especially when rivals are seen as enemies and choices no longer incremental but existential. Or perhaps a Democratic House could simply choose not to seat the Republican members elected, thus solidifying an even greater majority.

Democratic concern about GOP tactics in Texas and obstructionism of favored voting reforms put unrelenting pressure on Pelosi. Even if institutionalists initially resisted refusing to seat the Texas delegation, vociferous lobbying from the party's progressive Democratic base proved too much to resist, particularly if it meant holding on to the House, preserving the January 6 Select Committee, and shielding Biden from impeachment. Pelosi, though reluctant, could consider refusing to seat the Texas delegation, knowing her party would support her. Such an action, whether successful or not, would be another descent into norm-breaking oblivion. Pelosi could justify her actions by claiming she was preserving democracy. Republicans, some of whom backed the Big Lie, would then accuse Pelosi of destroying democracy. Whether the Texas delegation was seated or not could ultimately be irrelevant.

That process of vanishing could begin, and look something like this.

Provoked by the denial, successful or not, of congressional representation, Texas, which had just reelected Republican governor Greg Abbott by a fairly wide margin, announced it was prepared to take unprecedented action to halt this usurpation of power. Republican-led states, where some certifications were being held up, vowed to join Texas in whatever protest it deemed necessary. Republicans resurrected the words of Texas GOP chair Allen West after the U.S. Supreme Court rejected Texas's lawsuit to invalidate election results in six states, thereby overturning the 2020 election: "Perhaps law-abiding states should band together and form a Union of states that will abide by the Constitution."

After a brief debate, Republicans worked with Abbott to enact a resolution of refusal. The terms were simple. The Republic of Texas (as it still calls itself) would no longer compel individuals or businesses within Texas to pay federal tax revenue and, further, would block any efforts by federal officials to collect said revenue. Texas said the grant of immunity from paying federal taxes would last until Pelosi seated the full Texas delegation, halted all election litigation, and delivered unto Republicans majority control in the House of Representatives.

There were some knotty details to sort out. Texas provisionally allowed the federal government to continue operating fifteen military bases and twenty-nine ports of entry. It informed Washington it was preparing to take possession of military facilities and ports of entry for the sovereign republic of Texas if the impasse was not swiftly resolved. Travel restrictions, Texas menacingly warned, would accompany these repossessions.

Sympathetic states (possibly states like Alabama, Arkansas, Mississippi, Missouri, Oklahoma, South Carolina, South Dakota, and Wyoming) followed suit. Each state wrote its own resolution of refusal differently, but the march away from Washington was clear.

America being a diverse place, there were states with other sympathies and they sided with the Democrats. California, Oregon, Washington, New York, Vermont, Connecticut, Massachusetts, Hawaii, Illinois, Minnesota, and Delaware banded together as a compact against doing business with or recognizing the rights of visitors from Texas or any other state that joined its revenue-withholding gambit. This was a toothier form of boycotts that arose in earlier disputes over abortion and voting laws. States were merely intensifying the sense of separation, pressing up against the Interstate Commerce Clause along the way. Every step in the escalation raised arcane legal questions, but the impetus to pull apart and strike poses, fueled by grassroots political energy, overrode them. Banding together against Texas, the rival states said, was protection against secession, fascism, vigilantism, intimidation, voter suppression, and redistricting "violence." Democrats believed it as surely as Republicans believed their equally florid rhetoric about patriotism, treason, subversives, socialist radicals, and BLM mobs.

Whether from a single galvanizing incident—a gunshot and death—or the culmination of less-violent but no-less-shocking incidents over time, a "national divorce" began. The approach was economical, but the effect was spiritual. A great, slow-moving cleaving came over America. The federal government tried to be patient. It changed nothing, of course, for the states that did not adopt resolutions refusing to pay tax revenue. Initially, the federal government took no action against those that did. Washington had plenty of practice dealing with non-cooperative states or resistance to federal requirements to receive revenue transfers in lieu of policy changes. It had far less practice with states flatly denying revenue and seeking to block collection thereof. The Civil War was an armed rebellion, an opposing force against the Union. This was less stark and more procedural. It was a rebellion, if you will, of accounting and shared resources. Uncle Sam was stunned and struggled for recourse.

As was discovered, it takes a great deal of energy and personnel to erect barriers within a once-unified nation. The matters to which states now turned their attention were related to protection and isolation. Travel wasn't exactly halted because the attitude of boycott began to be translated into procedures of suspicion. States started to monitor themselves in relation to one another and therefore wanted to more closely inspect the movement of people, goods, and services. Definitions of contraband expanded exponentially and something akin to paranoia regarding motives about "other" states began to seep into laws and habits. This naturally led to unraveling of intertwined limbs of commerce that once profitably joined all fifty states. This meant increasing the security state—state by aligned state—at the expense of almost all else. All those fears about things getting militarized during COVID finally came to be—long after the pandemic had subsided. It was not the virus that cut down American democracy. It was a bastardized vision of protecting democracy that dealt the mortal blow.

Armed borders kept things in and kept things out, as armed borders almost always do. States for a time appeared satisfied, especially because Washington seemed stupefied. Federal courts, as it turned out, could not force states to do much of anything. There was no national military force large enough or motivated enough to storm Texas or any other state for revenue earmarked for Washington. National Guard forces became true militarized arms of the state—each state.

With legal disputes now separating one state from the other, America began to slowly disappear. Stock prices fell. More worrisome, America's bond rating suffered, and interest rates rose—destabilizing the Federal Reserve. Texas said it might create its own currency. Simple transactions became complicated and confusing. Naturally, there were, for a time, regional winners, but the overall trajectory, reflected in bond markets and declines in foreign investment, was of an increasingly sluggish national economy. America was no longer a sure bet, the dollar less reliable as the safest global currency. States acted as small nations and transacted business for their nation and against other nations—places that used to exist as white stars on the same field of blue but now flew their own reimagined economic and cultural flags.

States that didn't join either compact struggled for identity and good relations with both state compacts. Much energy and time was wasted in all directions. Other things began to slowly crumble too. Federal subsidies for infrastructure, scientific research, agricultural innovation, flood control, and weather forecasting atrophied. Decay took a noticeable, pitiable turn toward rot, leaving mid-twenty-first-century children to wonder what this thing was their grandparents remembered with such mourning . . . what was it called, again . . . the United States of America?

Perhaps most disturbingly, into the void left by a unified American nation—the world's formerly oldest and longest-enduring democracy—stepped the opportunistic nations steeped in autocracy. Russia, North Korea, Iran, and most notably China, already transfixed by Russia's invasion of Ukraine and its aftermath, began to wonder if America could still lead the free world or if it had become only a collaborative partner with Europe. The great question of authoritarianism vs. democracy, to which America had always acted as if it knew the answer, seemed up for grabs in Beijing, Pyongyang, Tehran, and Moscow. The lessons of Ukraine were far from settled but America looked not only distracted but on the verge of some form of disintegration. Autocrats began to wonder how best to pounce. Our allies, and the free people of the globe, were even more shaken than they were after the Capitol riot. Would America recede? Would they become more vulnerable? Was America devouring itself at the expense of all it had fought since the end of World War II to protect and preserve?

We have just tried to paint a narrative picture. It is not of a world blown up, not literally anyway. We are not describing an invasion where civilians are slaughtered as they were in Ukraine and vestiges of civilization and order fray. Ours is not a story of bunkers, stockpiles, and gaunt survivalism. It is not a story of militias in cabins or vigilantes in convoys. It is a potential story of national suicide committed gradually and with self-justifying intent, on paper—no bullets or bayonets required. It is a story about the death of America as a place, an ideal, and a home for liberty, prosperity, and law. It is a story the component parts of which are with us now. It is a story that intentionally leaves out widespread bloodshed—because our darkest fears are already bad enough. It is a story that fills in blanks we ourselves have created, blanks that will be filled one way or the other—through cooperation or confrontation. We must confront and extinguish election-denying cynicism. We must commit ourselves to casting and counting votes without fear or favor. We must do as generations did before—believe in democracy as we believe in ourselves.

The great cleaving could be closer than we think. Our next civil war is stalking us. We can stop it. We must stop it. Or we, as an ideal and as a spirit will, in Abraham Lincoln's words, surely perish from this earth.

2

JANUARY 2017

THE 2016 campaign was unique for a variety of reasons, putting unforeseen stresses on our democratic system. President Barack Obama had served two terms and was leaving office. Republicans controlled both chambers of Congress. A former entertainer and self-proclaimed billionaire somehow emerged from a crowded field of establishment candidates to capture the Republican nomination for the presidency. While the sitting vice president, Joe Biden, briefly considered a run for the Democratic nomination, the battle to succeed President Obama came down to a surprisingly close race between the former First Lady and secretary of state, Hillary Clinton, and the junior senator from Vermont, Bernie Sanders, running to her left.

While initially it appeared as if Republicans might be fractured because of their unusual primary battle, the party rallied behind the nominee, Donald John Trump. The Democrats, initially thought to be more unified, discovered that after Clinton secured the nomination, there remained substantial fissures in the party, with many on the progressive wing feeling unrepresented. By August, the battle for the presidency was set—Trump running with Governor Mike Pence of

Indiana, and Clinton with Senator Tim Kaine of Virginia. Had this merely been a political campaign pitting a reality TV star against a former First Lady running to become the first female president of the United States, that would have been enough. But there were many disturbing aspects happening behind the scenes and before our eyes.

It began even before the conventions. Unbeknownst to most of the country, anti-democratic foreign adversaries began interfering in the election, intending to destabilize American democracy by further dividing us. These efforts primarily originated in Russia, led, it appears, by elements of the Russian GRU (Russian military intelligence). They had two primary prongs.

First, waves of disinformation on social media attempted to inflame anger and widen divisions between Americans. Leveraging attitudes about race, religion, and other issues, the Russians targeted us, to make us believe our neighbors and fellow citizens were our enemies, rather than the autocrats that sought to weaken America to consolidate power and line their own pockets. One example of this—Russian troll farms were connected to efforts to encourage angry protests both for and against racial justice efforts such as Black Lives Matter, in places like Houston, hoping angry protesters would conflict with each other.

Second, and as importantly, cyberattackers from Russia sought to gain access to election infrastructure. Almost all of these efforts failed. Primarily they were likely probing for vulnerabilities. But one succeeded. Its success was telling.

In June and July, 2016, Russians gained access to the statewide voter registration database run by the Illinois State Board of Elections. The attackers obtained access to this system and were inside the database for approximately three weeks. It's important to note that, unlike ballots themselves, voter registration records are not secret or anonymous. In fact, there are regular measures to back up databases and confirm the information within them. So, if anyone attempted to tamper with voter records—deleting or altering a significant number of them—it's almost certain that effort would have been detected.

However, such an attack on a voter registration database, altering many voter records, could cause substantial chaos, particularly if conducted right before a major election. As voters attempted to vote, they could find themselves no longer on the voter list, requiring them to cast provisional ballots. And if this attack were conducted close to an election, and if the numbers of voter records changed was very large, it's possible a state could run out of provisional ballots, yielding even greater chaos. Best case scenario for the attacker—it would be highly unlikely to change the election outcome, but rampant chaos during voting would lead to frustration and a severe reduction in voter confidence.

But this was months before the November election, and the Russians did not attempt to alter or delete data—it appears they just explored and probed. And after a few weeks, not having been discovered, probing only a small number of records at a time, they suddenly amplified their efforts, exponentially increasing the number of records they were looking at, but still avoiding any changes in the voter data. However, the sheer magnitude of their intrusion almost guaranteed they would be discovered.

And discovered they were. Immediately after the escalation, administrators detected the Russian intrusion and shut access to the entire system down. No voter records were affected, but the nature of this attack suggested that wasn't the objective. First, this was Illinois. Not exactly a swing state. If the Democratic candidate lost there, it would have raised immediate questions. If it were discovered that Russia was probably behind an attack on actual voting in the United States, war could have been a possible outcome. Second, this was months before the election, with plenty of time to repair any damage done by the attack, well before voting began.

But if changing the election outcome was not the goal, what was? The Russians were in the voter database of a large state. Their presence was undetected for weeks. Who knows how long they could have remained lurking, slowly accumulating intelligence, before they were detected? But they chose not to remain undetected, suddenly amplifying their presence in July. Why? There's only one plausible explanation—they wanted to be detected.

There were a handful of other attempts at hacking into election infrastructure. It appears cybercriminals, likely based in Russia, intruded into Arizona's online voter registration system. There were a small number of rumored attacks elsewhere, though these attempts were sporadic, and none of them had an impact on the actual casting or counting of ballots. There remains not a shred of evidence to suggest that the election infrastructure was affected in any way in 2016 (or in any other presidential election).

But changing the outcome of the election was never the goal of our enemies. They wanted the government, the media, and the American public to know they had gained access to election infrastructure, and to believe that efforts to destabilize our elections were far more widespread than they actually were. The targets of these attacks were not so much the databases and infrastructure itself, but the confidence and trust of the American people in their own system of elections.

It was in this context that Trump, intentionally or inadvertently, began to support the narrative being pursued by Russia and others. In early August, perhaps in anticipation of losing the election, as most polls showed him trailing, Trump began speaking about the election being "rigged." Throughout the fall, he continued to raise doubts about our system of elections. And then there were the well-documented efforts to hack into the emails of the Democratic National Committee. These efforts, apparently led by Russia with complicit groups like WikiLeaks involved, resulted in embarrassing leaks exposing the hardball inner workings of the Clinton campaign and Democrats, further deepening intraparty division. Republicans did not go unscathed. Though unrelated to computer intrusions, a massive complication arose with revelations about Trump's behavior, most memorably the *Access Hollywood* tape. Trump had to apologize and beat back calls that he withdraw from the race, after which the false rhetoric about election "fraud" and "rigging" only seemed to increase.

At the last minute of the campaign, as if the American electorate was not sufficiently inundated with divisive messages that raised doubts about our democracy, came the "October surprise"—the letter from FBI Director James Comey to Congress on October 28, 2016, less than two weeks before the election, indicating he was reopening the investigation into Clinton's private emails while secretary of state and security concerns surrounding them. Controversy further swelled around the Clinton campaign—controversy that the Trump campaign and our foreign adversaries were all too willing to exploit to their advantage.

Even with the added tumult, it still appeared that Clinton was highly likely to win the presidency, thanks to a continued significant lead in the polls, the perceived weakness of the Trump candidacy, and the "blue wall" of Michigan, Pennsylvania, and Wisconsin that had voted consistently with the Democratic candidate since the presidential election of 1992. Clinton's campaign planned a massive celebration in the Javits Center in New York City, to commemorate not only her victory, but also the breaking of the glass ceiling with the election of our nation's first woman president. With those expectations in place, the nation waited through Election Day and Night.

There was some manner of shock as the results started coming in. States thought to be toss-ups, like Florida and Ohio, were called fairly early for Trump. The victories weren't large—Florida in particular was a thin margin of victory of less than 113,000 votes—but it was enough to make the call. States expected to be safely in Clinton's column, including the "blue wall" states, were close, with early, if narrow, leads for Trump, and ballots from Clinton strongholds in those states still to be counted. But as Clinton's path to victory narrowed, the nation began to realize the unthinkable was about to happen. At around 2:30 a.m. Eastern Standard Time on November 9, 2016, the networks called Pennsylvania for Donald Trump, and he was declared to have won the presidency.

The margins in several states that gave Trump a win were comparatively thin: Arizona won by less than 92,000 votes, Florida by just over 1 percent, Wisconsin by less than 24,000 votes (0.77 percent), Pennsylvania by just over 44,000 votes (less than 0.75 percent), Michigan by barely over 10,000 votes (less than 0.25 percent). And Trump lost the popular vote by a relatively large margin to Clinton—nearly 3 million votes, constituting a lead of more than two percentage points for the former secretary of state.

Despite the narrow victories, the popular vote defeat, and the surprise nature of Trump's victories in states given the polling, Clinton conceded on November 9, 2016. Every one of the close states, except for Pennsylvania (which switched to statewide auditable paper ballots for the 2020 presidential election), had paper ballots statewide that could be audited and recounted. In fact, Green Party candidate Jill Stein requested (and paid for) recounts in Michigan, Pennsylvania, and Wisconsin, and those recounts confirmed the narrow victories for Trump. While some questioned the validity of the election, the elections were accepted, certified, and recounted where necessary. The Obama administration cooperated in the transition, and with some minor drama during the joint session of Congress to certify electoral votes, Donald Trump was declared the winner and took office on January 20, 2017, despite the unexpected and narrow character of his victory.

Everything you just read actually happened. It was true on November 9, 2016, and it is true today. But what you are about to read is fantasy. It did not happen. It could not happen. Thanks to the institutions and people of integrity in both parties in 2016–2017, it would not happen. Up until Election Day, all of this actually occurred, but consider an alternative universe where, post–Election Day, the wheels came off.

Imagine a world where, instead of conceding on November 9, 2016, Secretary Clinton announced that her campaign had identified significant irregularities in Arizona, Florida, Michigan, Pennsylvania, and Wisconsin, and she wasn't ready to accept the results. Even though the results were unofficial, and election officials in those states were reconciling and confirming vote totals, and often auditing the results, Clinton and her campaign claimed widespread malfeasance, foreign interference, and sent every lawyer with a "D" next to their names to these states to raise concerns, spread rumors, and work the press.

Imagine the Obama administration deciding that Trump could be a threat, particularly given the apparent support offered (to be confirmed later by a bipartisan report from the Senate Intelligence Committee), whether solicited or not, to the Trump campaign by the Russian government, and the fact that several people affiliated with the campaign were under investigation for improper foreign contacts. In such a light, rather than agreeing to cooperate in the transition to the Trump presidency, the Obama administration decided to allow the process to play out, in court proceedings and in the court of public opinion.

Imagine how skilled the "A" team of Democratic lawyers would have been in such a scenario, bringing court case after court case challenging the process in the questioned states, and pointing out that in all of those states, Republicans controlled the election machinery. Republican secretaries of state ran the election infrastructure in Arizona, Florida, Michigan, and Pennsylvania. Even in Wisconsin, the nonpartisan Election Commission was built to spec by the Republican legislature only a year earlier, giving the legislature far more control over election processes.

Imagine that, given vote margins well outside of typical recount reversal, Democrats lost most of these cases, but raised enough

concerns in the media, including social media, that most Democrats didn't believe the results. How could they concede, given the
alternative of a Trump presidency, and his defeat in the popular
vote? Circulating in left-wing media, on Facebook, Twitter, and
elsewhere, were conspiracy theories purporting to connect Russian
interference with state voter databases, widespread fraud, or
attacks on voting machines. Tens of millions of sincerely disappointed and concerned Clinton supporters, scared of the prospect
of Trump in the White House, refused to believe he won the election, and dozens of overnight social media "celebrities" gained a
following, and perhaps even a financial windfall, by telling those
Americans lies that were just what they wanted to hear—that Clinton didn't really lose.

Imagine a Democratic base completely riled up, with ill-informed
questions about the integrity of the 2016 election being constantly
drilled into them from every corner of their media world. These
questions rang louder when considering how much better Republicans did in these states up and down the ballot—in statewide, state
legislative, and congressional elections—than had been anticipated
by the polling. The Obama administration and Democratic members of Congress got bombarded by demands to do something, anything, to block Trump: begin an investigation or seize and investigate
voting machines from the Republicans in charge of elections in the
challenged states.

Imagine marches, rallies, and protests occurring in every major
American city, demanding the White House fix what felt like an
assault on democracy. Counter-protests of Trump supporters
appeared at each, and in some cases, violence broke out. In some
cities, riot squads were called up, as tear gas and other crowd-control
measures were required. To those protesting, Trump was an existential threat to American democracy, potentially a puppet of the Russians, who had lost the popular vote by millions. And now millions
of Americans became convinced by fringe activists, charlatans, and

profiteers that Trump couldn't possibly have won the electoral votes necessary to take office. While the country descended into chaos, President Putin in Russia, President Xi in China, the Ayatollahs in Iran, and Chairman Kim in North Korea sat back and enjoyed the show.

Imagine in this environment, under extreme pressure from his Democratic base as well as some members of Congress and facing the prospect of rampant and uncontrollable violence in the streets, President Obama felt the need to encourage Attorney General Loretta Lynch to launch an investigation into allegations of widespread election fraud. Perhaps he might sincerely believe this could answer questions about the election, put the issue to rest, and restore order. But this was a whiplash decision, reversing decades of Justice Department independence, particularly when it comes to interference in an election, particularly post-election during the counting and certification phase. Even in 2000, especially in 2000, with the apparently losing presidential candidate being the sitting vice president, the Justice Department had rigidly held to its non-interference directive. This is David Becker speaking—as a trial attorney in the Voting Section of the Justice Department in 2000, we were given firm instructions not to engage, interfere, investigate, or even comment on the ongoing dispute in Florida. Traditionally, legally, and morally, those challenges would and should be left to the campaigns, fortified with teams of lawyers capable of resolving disputes through the judicial process.

And imagine that, in such an environment, as fanciful as such a suggestion might have seemed, the spouse of a liberal Supreme Court justice, who had many connections throughout Washington, texted her acquaintance Denis McDonough, President Obama's White House Chief of Staff, urging him to do something to stop Trump from taking office as a result of a "stolen election." She knew better than most that the White House could do more to interfere with the transition, and seek to prevent or delay Trump's taking office, or investigate possible wrongdoing. And though she held no official title in Washington, she was well known to powerful Democrats by virtue of her husband's position.

Under all these pressures from a variety of sources, even greater than 2000, imagine the DOJ and the Obama administration succumbing and initiating an official federal investigation, raising serious issues of federalism with regard to the states' administration of their own elections. That they eventually found nothing became irrelevant, as rumors and conspiracy theories circulated on social media—further fanning the desperate hopes of Clinton supporters. Of course, our adversaries helped amplify both ends of the confusion, spreading lies to both sides. It was so easy. They did not even need to create false or divisive content anymore—they only needed to create bots to further spread malicious content created by Americans, for Americans.

Then imagine that in this environment, the election officials kept doing what they do best—their jobs. They counted, recounted, and audited ballots, all with transparency, and with observers from both campaigns watching. Every single count and recount confirmed the results. There were minor mistakes here and there, as there are with any major election, but no evidence whatsoever of widespread fraud even close to sufficient to alter the outcome. Some in the Clinton campaign tried to inflate the importance of these small errors, but when forced to present evidence that could raise questions about the outcome of the presidential election, courts consistently found the evidence lacking, and ruled in favor of the state election officials and the processes established, and largely unchallenged, before the election. By early December, the states had all certified their results, consistent with the laws that existed before the election, the election results as confirmed, and the orders of the judiciary. Efforts to raise issues even before the United States Supreme Court failed, without any evidence that the states, exercising their powers under the Constitution, were flawed in their processes or certification.

Imagine that as the states began delivering the slates of electors to the National Archives, as required by federal law, some rogue Democratic members of the state legislatures in the five disputed states decided to throw a Hail Mary. They conceived of a plan to file alternate slates of electors from those states with the Archives, and hoped that they could convince Vice President Biden, a vocal supporter of Secretary Clinton, to lead a process whereby those false slates, representing the opposite of the duly certified results, would be considered instead of the real electoral slates. This was the longest of long shots, given that both houses of Congress were controlled by Republicans, but perhaps it could throw enough confusion and chaos into the mix where a miracle could happen.

In pursuit of this plan, imagine in Arizona, Florida, Michigan, Pennsylvania, and Wisconsin, the "electors" for Secretary Clinton met, "certified" their votes, and sent them to the National Archives. But at this point, the Obama White House, having seen no evidence of widespread fraud, having seen court after court confirm the results, and with the certified electors duly delivered to the National Archives, announced publicly that they would cooperate in the transition to President-Elect Trump, even calling him, for the first time, by that title. Even Clinton, at this point without any further legal recourse, held a press conference announcing that, though she believed there were significant problems with the election, she was conceding for the good of the nation, and wished President-Elect Trump well as he served what she hoped would be his better angels. But this didn't satisfy the tens of millions of Americans—over two-thirds of all Democratic voters—that the election was accurate, and that Trump truly won. It didn't help that Trump himself was spreading deceit within the country by alleging widespread fraud, in the opposite direction, which he claimed had denied him his popular vote victory.

Imagine that a few extremely blue states, perhaps led by California, Massachusetts, and New York, all of which were won by Clinton by more than 20 percentage points, decided to organize a last-ditch lawsuit under the U.S. Supreme Court's "original jurisdiction." Such original Supreme Court jurisdiction is reserved for lawsuits between the states, and would require the Court to hold a trial seeking to find that election rules and processes in other states—red states won by Trump—were unconstitutional. Further, the plaintiff states sought a ruling that all the presidential votes in those states—whether they voted for Clinton, or Trump, or someone else—be thrown out and ruled invalid for purposes of the electoral vote totals. In such a scenario, under the warped, anti-federalist theories being pushed by these states, with the challenged states' electoral votes excluded, Clinton would win a majority of the remaining Electoral College votes. The Supreme Court did what it should do with such nonsense, dismissing this case almost immediately, and unanimously.

Imagine that on January 6, 2017, protests around the country become more violent and desperate. In the eyes of the protestors, America was about to hand the keys to the White House, along with the nuclear football, to a man compromised by a foreign enemy and supremely unfit to hold office. This was not a matter of a difference in political philosophy for them; it was an existential threat to pluralistic democracy in the United States. Minorities and historically oppressed groups were afraid for their futures and convinced that Trump had not earned the actual right to take the oath of office on January 20, 2017. As much pressure as possible was brought to bear on Vice President Biden, but he made it clear that he intended to do his duty as prescribed by the Constitution and presided over the official election of Donald J. Trump as president of the United States.

Imagine as sincere activists, joined by more than a few profiteers and con artists seeking to capitalize on this national chaos for their own benefit, planned a massive rally on the National Mall for the morning of January 6. While most elected Democratic leaders avoided this rally, and any other attempts to subvert the constitutional and peaceful transfer of power, there were a handful that saw this as an opportunity. A small number of elected Democrats, most of them formerly obscure, exploited the anger felt by Clinton supporters, riding that divisive wave to prominence and profit. Some spoke at the rally, further inflaming the angry spirit pervading the moment, as the clock inched closer to 1:00 p.m. Eastern Standard Time on January 6, 2017.

This did not happen. It could not have happened. It would not have happened. Secretary Clinton did as every other candidate in America's modern history has done—Romney, McCain, Kerry, Gore, Nixon, Dewey—she ran her race, legitimately raised concerns through proper channels, including the courts, and conceded to the winner of the Electoral College. President Obama, Vice President Biden, Attorney General Lynch, members of Congress, members of the Supreme Court and their families, all did the same. They respected the rule of law, and despite the serious concerns some of them had about Trump's fitness for office, did their duty.

For those readers of this book who might have supported Trump in 2016 and/or 2020, consider the above and ask yourself, is this the way the 2016 post-election period should have played out? Because as you'll see in the pages to come, the lead-up into January 2021, as orchestrated by President Trump, was not just as bad. It was far, far worse.

3

JANUARY 2022

AMERICA'S 250th birthday is four years away. Whether America celebrates its tricentennial in 2076 will be determined by what happens between now and its semiquincentennial in 2026.

When the history of America is written, either at that 300th birthday or from the vantage point of collapse on or around its 250th, January 2022 will be seen as the most consequential of many months of renewal or dissolution. January 2022 was significant because it was during that month we learned the full extent of the debasement of democracy that occurred in the lead-up to January 2021. January 2022 was not so much about itself, but about the same month in the previous year.

Even for a country accustomed to convulsions of politics and law, this was an acutely convulsive time. Forces long set in motion began to collide and new ones jostled for public attention, all centering around the definition of democracy, protest, justice, and accountability. January 2022 also revealed, with startling details, what America, at least one part of it, had become. A Monmouth University Poll, released January 27, showed 32 percent of the nation believed President Biden "only" won by fraud while 17 percent said there was "a path to reverse" the election and replace Biden with former president Trump. National sentiment was torn about which was a bigger problem, election fraud, defined as votes being cast in the name of ineligible voters (41 percent major problem), or voter disenfranchisement, defined as eligible voters being denied a ballot or not having their ballot counted (49 percent major problem). Polling data aside, events in January also pointed to what America could become, provided it could pierce clouds of partisan obfuscation about real and fanciful threats to democracy.

January 2022 quite helpfully provided organizational coherence for this book. This project started as a modest celebration of 2020 election workers, the unsung guardians of democracy who protected the vote under trying and uncertain circumstances. But as America tied itself into tighter knots about what happened in 2020, this project shifted to a survey of the titanic forces pulling at America's democratic future, forces threatening to destabilize what we originally sought to celebrate—the resilient, transparent, diverse, and accountable way America casts and counts votes.

JANUARY AND THE LIGHTNESS OF FRAUD

January raised issues, more than a year after the election, about what fraud was or wasn't. The persistence of doubt about election 2020 cannot be wished away. Many if not all of the most lurid early allegations of corruption (bamboo ballots, industrial-scale vote flipping, hidden caches of ballots) had been proven false and abandoned. But questions remained in the minds of many about specific procedures (drop boxes, mail voting, and voter verification) and their legal basis. These are not crackpot questions. We will delve into them. Our goal: clarify the methods, explain the law, and illustrate the difference between the evolving and somewhat-esoteric world of election administration versus "shenanigans" (a word that comes up a lot) designed to help advantage one political party over another.

One way to think about this distinction is that once election rules are established, under the rule of law, it is up to the political actors (parties, candidates, grassroots coalitions) to adapt in pursuit of victory. Complaining about election rules after a candidate has lost is the worst sort of sore-loserism, and cannot be sustained. It has no legally recognized validity in our history, which is why state and federal courts rejected cases in 2020 alleging fraud or malfeasance when evidence showed rules were followed.

Importantly, in the run-up to Election 2020, America saw unprecedented litigation—more than 400 lawsuits filed and settled over a multitude of new voting methods and mechanisms. Those lawsuits did as they were intended—set rules and guidelines for election officials, election workers, voters, and all political players. The Trump campaign, Republican National Committee, and state Republican parties won a fair share of these pre-election cases. Joe Biden's campaign, the Democratic National Committee, and Democratic state parties, of course, won others. Some election rules, known well before the election, went unchallenged. But both sides knew how this monumental election would be conducted because both sides fought tenaciously over rules in all the closely contested states. There was no shortage of pre-election scrutiny. In fact, the 2020 election was the most scrutinized, publicized, and litigated election in American history, by a large margin.

JANUARY AND THE ATTEMPTED ELECTION OVERTHROW

January 2022 also exposed the depths of then-president Trump's plot to subvert the 2020 election. Thunderous details emerged about counterfeit slates of electors organized by Trump personal attorney Rudy Giuliani and abetted by the Trump reelection campaign. Efforts to harass election officials were revealed to have been coordinated by those with close ties to Trump, including by Bernard Kerik, the former New York City police commissioner who became a Trump election-denying ally. Subpoenas were issued for a raft of top White House officials, including Ivanka Trump. In the January 6 Committee's January 20 letter to Ivanka Trump, it raised several startling questions, including what Trump said to Vice President Pence before Congress assembled to certify legally submitted electoral votes. The letter pointed to revelations that would unfold throughout 2022:

> You were present in the Oval Office and observed at least one side of that telephone conversation. General Keith Kellogg [then national security adviser to Pence] was also present in the Oval Office during that call and has testified about that discussion, as follows:
>
> Q: It's been reported that the President said to the Vice President "you don't have the courage to make a hard decision." And maybe not those exact words but something like that. Do you remember anything like that?
>
> A: Words—I don't remember exactly either, but something like that, yeah. Being like you're not tough enough to make the call.
>
> Q: Another report of this call is that Trump said "Mike, it's not right. You can do this. I'm counting on you to do it. If you don't do it, I picked the wrong man four years ago. You're going to wimp out." Do you remember anything like that?
>
> A: Words like that, yes.

The letter to Ivanka Trump said Kellogg testified about what she said to him after hearing the call:

> "Mike Pence is a good man."
> I said "Yes, he is."

The committee outlined other questions: "The Committee has information suggesting that President Trump's White House Counsel may have concluded that the actions President Trump directed Vice President Pence to take would violate the Constitution or would otherwise be illegal. Did you discuss those issues with any member of the White House Counsel's office? To your knowledge, were any such legal conclusions shared with President Trump? Similarly, in the days before January 6, a member of the House Freedom Caucus with knowledge of the President's planning for that day sent a message to the White House Chief of Staff with this explicit warning: 'If POTUS [meaning President Trump] allows this to occur . . . we're driving a stake in the heart of the federal republic.'"

Part of the plan was to use fake slates of electors to stall the counting of electoral votes on January 6, 2021. Later in January, federal and state investigations were launched into those who created the fake electoral vote slates. It appeared to be a premeditated attempt to defraud the electoral vote process. The goal was to delay Biden's certified victory and, eventually, erase it through a vote in the U.S. House of Representatives or through acceptance of bogus electors from seven states.

It was also learned an executive order had been drafted for President Trump to use the U.S. military to seize ballot boxes and declare a national emergency—all to preserve his presidency. The order, dated December 16, 2020, was riddled with conspiracy theories about voting systems, misinterpretations of voting results, and groundless allegations about foreign interference. It read in part:

> Effective immediately, the Secretary of Defense shall seize, collect, retrain, analyze all machines, equipment, electronically stored information and material records required for retention. Within seven days of commencement of operations, the initial assessment must be provided to the Office of the Director of National Intelligence.

Relying heavily on claims made by left-leaning activists in an unsuccessful case brought before the election to decertify the Georgia voting machines, the draft executive order provided seven days for an "initial assessment" of alleged fraud and foreign interference. But it foresaw a never-before-seen delay in adjudicating a presidential election:

> The final assessment must be provided to the Office of the Director of National Intelligence no later than 60 days from commencement of operations.

Further, the draft executive order called for "the appointment of a Special Counsel to oversee operation and institute all criminal and civil proceedings as appropriate based on the evidence collected and provide all resources necessary."

The draft order can only be described as chilling. It provided, for the first time, true insight into how close America came to coup d'état through the armed seizure of ballots, through U.S. soldiers grabbing election equipment on the basis of myths, lies, misconceptions, and a deeply warped interpretation of presidential power, all leading, one suspects, to a delay in the transfer of power, and ultimately, installation of the losing candidate into the White House—a dictatorship in draft form.

"This is not the kind of thing that happens spontaneously and it's not the kind of thing that happens just because one person decides to make it happen," Maryland Democratic representative Jamie Raskin, a member of the January 6 Committee, told us. "The events of Jan. 6 were the culmination of weeks and weeks of planning and months of propagandizing the public. It took a very large number of people to conduct a violent insurrection and to attempt a political coup against the government."

The revelations forced America to comprehend in ways it had not before that there was a multi-layered plan, no matter how disorganized and legally dubious, to overthrow an American election—and that plan had percolated inside the Oval Office. This was not a concoction of the left. In fact, Trump White House documents and interviews with Trump White House personnel showed reality was far worse than original accusations from leftist opponents of the former president. One of Trump's lawyers, John Eastman, despite being accused of attempting to corruptly overturn the 2020 election, met with Wisconsin Republicans in mid-March 2022 to discuss decertifying electoral votes cast for President Biden. "President Trump has gone to war with the rule of law," Liz Cheney told us. "I think that that's absolutely the case."

In the pages ahead, we will ask and answer questions about the validity of Election 2020 that coursed through this soft coup—things like mathematical improbabilities, access of poll watchers, methods of counting ballots, mail-in vote security, and much more. As important, we will highlight the dangerous legal theories team Trump toyed with to preserve his defeated presidency—not because they worked but because they could resurface in attempts to challenge or undermine election results in the 2022 midterms or 2024 presidential election.

Fears about what Trump might do in 2024 should he become the GOP nominee prompted bipartisan interest in late January to amend and clarify the Electoral Count Act, which in vague and sometimes conflicting language, established the process by which Congress certifies slates of electoral votes. Trump sought to exploit some of the Act's blurry language on procedure as he leaned on Pence to intervene. The push for new legislation sought to clarify the role of the vice president, increase the number of lawmakers required to protest certification, and provide federal protection to election workers. On January 30, Trump erased all doubts about his 2020 intentions, writing, bizarrely, that:

Democrats and RINO Republicans [RINO stands for Republicans in Name Only] . . . are desperately trying to pass legislation that will not allow the vice president to change the results of the election. . . . Mike Pence did have the right to change the outcome and now they want to take that right away. Unfortunately, he didn't exercise that power, he could have overturned the election.

To be clear, Pence did not have that power. The Electoral Count Act does not empower the vice president to change the outcome of a national election, nor could such a provision be reconciled with Article II or the Twelfth Amendment of the Constitution. But its convoluted language, written in 1887, has left room for interpretation as to how far Congress can go to resolve disputes within a state over electoral votes.

The ECA was meant to minimize and ceremonialize the role of Congress, placing primary dispute resolution powers within each state. But Trump and some of his advisers insisted, wrongly, that they had the power to decide if electoral votes were disputed and that Pence could rule accordingly. That power does not exist. The ECA is not a constitutional "cheat code" that allows members of Congress, or the vice president, unhappy with the rules or the outcomes in the states, to decide to ignore those outcomes. In fact, such an interpretation would be about as contrary to federalism and the conservative ideal of states' rights as one could imagine.

Nevertheless, having invented a power that never existed, Trump in January 2022 acted as if bipartisan efforts to clarify that truth somehow validated his erroneous premise. He then conflated that further to suggest a right that plainly did not exist was being taken away. This is a type of offense peculiar to Trump—one built entirely on fiction but one that decidedly benefits him. To be clear, you cannot take away a right that did not exist. But Trump made clear what his intentions were, whether he fully understood that or not. Though his apologists contend Trump merely wanted to investigate allegations of election improprieties, Trump said out loud what he really wanted—Pence to overturn the election.

January 2022 also brought federal charges of seditious conspiracy against some of the January 6 rioters. The charges were the first of their kind brought against Americans since 2012—in a case that failed to win a conviction against the far-right Hutaree militia. Federal prosecutors had successfully charged "Blind Sheik" Oman Abdel Rahman and nine others with seditious conspiracy in 1995 after uncovering a plot to bomb the United Nations and other New York City landmarks. Puerto Rican nationalists, seeking independence from the U.S. government, were convicted of seditious conspiracy in 1954 after entering the U.S. House chamber and firing dozens of shots from semiautomatic pistols, injuring five lawmakers.

Many seditious conspiracy prosecutions have failed, largely because their seditious planning and discussions did not materialize—thereby being judged protected speech under the First Amendment. But an attack occurred on January 6, giving seditious conspiracy allegations clearer connection to actions threatening government functions. The charges were the first to examine whether a larger conspiracy of funding, mobilization, and organization was behind that Capitol riot. At minimum, it was shocking to see evidence in the first indictment that the alleged conspirators stockpiled weapons inside hotel rooms across the Potomac River in preparation for an armed assault that, quite fortunately, never came. All defendants are presumed innocent until proven guilty, but the mere allegation of seditious conspiracy conjured fears of democracy on a war footing.

In that same month, a request by the Fulton County, Georgia, district attorney was approved to impanel a special grand jury to investigate whether Trump engaged in "criminal disruptions" when he asked Republican secretary of state Brad Raffensperger to help him "find" enough votes to overturn Biden's statewide victory. The grand jury was necessary, Fulton County District Attorney Fani Willis said, because "individuals associated with these disruptions" (meaning Trump and his attorneys) had engaged with Raffensperger, Georgia's attorney general, and the U.S. attorney for the Northern District of Georgia. That left the DA "as the sole agency with jurisdiction that is not a potential witness" to the underlying offense. On January 29, at a rally outside of Houston, Trump made a reference to the Fulton County prosecutor in an unsettling way. "If those radical, vicious, racist prosecutors do anything wrong or illegal, I hope we are going to have in this country the biggest protest we have ever had in Washington, D.C., New York, in Atlanta and elsewhere because our country and our elections are corrupt." Fani Willis is Black. As is New York attorney general Letitia James, whose 2021 and 2022 investigation into potential Trump tax and insurance fraud appeared to pose significant legal jeopardy.

Some Republicans distanced themselves from Trump's remarks. Willis, the Fulton County DA, sought FBI protection for her and her employees. Trump did not explicitly call for violence, but January 6 proved he does not have to—that his most ardent supporters need only cues about corruption and racism to take matters, sometimes violently, into their own hands.

On January 28, a commonwealth court in Pennsylvania ruled a 2019 law that allowed universal voting by mail violated the state constitution. Trump hailed this a significant development, even though it undermined other allegations of questionable election 2020 procedures. The law legalized no-excuse voting by mail. It had been a bipartisan compromise between Republicans, who wanted to eliminate straight-ticket voting in Pennsylvania, and Democrats, who wanted to expand voting by mail. Every Republican in the State Senate, and all but two in the State House, had voted for the bill. (Support among Democrats was more split.) Pennsylvania's constitution requires in-person voting, so, technically, the 2019 law did not comply, according to the lower court. The Pennsylvania Supreme

Court will be reviewing this ruling, and some commentators believe it is likely to be overturned.

It was odd to see Trump highlight this development because in many other states he and fellow election deniers questioned any pandemic-related voting change that had not been approved by a legislature and governor. Obviously, the Pennsylvania law in 2019 met this criteria, and aspects of the law were litigated by both campaigns and determined months before the election. The glaring inconsistency would be repeated over and over in 2022—complaints about Election 2020 were not about actual fraud, improper votes, or illegal procedures. They were sour grapes. Trump and company hated losing, hated the fact they couldn't win legitimately even though they knew the rules and procedures. It wasn't that there was a problem with the election. There was a problem with the Trump campaign. And that, the former president, smoldering in wounded vanity, could not abide. This was the only election-denying constant that shone through in 2022.

JANUARY AND THE SUPREME COURT

As if this were not enough, the U.S. Supreme Court rejected Trump's efforts to block the House Select Committee investigating January 6 from obtaining documents, phone logs, text messages, and other evidence about what Trump and key advisers did as marauders invaded the U.S. Capitol. The decision opened an unobstructed view into Trump's mindset, words, and actions on one of the ugliest days in American history. The documents also allowed investigators to assess how Trump's post-election moves to install loyalists in top positions at the Department of Justice and Department of Defense fit into the larger plan to topple election results.

The Biden administration had never backed Trump's assertion of executive privilege to shield the records and the high court agreed with a federal appellate court on two key points—the congressional investigation had a legal basis and executive privilege did not protect efforts to subvert democracy. Another bizarre twist, as if January needed another, was the warning issued by Newt Gingrich, former House Speaker and Trump adviser, that members of the January 6 Select Committee could be arrested if Republicans won control of the House in the 2022 midterm election. "This is all going to come crashing down," Gingrich said January 24 on Fox News. "They're the ones who, in fact, face a real risk of jail for the kinds of laws they are breaking." By way of reply, committee member Liz Cheney, Wyoming Republican, said, "This is what it looks like when the rule of law unravels," and fellow committee member Zoe Lofgren, California Democrat, said, "I think Newt has really lost it."

As if to remind everyone in America what was at stake, Supreme Court Justice Stephen Breyer, on January 27, formally announced he would retire at the end of the Court's term in June. In the Roosevelt Room he stood with Biden to summarize his decades of wrestling with American law and politics.

> I sit there on the bench, and after we hear lots of cases—and after a while the impression—it takes a while, I have to admit but the impression you get is, you know, this is a complicated country; there are more than 330 million people. And my mother used to say, "It's every race. It's every religion." And she would emphasize this: "And it's every point of view possible." And it's kind of a miracle when you sit there and see all of those people in front of you— people that are so different in what they think. And yet, they've decided to help solve their major differences under law. [Breyer then took a pocket-sized copy of the Constitution from his jacket.] People have come to accept this Constitution and they've come to accept the importance of the rule of law. I'll tell you what Lincoln thought, what Washington thought, and what people today still think: It's an experiment.

The experiment felt delicate and fragile as Breyer spoke in the same room, where roughly one year before, a plot was hatched to strangle that experiment. The plot sought to cancel millions of American votes and impose an illegitimate result—the second term of a presidency defeated in the popular vote and via the Electoral College. Breyer's buoyancy appeared an antidote to the numbness of January's soul-crushing headlines. He spoke for America and to America—specifically to young Americans.

> I'll tell you something. You know who will see whether that experiment works? It's you, my friend. It's you, Mr. High School Student. It's you, Mr. College Student. It's you, Mr. Law Student. It's us, but it's you. It's that next generation and the one after that—my grandchildren and their children. They'll determine whether the experiment still works.

As reassuring as Breyer may have been, on January 29, at that rally outside of Houston we mentioned earlier, Trump said that if he were to be reelected in 2024, he would seriously consider pardoning January 6 rioters. "If I run and win," Trump said, "we will treat those people from January 6 fairly. And if it requires pardons, we will give them pardons because they are being treated so unfairly." At the time Trump spoke, more than 750 people had been charged in the Capitol riot. Those initially charged faced misdemeanor and felonies. More than half had pleaded guilty by January 2022, and many blamed Trump for misleading them with false rhetoric about a stolen election. Many of these early cases were likely to run their course before Trump, should he be reelected, would be able to order pardons. Some Republicans distanced themselves from Trump's remarks. More charges stemming from the riot were anticipated. With all cases unresolved or pending, Trump's statement injected an unwanted variable into calculations defendants and prosecutors might make on plea deals

or negotiations around plea deals, or other questions about testi-
fying or cooperating with investigators. Rule of law. Part of the
experiment.

JANUARY AND INDICTMENTS
FOR THREATENING ELECTION WORKERS

There would be more in January 2022. A man in Texas was arrested
on federal charges for allegedly threatening to kill Raffensperger
and two other Georgia election officials because they were, in his
words, "lawless, treasonous traitors." At about the same time,
Republicans in three states (Georgia among them) proposed the creation of a special police force to monitor elections—not to protect
poll workers or election officials, but to investigate those election
officials themselves, all under the pretext of ferreting out fraud.
This idea was not only laced with irony but was, from the perspective of how rare actual vote fraud is, performative.

The dizzying developments spoke to crucial issues this book tack-
les: what changes will alter the political and legal terrain for the
2022 midterms and the 2024 presidential election; how Trump's
attempt to subvert the 2020 election might delegitimize future elections; how the 2020 election was actually conducted (as opposed to
how it is maligned); what genuine misunderstandings about election procedures persist and how they can be explained; and, lastly,
how nonpartisan election professionals and election workers continue to find themselves in the threatening crosshairs of manufactured election rage.

JANUARY AND VOTING RIGHTS

The dawning of the year 2022 also brought a debate over voting
rights to Washington. Biden marked the one-year anniversary of the
Capitol rebellion by saying democracy is fragile but that its

guardrails held. For the first time, he detailed Trump's destabilizing role, not knowing that within that very month more disturbing details would emerge. Biden also made plain he would push for his version of voting rights legislation in the coming days.

Five days later, Biden compared Republicans who disagreed with him on a Democratically drafted expansion of federal voting legislation with the vilest bigots of the segregated South. "Will you stand with election subversion?" Biden thundered from the campus of Atlanta University Center Consortium, days before Martin Luther King's birthday and national holiday. "Do you want to be on the side of Dr. King or George Wallace? Do you want to be on the side of John Lewis or Bull Connor? Do you want to be on the side of Abraham Lincoln or Jefferson Davis?" The speech drew significant criticism from many corners of American punditry.

Senate Republican Leader Mitch McConnell, who warred with Trump in 2021 and has done more than most Republicans to defang doubts about the 2020 election, called Biden's speech "profoundly unpresidential." From the Senate floor, where McConnell speaks regularly but not often memorably, the GOP leader laid down his own view. "The sitting president of the United States compared American states to 'totalitarian states.' He said our country will be an 'autocracy' if he does not get his way." McConnell spoke in characteristic cadence, more drone than drawl. "Twelve months ago, this president said that 'disagreement must not lead to disunion.' But [January 11] he invoked the bloody disunion of the Civil War to demonize Americans who disagree with him. He compared a bipartisan majority of senators to literal traitors."

At a White House press conference one week later, Biden angrily denied comparing Republicans to Bull Connor or Jefferson Davis (which he plainly did). When asked if the 2022 midterms would be legitimate if, as was certain, pending voting legislation failed to pass, Biden equivocated. But it was clear that any attempt to make the Democrats' voting rights push bipartisan had failed miserably.

We will tackle all of what January 2022 brought to the debate about democracy's future. It was clear to us in the moment and clearer in each subsequent month that January represented a tidal shift, that everything that came after would be new, either refreshing or numbing our understanding and application of democracy— with incalculable consequences for America and the world.

We will methodically describe what happened in 2020, why it looked suspicious to some, and why, in the end, it wasn't. We will enumerate all the dangerous ways in which Trump tried to kill Election 2020 and how close he came to "driving a stake in the heart of the federal republic" (in the words of House Republican Chip Roy from Texas, who begged the White House to stop its electoral vote scheme). We will carefully analyze state laws passed after 2020 and highlight dangerous trends (such as disempowering elections professionals and elevating partisan overseers).

WHAT JANUARY 2022 MEANS

These are tumultuous times for democracy and our debate about its direction. No book can capture every tremor or trauma. We attempt to describe clearly and simply where we have been, where we are, and where we are heading. As the first chapter makes abundantly clear, we harbor deep but not debilitating fears. Oddly, we would be more afraid if there was less rancor, if we seemed resigned or doomed. We are arguing. We are tussling. That democracy is a crackling topic gives us hope, even amid inflamed passions and smoky disinformation. America is on alert but to what, precisely, it is not quite sure. Political posturing isn't helping much. As a journalist and election law specialist, we humbly suggest we can help.

We make this solemn promise. This book will not take sides. We do believe one overarching truth: Trump's bid to overturn the 2020 election was an assault on the Constitution and the voters. We do not regard this as an opinion. There is nothing comparable in our history. No president ever contemplated what Trump contemplated. Every previous president or nominee rejected Trump's schemes and his rhetoric. Moreover, there is nothing in our history of presidents or nominees even toying with the array of election excesses Trump attempted to normalize. Trump tried to assume powers not only that he did not possess, but that no previous president even wondered if he had, let alone pondered wielding. From this we will not avert our gaze, because history will not either. This will in no way blind us from recognizing as legitimate every Republican elected on the 2020 ballot or from fully acknowledging that Republicans out-performed expectations in state legislative races, congressional races, and Senate races. Pre-dating 2020, we readily acknowledge Republicans legitimately won very close elections and did so using almost the same procedures to cast and count votes used in 2020. We will not describe every post-2020 change to state election laws as suppressive. We seek to clarify, not inflame; educate, not aggravate. We write for the great ideological middle of our country, tens of millions of souls who want to know what works and why, whose fight is for America and not with other Americans.

Our 250th birthday is coming up. It may seem impossible to confidently predict we will make it to our 300th birthday. Consider this. Did America's bicentennial look like a sure thing in 1966 when war in Vietnam was accelerating and race riots flaring? What about 1968 when angst over Vietnam toppled the presidency of Lyndon Johnson and assassinations claimed the lives of Dr. Martin Luther King and Robert F. Kennedy? Or when, that very same year, police officers and national guardsmen clubbed and arrested hundreds of protesters outside the Democratic National Convention in Chicago? Did our bicentennial seem certain six years later, in 1974, when President Nixon resigned over Watergate and it was learned that federal agencies, under Democratic and Republican administrations, had illegally surveilled anti-war and civil rights protesters? Did preservation of democracy appear certain? For most Americans it did, despite the painful disagreements. Many books and articles of the time described America as divided as it had been at any time since the Civil War—and that was before the political earthquake known as Watergate.

We are not resurrecting past traumas to tranquilize current anxieties. We know the fundamentals of democracy are tested as never before and that our current strife looks and feels bad, nauseating even. We know as bad as events were in the 1960s and 1970s, we did not, as a people, disparage our own elections or wonder if the way we counted votes was a hidden tool of sabotage. That some of us do now is a debilitating sickness, one we hope to slow. We have been sick before and healed even though the issues that divided us were starker—in the 1960s, as just one example, life or death in Vietnam, segregation or freedom in the South.

The nation seems to be searching for a modern meaning of democracy, one where participation and technology create new access and with it, some alteration of past patterns. These new approaches, especially ones rapidly fashioned during the pandemic, were disorienting to some. We do not fault those whose discomfort leads them to harbor doubts. We only suggest that one look at the fact that current voting methods are already safe, secure, and verifiable. We will offer evidence that sloganeering about "election integrity" and "forensic audits" are, more often than not, money-making schemes and grifts, harming the integrity of our systems.

We are confident in the future so long as all of us remember what democracy requires—the tireless work of hundreds of thousands of our fellow citizens, spanning every possible political philosophy. It requires that those who campaign and lose must accept a fair defeat with grace and dignity, not because they want to but because it makes our country stronger. A politician who concedes is not a wimp or a sellout. A politician who concedes is part of the mortar in the ever-enlarging house of American democracy. "The time when an election is final is as important as the victory statement," historian Doris Kearns Goodwin told us. "Maybe more important than the victory statement by the candidate because it resolves that an election has happened. The people have spoken. We believe in the honor of the institutions we have created." A concession is a gift, an offering, if you will, to every citizen, every voter and non-voter.

There is reason to believe that reason can prevail. We seek to explain what works, what is true, and what is best about democracy—not the politicians we elect, but the process by which we do it and the semi-saintly among us who do America's unsung work. The better we understand how our democracy works, the better we can protect it until our 250th birthday and beyond.

part
two

4

ELECTION 2020 AND THE TRUTH

THE Big Truth: democracy is made up of millions of little truths, intimate and interlocking truths. Truths found in the votes cast by Americans in person or by mail. Truths found in the citizenry that voluntarily counts those votes and dutifully reports the results. Truths found in election officials who scrape together the means by which elections are held, public servants who create the voting precincts, buy the equipment to tally the votes, and manage the process of moving the votes along the line to be tallied and certified . . . so that they may be transparently confirmed and trusted. Truths found in this collaborative exercise of civic virtue are more obvious and verifiable than they have ever been in our history. The Big Truth is a variation of *E Pluribus Unum*—from many one. From millions of little truths we form a Big Truth, one we should celebrate, and almost always have before, but somehow now can't, or that troubles us or feels less settled than it should. This book is about those little truths and The Big Truth. It is devoted to the people who make each little truth meaningful so that The Big Truth may flourish.

PAPER BALLOTS AND OBSERVERS

Here is a truth that matters more than you might suspect. The 2020 election had more paper ballots than any national election in our history. Paper ballots are a hedge against hacking. You can't hack paper. Paper ballots are the fingerprints, almost the DNA, of a verifiable election. All of the so-called disputed swing states used them. In fact, around 95 percent of the voters in our nation voted with them in 2020. And paper ballots are required for effective audits, confirming the results. Thanks to the pervasiveness of paper ballots in 2020, more states audited those ballots and confirmed the results than ever before, including all of the swing states.

Another truth was vote counting had never been more visible or scrutinized. Despite what you may have read or heard, poll watchers and observers were present at all desired locations and in accordance with state or local laws. Many vote counting locations even livestreamed the process around-the-clock. Never before had ballots been counted as visibly and verifiably. Court records on this are clear. In Pennsylvania, the only place where any serious discussion of poll watching or vote-counting observers occurred, the only intervention was to move observers from ten feet away to six feet away. That court record does not suggest poll watchers or observers were excluded. There is no credible allegation in any other state of that either. This is one of the many unfortunate contradictions of the 2020 election. We never had more observers and yet we've never had more doubt about what those observers saw.

Part of The Big Truth, and it is one of many sad truths, is that this process, undertaken to increase confidence in election results, fell short for some. This spoke to a general atmosphere of mistrust so deep that even when people could see something, they were not always prepared to believe what they saw—or believe it over allegations from critics with whom they were already politically aligned. That this transparency did not help is no reason to abandon it or question its future value. It must be preserved. Some in our country were fed lies about the election, and their skepticism and fanaticism deepened even as the livestreams played blandly on. For those predisposed by the losing candidate to find conspiracies around every corner, watching people count votes did not necessarily increase confidence, not when the watchers had already made up their minds. What it did do, however, was contribute to the exposing of election workers to identification, vilification, and bullying—all of which happened in 2020 and continued well into 2022. A Justice Department task force was established for the first time ever to prosecute such crimes. Hundreds upon hundreds of cases of harassment and threats were reported, and by the end of January 2022, two separate federal indictments had been filed.

Confirmation bias is one of those phrases that sounds elitist and academic but really isn't. All it means is that you fit all evidence and observations into any preexisting beliefs you may possess, whether warranted or not. This is the 2020 election. For those who doubt it or are certain it was stolen or hacked or rigged, the notion that it would be was planted at least in the summer of 2020 and its wellsprings may go back to Trump's preposterous assertion that he won the popular vote in 2016 but that "victory" was erased by 3 to 4 million votes cast by "illegal aliens." That did not happen. No matter. The idea of fraud afoot was injected into the psyche of Trump loyalists. The rest of us moved on. They did not.

The Big Truths we seek to elevate here are about the election system—our election system—and the people within it who produced the result. It is that system and those people who deserve a stout and rigorous defense. To respect the system and those people can and should be an act of nonpartisan appraisal. We don't ask for blind allegiance or dog-eyed devotion. We only ask for fairness, logic, and decency. We invite you to come with us to judge for yourself if what happened is worthy of your future confidence and trust. We will offer evidence and explanations about elections, not about politics. You may believe our politics is broken. Whether that is true, we wish to show how our elections are not. We look for a conversation where we judge them differently. Elections are about the process by which we cast and count votes. We believe there is reason for confidence in both—whether you are satisfied with the result or not. If you are a baseball or football or basketball fan, we suspect you still love the sport even when your team loses. We ask for the same sense of balance.

TRUMP VOTERS ARE PISSED OFF

To achieve this sense of balance we must acknowledge another important and painful part of The Big Truth—Trump loyalists are pissed off, royally pissed off. They believe Trump—as candidate, nominee, and president—was hounded and undermined at every turn. Whether these feelings are justified isn't particularly relevant. It is a fact that Trump's 2016 victory is the only one in our history to be met with so much horror, contempt, and curdled disrespect. It was a shocking upset, and represented the only time in modern history where a president was elected despite losing the popular vote by such a significant margin. In addition, we knew at the time that, while there was no evidence of fraud or ballot tampering that altered the results, which were legitimate, there were efforts by our adversaries, particularly Russia, to interfere with the election and sow discord through disinformation, for their preferred candidate.

This is Major Garrett speaking here. I have spent more than seven years covering Trump. I have what I regard as a better-than-average sense of Trump supporters, having met hundreds upon hundreds at more than a hundred rallies across the country. I know how deeply this denial of Trump's victory stings. It comes off as a dismissive taunt from doubters and critics and cynics who don't see Trump or his agenda the way they do—as something that was missing and overdue. Trump's 2016 victory was the most improbable in

American political history, a daring, no-holds-barred takedown of one of the nation's best-known, best-funded, and most-successful political machines. Trump defied all political experts, won the presidency, and marshaled an unprecedented political movement that, despite heavy resistance, media criticism, investigations, a pandemic, and myriad unforced errors nevertheless grew in size and potency—attracting 11.2 million more votes in 2020 than it had in 2016.

Setting aside ideology and party loyalty, Trump's victory and presidency was a shattering, discombobulating shock to the system. Trump wanted, he *craved*, credit for toppling the established order. And yet notice and praise, respect and analysis of this achievement came sparingly or not at all. It fell to his already converted ranks to stand by his side, take up the call, defy the forces arrayed against their leader. This energy is real and vital to understanding persistent doubts and disbelief about the 2020 election. The battle lines were drawn, and in the minds of Trump supporters they are certain *they* didn't draw them—doubters and haters did. As but one example, Trump and his supporters believe he was set upon instantly with the Steele dossier, National Security Adviser Michael Flynn's clumsy lies, the recusal of Attorney General Jeff Sessions, and the appointment of Special Counsel Robert Mueller—all of which denied Trump a presidential honeymoon and hobbled his ability to govern and acquire, if he could, new political capital.

In chapter one we introduced you to Kathy Bernier, a Wisconsin state senator, hearty Trump supporter, and among the most conservative voices in that state's legislature. Bernier, with more than forty years of experience with Wisconsin elections, regards 2020 as a disappointing but verified Trump defeat. But she burns about the treatment of Trump. "Democrats don't get away free and clear. No one has spoken out about the 'Russian collusion' and all the things that went on for the entire term of President Trump on a lie. Democrats are just as guilty as the Republicans for perpetuating misinformation and outright lies." We spoke to Bernier as she was catching flack from fellow Republicans for calling for an end to all investigations of 2020. "President Trump had a lot of good policies. I loved his policies. I loved his work ethic and we can disagree with our own political party. Trust me, there's a lot of Republicans that don't agree with me right now. But we should be free to speak our minds. And the same thing holds true for Democrats. They haven't. I haven't heard any Democrat speak up and say the [Steele] dossier was wrong. What happened through that and the Hillary Clinton campaign was flat-out wrong. We need to recognize right from wrong. And in this society right now, it's all a blur and we're going to support the people who lie to us—come hell or high water. And that's not right."

Before we get too far down this rabbit hole, let's remember Trump did plenty to befoul his transition, undercut his ability to govern, and limit the acquisition of political capital. (You can read all about it in Major Garrett's book *Mr. Trump's Wild Ride*.) That being said, when Trump talks about the swamp or the deep state, these metaphors matter to a faithful who believe that *from the jump* their political hero, their courageous outsider and truth-teller, was abused and mistreated—without repercussion or shame.

To Trump and his believers, this was a unique assault not only on Trump but the presidency. This belief is so deeply rooted in the psyche of Trump supporters that it is accepted wisdom, a dividing line between what it means to be a Republican, a patriot, an American. Within the Trump movement there are many sub-motivations: nostalgia for an America that seems to be slipping away, either via new demographic trends or secular cultural trends; anxieties about the digital economy and its dislocations; and, undoubtedly, the emotional trauma associated with acknowledging our nation's racist history. "There are some deep political tectonics shifting in the country," Raskin told us. "There are not many nations and there are not many societies in history where political power is shifted from one dominant racial or ethnic group to another without violence or traumatic political conflict." These strands create a political cord with surprising tensile strength. And it has a language and set of oversimplified certainties: either you believe Trump was railroaded and the railroading forces—the media, Big Tech, liberals, academics, RINOs, corporatists—must be stopped, or you don't. To Trump and his followers, opponents' references to constitutional, legislative, or presidential norms are pieties of convenience, tools used only to demonize and minimize Trump— even when they clearly are not. After all, if we revere Washington, Jefferson, Jackson, Lincoln, Theodore Roosevelt, Wilson, Franklin Roosevelt, Truman, Kennedy, Johnson, Reagan, and Obama—and we do—then we must revere the constitutional, legislative, and presidential norms they helped create, sustain, and convey. Trump's uniqueness does not give him free rein.

DEEPER GRIEVANCES AND ELECTION 2020

Those who defend Trump know he is different. But they don't believe each difference is evidence of wrongdoing or malice. To the contrary, allegations of this kind tend to reinforce that Trump, probably, is onto something and maybe high time. If norms prevailed, Trump and his followers believe, the worst would not be assumed. But in a world where norms were abandoned—note Trump supporters believe it was not Trump who abandoned them first or at all, but his rivals—new tactics, up to and including violence, may be justified to defend Trump and Trumpism. The sense of alienation and rage hardened in 2021 and early 2022 as revelations from two federal investigations—one into surveillance of Trump 2016 campaign associates the other into Hunter Biden— raised serious questions about unethical behavior and possible criminal violations. To Trump supporters one story, that of Democratic ties—up to and including Hillary Clinton's presidential campaign—to the inflammatory Steele Dossier was buried or minimized. Trump supporters believe the same about Hunter Biden's laptop, first dismissed as potential Russian disinformation in the fall of 2020, but in 2022 confirmed as evidence in a widening investigation into potential financial crimes. A frequent refrain in chatrooms, interviews, and social media postings is that whatever Trump supporters have said or done pales against what has been done to them and to *him*. They perceive their reaction to this as righteous, battling injustice and wickedness—in essence a provocation. Provocateurs will pay. No price is too steep. No damage too deep. They are in the depths. And some Trump supporters speak of pulling the nation into the void. A C-SPAN microphone recorded that aggrieved rage on January 6 when an unknown Trump protester, deep inside the U.S. Capitol, screamed, "We own this place! We own you!" Another protester, his voice taut with agony, shouted, "The government did this to us. We were normal, good, law-abiding citizens and you guys did this to us. We want our country back!"

This spirit continues to this day. It could be found in early 2022 surveys showing Trumpist Republicans found the January 6 riot at the U.S. Capitol either mostly peaceful or a justifiable reaction to a greater assault on democracy. It can be found in the censures of Reps. Liz Cheney and Adam Kinzinger in early February 2022, and the Republican National Committee's characterization of January 6 as "legitimate political discourse." The dichotomy is telling and logically iffy. Either January 6 was almost nothing, meaning a small protest with a few rowdy tourists and colorful characters, or it was a clanging blow for freedom to protect a wronged president from an unjust ouster. It cannot possibly be both, unless the point is to absolve Trump and Trump protestors. A separate conspiratorial concept, abetted by Trump early in 2022, was the riot was a federal law enforcement setup, an inside job. Finding a way to rationalize January 6 has been a never-ending quest for Trump supporters—much as election denialism has been. We only point out that both have one thing in common, a shifting story line that evolves when a previously erroneous explanation collapses. To observe this is to take Trump and his supporters seriously and merely tabulate the hopscotch nature of their explanations.

This is part of The Big Truth that we, as a nation, must comprehend. Beliefs about what did or did not happen in the 2020 election are not just about the results. Beliefs of a rigged or stolen election are as much about a collection of grievances that have taken on a quasi-religious fervor in some quarters and a militaristic mindset in others. The 2020 election is a proxy for the future of Trumpism, which, in the minds of millions of Trump supporters, is a distorted proxy for the future of America, of patriotism, liberty, the Constitution, and the republic itself. Which makes the response to its aftermath all that more dangerous.

This is not to apologize or excuse Trump or Trumpism. It is a recognition of what this debate is about to tens of millions of Americans. It is, at its core, much less about the mechanics and mechanisms of casting and counting votes and much more about their devotion to Trump, their fury at the abuse they perceive he (and by extension they) suffered at the hands of his political enemies, and their certainty that belligerence is the only suitable response. Belligerence or be rolled. Belligerence or lose what you believe America is and represents. It is the manifestation of a multitude of perceived grievances against Trump, and more importantly, against themselves.

Here is another Big Truth. Trump supporters, by all accounts, have come to care more about election denialism than almost any other issue. Their concerns about the election compete with and in some surveys exceed immigration or crime. Expressing doubts about the 2020 election was the 2021 litmus test. In early 2022, that appeared to be insufficient. Republicans vying for Trump's endorsement, or the backing of his movement, had to say the election was stolen and suggest, as Republicans did at the Trump rally outside Phoenix in early 2022, that criminal charges must be brought—against whom and for what it was not clear but was a crowd-pleaser just the same. Trump may run in 2024; he hinted strongly in this direction in late January 2022 when, while teeing off at one of his Florida golf courses, he described himself as the forty-fifth and forty-seventh president. At this moment, in early 2022, he could harness the energy of his loyal base more profitably for himself and the Republican Party.

When Ricky Hatch—the Republican Weber County, Utah clerk and auditor—spoke to us about election denying fanaticism from Trump-polarized Republicans, he admitted to having, on occasion, let conspiracy venting and repeated falsehoods go unanswered. Other Republicans, he told us, play along with The Big Lie in their states or in Congress, fearful of being targeted for ouster.

"It is a super-vocal minority that just believes it to their core," Hatch said. "Very small, very vocal, and very aggressive. And they will say 'I will get you out of office over this.' They are like bullies and you just nod in agreement and don't say anything. I have felt that myself."

Hatch has turned a corner and now will speak in any venue about the accuracy of the 2020 election and the security of American elections.

"I have to push back or we are going to destroy our fundamental trust in elections. I know the truth."

For good and for ill, Trump is the most consequential political figure of this millennium and possibly the most important in fifty years, for almost all the wrong reasons. Any Republican elected in 2016 would have cut taxes and federal regulations, nominated conservatives to the Supreme Court, and tried to repeal Obamacare. None would have dared toy with democracy as destructively as Trump did before he was elected, while he was president, and as he was heading out the door. At this stage of his political career,

Trump's importance lies in his capacity to do irreparable harm, his willingness to undermine or destroy faith and belief in elections.

HOW DEMOCRACY WORKS—AND WORKED

The biggest of the Big Truths is that Election 2020 was one of the greatest American accomplishments of recent history. Turnout was historic. Health risks were real. Procedures were changed to accommodate legitimate fears about voting in person and in concentrated numbers. Voters were given unprecedented choices. Again, verifiable paper ballots were used and served their purpose—to act as a fail-safe and transparent proof against fraud. And around 95 percent of voters used them. We forget now but primaries in 2020 and the general election occurred before vaccines were available. These mass gathering events had to adapt to the pandemic. We may forget now but the tools available were limited: social distancing, mask-wearing, hand sanitizing. That's all we had. To allow people to vote and vote safely, precautions were taken. Yes, primaries in the teeth of the pandemic were a bit messy. What wasn't in the spring of 2020? Many primaries were delayed for safety reasons. In some states, voting lines were long. Polling precincts in some urban areas were understaffed. Voters were sometimes confused about which precincts were open. Under great pressure, election and public health officials tried to balance risks and did an admirable job. Our democracy persisted against heavy odds. Much was learned.

Primaries helped election officials learn how to adapt and develop best practices. This is what America has always done during a crisis. We innovate and find new solutions under pressure. Yankee ingenuity is an old phrase, but it speaks to a cultural characteristic we used to cherish—doing new and hard things under stress, without a road map. Why this time do we scorn that which we used to celebrate? Why can't we see the achievement for what it was? Because to do so would require us to believe in the very institutions we have created to help us govern ourselves. To a large and worrisome degree, we have stopped doing this.

This book cannot solve that problem. But it can suggest that we, as a nation, are doing the work of our adversaries—attacking ourselves and weakening our institutions. We have become angry and intolerant of one another and indifferent to the institutions and mechanisms *we* built to mediate and soften *our* political differences. Democracy is not a habit of humanity. Despotism is. Democracy is an invention, an experiment that has always required more effort than all known alternatives. Free people, diverse in race, religion, national origin, sexual orientation, and so many other ways, disagreeing and resolving differences peaceably for the common good, is an ideal, not an edict. Ideals require participatory belief and faith in those in whose hands the machinery of that ideal has been placed—meaning, to put it simply, one another. We administer elections ourselves. We—ourselves, our families, our neighbors, our fellow citizens. We people neighborhood precincts with, yes, our neighbors. Elections, each and severally, represent mini exercises of our democratic ideals. They are acts of civic prayer, and the altar, if you will, is the voting booth. It, like all altars, is a place of practiced faith, strengthened not by blind allegiance but by active maintenance. Abandoned altars crumble, as do ones abused and assailed.

We are at a point of maximum peril for our democracy. We are assailing and abusing elections in new and calamitous ways, shifting the battleground from debate and persuasion *before* an election to doubts, criticism, and rejectionism *after* an election. Historically, the blood sport of politics occurred before elections. We now risk blood spilled after them.

CLOSE ELECTIONS—WE'VE HAD THEM AND SURVIVED

Our young country nearly collapsed under the weight of rivalry and intrigue after the election of 1800, which produced Thomas Jefferson's presidency only after last-minute forbearance from federalist leaders. Andrew Jackson's loss in the election of 1824, the first in which the winner of the popular vote did not prevail, similarly threatened to wreck the nation and would have, had Jackson, the victim of a "corrupt bargain" between eventual winner John Quincy Adams and Henry Clay, not licked his wounds and focused on winning decisively four years later. Both elections required contingent elections in the House of Representatives. Both were cauldrons of intrigue. Both put the fragility of our democratic republic in peril. But at no point did any of the leading figures question the validity of the votes cast or the cumbersome method of resolving the ambiguous result. To preserve the national experiment of democracy, nominees and eventual presidents (Jefferson and Jackson), as well as other factional leaders, followed the convoluted rules and accepted the outcome without libeling the system. That we have grown into the world's longest functioning democracy (despite the danger we are mindlessly courting now) is not a testament to the inherent resilience of our election system but to the forbearance of early political leaders who prioritized its strengthening above all other considerations.

Forbearance. It arrived again in 1876 when Congress formed a special committee to resolve contested voting results in Florida, South Carolina, and Louisiana. Once again, the process was messy and the popular vote winner, Samuel Tilden, did not prevail. Rutherford B. Hayes won after the committee awarded him all three disputed states, and an informal agreement was struck to end Reconstruction in the defeated former Confederacy. As had happened before, Tilden and Hayes stayed out of the controversy and allowed the process to proceed. There was considerable backroom maneuvering but neither Tilden nor Hayes questioned the rules nor the methods of obtaining a result. Following precedent, they sought to strengthen the system, not weaken it. Much fault can be found in all three of these elections, but the legacy of each is that key figures operated within the known rules and did all they could to offer support and belief in a peaceful and workable conclusion—in other words, they exercised ambition to a point and then set it aside in service to America's democratic experiment.

The same can be said of the 1960 presidential election. In terms of popular vote, the race between Republican Richard Nixon and Democrat John F. Kennedy was much closer than 2020. Kennedy won by 112,827 votes out of more than 68.8 million cast. Nixon won 59 percent of the nation's counties while Kennedy carried 38 percent, but as was true then and is true now, concentrations of voters within counties proved decisive. Something else happened with relevance today. Kennedy appeared to have won Nixon's home state of California by roughly 37,000 votes when all precincts were reported. But when all absentee ballots were counted *a week later*, Nixon won by some 36,000 votes. Democrats never questioned this reversal. The Republican National Committee, however, challenged the results in eleven states. That scrutiny led to one reversal. Hawaii was certified for Nixon based on a 141-vote victory. But a recount, conducted in late December, concluded Kennedy won by 115 votes. A Hawaii circuit court ruled Hawaii's electoral votes should be awarded to Kennedy. The certificate awarding the state's three electoral votes to Nixon had already been sent to Congress and the National Archives. On December 30, 1960, the circuit court said another certificate had to be produced, one awarding electoral votes to Kennedy. When Congress convened on January 6, 1961, Nixon, presiding as vice president, was presented with two sets of electors. Knowing of the recount and the circuit court affirmation of the process, Nixon sought and obtained unanimous consent for the awarding of Hawaii's three electoral votes to Kennedy. Despite intense party pressure, Nixon never contested the election.

In 2000, genuine doubts about voter intent and vote counting procedures in Florida produced the longest election challenge in modern history—resolved by the Supreme Court's decision to stop the recount in two Florida counties, thereby preserving George W. Bush's narrow (537 votes out of 5.8 million cast statewide) margin of victory over Vice President Al Gore. Forty-seven cases were filed over the course of thirty-six days of nonstop, televised drama. Barry Richard, a registered Democrat with deep experience in Florida and national election law, was part of Bush's legal team. "Things were very different in 2000," Richard told us. "We didn't have a history of litigation of presidential elections. Nobody was lawyered up. Things are much different now because now the candidates create nation-wide legal structures well before the election. They have lawyers in every state, multiple lawyers in every state." This is an important distinction. As we have noted, Trump and the RNC were well represented, as were state Republican parties and third-party groups sympathetic to Trump, in all manner of 2020 pre-election litigation.

In 2000, Gore tried to win approval for a limited recount in counties where Democrats outnumbered Republicans and questions of voter intent appeared difficult to resolve. This led to examination of hanging chads and dimpled ballots, voting methods long since abandoned, largely because of the 2000 fiasco. Florida secretary of state Kathleen Harris certified Bush's victory. "From there on," Richard told us, "the Gore team was trying to get the courts and ultimately the Florida Supreme Court to overturn that. The Bush team was trying to avoid that. The best that Gore could hope for was that the Florida Supreme Court would order a different delegation, in which case that would have been two delegations going to Washington, where Congress would have to attempt to decide which one would be seated." After the 2000 election, the Senate was tied 50–50 (sound familiar?) and the House was controlled by Republicans. If the House and Senate had split on which delegations to recognize, the decision would have reverted to Florida Republican governor Jeb Bush, younger brother of George W. "So, you can see, the path for Gore was very slim," Richard told us.

On equal protection grounds, the Supreme Court ruled in Bush's favor, arguing on a onetime basis that a limited recount would deny all Florida voters the benefit of a recount, and at that point, a full statewide recount was impossible before the Electoral College deadlines, according to the Court's majority. "There was very little in that case that had much precedent," Richard said. "It was based upon a given set of factual circumstances. They said we are not making any universal rules here." Gore accepted the crushing defeat and appealed for unity.

"First of all, the lesson is when you get to December 14th it's over," Liz Cheney told us. "When the Electoral College meets, it's over. That's the end of it. And the way that Al Gore handled that, you know, I think many people believe his concession speech was one of his finest speeches ever. We (the Vice President-Elect Dick Cheney and family) happened to be at the vice president's residence the day that Al Gore had to go certify the electoral votes. And I remember we walked in and he greeted us and he said, 'I'm wearing a suit because I'm going to go certify your victory as vice president of the United States.' You have to put people in positions of public trust who understand that, fundamentally, your most important obligation is the defense of the constitutional structure, framework, and our institutions. And your oath to the constitution. Every president until Donald Trump understood that."

It is worth noting, especially in the context of doubts about the 2020 election results, that there were six states with certified results of a margin of victory in 2000 smaller than the narrowest 2020 margin (Arizona's 10,457 votes). Those states were: Florida (537), New Mexico (366 votes), Wisconsin (5,708 votes), Iowa (4,144 votes), Oregon (6,765 votes), and New Hampshire (7,211 votes).

Bush won Florida and New Hampshire. Had Gore won New Hampshire's four electoral votes, he would have won the presidency with 270 electoral votes, and Florida, with its confusing ballots and razor-thin margin, wouldn't have mattered to determining the occupant of the White House for the next four years.

THE BITTERNESS AFTER BUSH v. GORE

The Florida recount tested the country and left many Democrats embittered. Not for the first time was a president's legitimacy questioned in America, but the animosity and sense of alienation seemed to sink deeper. Within some Democratic and academic quarters, the bruising experience of 2000 metastasized into never-ending suspicions about election procedures and machinery. This gave rise to unfounded allegations in Ohio in 2004 that Diebold voting machines manufactured votes for Bush, propelling him to a slender second-term victory over John Kerry, who never questioned the results, machines, or procedures in Ohio.

In 2000 and 2004, House Democrats challenged certification of electoral votes. Neither Al Gore nor John Kerry acknowledged these symbolic protests. In 2005, Rep. Stephanie Tubbs Jones of Ohio and California senator Barbara Boxer objected to the certification of Ohio's electoral votes. The Senate defeated the objection 74–1. The House defeated it 267–31. It gained no traction but left a wisp of doubt. In 2017, a handful of House Democrats sought to contest certification of electoral votes. Hillary Clinton never endorsed the protest. No U.S. senator endorsed and in a memorable display of gavel-wielding gusto, Vice President Joe Biden loudly dispatched the objections to parliamentary oblivion. Clinton complained about the election and blamed outside forces, namely Russian bot farmers and FBI Director James Comey, but she never challenged the election process, the counting of the ballots, or the election professionals that oversaw that process.

Rhetoric is one type of sour grapes. Protesting across chambers in Congress is quite another. Whatever corrosive effects resulted from the scattered House Democratic protests in 2001, 2005, and 2017, they cannot be characterized as a coordinated attempt to nullify a certified national election. Republicans seek to treat them as morally equivalent. They are not. As we have learned, attempts to challenge certification of the 2020 election were part of a systematic effort to first delay and then thwart, through intervention of the House of Representatives, the will of the people.

We recount this history as a quick refresher on close and contested elections. It is also a reminder that never before 2020 did a nominee or sitting president question the validity of the system upon which election results were based. In some circumstances, evidence-based challenges were made in various courts—though they, too, were the exception, not the rule. Throughout our history, nominees and presidents upheld the basic principle that elections are fair, well administered, and as verifiable and believable as methods of the day could yield. Similarly, they took care to follow known rules and adhere to the legal and procedural methods of the time. Hotheads complained bitterly, of course. But nominees, those with the most at stake, did not indulge in attacks on the system itself. The political class over decades knew and practiced all manner of gamesmanship and vote-gathering. That was understood and appreciated as hardball politics. Both sides engaged in and marveled at new innovations, angles, and antics. Generally, the sense was all things evened out over time. The system continued and they fought fiercely within that system. Arguments about process existed, when they arose at all, on the margins. Party leaders and nominees refused to undermine democracy itself. Even if their partisans were enraged, nominees took care to modulate passions and tame wild accusations. Failure to do so, they feared, would poison the populace in uncontrollable and assuredly dangerous ways—much as is being done now.

On the cusp of the greatest power known to them, these political figures bowed before that civic altar. Even when it appeared they might have been cheated or deceived, they sought patiently and without rancor to discern the voice of the people, however confusingly it may have been articulated. This was true in 1800, 1824, 1876, and every close election that followed. Until 2020. What jeopardizes democracy now is 2020—not anything that came before. Until 2020, presidential nominees knew and practiced civic faith. They knew that to sow doubt, without evidence, about the validity of elections was to question something deeper. It was to doubt our original purpose and hard-fought improvements since. It was, in essence, to doubt America. Our system has, from the beginning, been built on the idea of mutual consent. At first, our conception of consent was limited to white men with property. But even that was revolutionary for its time. Gradually, we expanded those whose consent was sought and registered. But the idea of mutual consent never died. It can only perish when one part of America denies it to another, when victory is the definition of legitimacy.

HEADS I WIN, TAILS YOU LOSE

As we have seen, those who most ardently question the 2020 election do so convinced the only acceptable outcome is Trump's victory. No other outcome can or will be entertained. In service of this mindset, those who denounce the elections as wholly fraudulent indict, possibly without fully realizing it, their friends, neighbors, and the community at large. "It's really done at the precinct level," Georgia Republican secretary of state Brad Raffensperger told us, discussing the smallest level where the wheels of democracy turn. "And those precinct workers that you meet there, they are the people you see at the grocery store, they are the people in your church groups or out on the ball field with your kids playing Little League. Those are your neighbors and those are the people walking that line of integrity to their job with integrity. Not looking left or right, but just doing their job."

In Pennsylvania's Bucks County, Commissioner Bob Harvie described the tenseness of 2020 for his election workers—many of whom came from other county departments to pitch in. "You had 80 percent voter turnout, lines around the block just to get into the building," Harvie told us. "That was something they had never seen before. So, in light of all that and later, the pressure, just the constant working seven days a week." Preparations in the county began in August. "We didn't finish until January because they were still going through and verifying and auditing to make sure that we got everything right. There were eleven court challenges to the results here. We won all eleven." Harvie, who you may remember taught high school American history for a quarter of a century, furrowed his brow as he thought about the future. "I think if you wanted to destroy democracy, the first thing you do is turn members of that country against each other. And the second thing you do is get people to start doubting the validity of the elections that they vote and, you know, engage in. You do those two things and democracy falls apart."

Let us pose this question: If democracy is based on mutual consent and consent is withheld, can democracy persist? Democracy is not self-replicating. It is participatory and counterintuitive. It sends mixed and vexing signals. You can believe and organize, vote and write letters, knock on doors and speechify among friends and neighbors, you can work your ever-loving heart out and still lose. What's more, you must accept defeat peaceably and watch the victor wield power, even if you fear it will be wielded against your wishes and possibly against your interests. You do this, we do this, in furtherance of the greater good and to keep alive democracy and all it protects, animates, and elevates. This, we humbly observe, is not easy. If it were, democracy would have flourished centuries ago. It did not. We gave it New World relevance and prominence. We undermine it at our permanent peril. And that is what we are talking about—undermining and delegitimizing democracy. We are playing with a fire of unquenchable thirst. One fury will provoke another. The fire will spin savagely and scarcely any sacred instrument of America will be spared.

That is why we must understand what went right in 2020. We must come to know and celebrate the systems and people who shielded democracy from all manner of hazards, viral and otherwise. We must comprehend the beauty and heroism of common Americans who guarded our system, made it work, and produced the best election in history. And we must take stock of the gruesome abuse, trauma, and pain these decent Americans have suffered at the hands of election deniers who grotesquely accuse them of fraud, theft, and treason. We must open our eyes to an American story of heroism, of ordinary people doing extraordinary things under unimaginably difficult circumstances. We must stop stomping on the 2020 election and start elevating it to a place of prominence, maybe even reverence.

TRUST, BUT VERIFY

Again, we are dealing only in verifiable facts here. It is a fact that Joe Biden won, regardless of who anyone personally preferred. It is a fact that Democrats gained a 50–50 U.S. Senate, with Vice President Harris serving as a tie-breaking vote. It is also a fact that Republicans gained seats in the U.S. House, winning virtually every single swing district race, and increased their party's dominance in state legislatures. It is a fact that Election 2020 was a model for all future elections, an achievement worthy of an innovative, energetic, and ingenious people. This is the legacy of 2020—not backwater denialism, violence, and pitiless grievance. Let us come to understand what truly happened and why. Let us come to see the story of the 2020 election as it truly was, not as it has been ceaselessly slandered from afar.

First, the 2020 election was a record-breaker in many ways. It was in unintentional ways the perfect place for some manner of confusion to take root and perhaps to harden into suspicion. Under placid circumstances, national elections are gigantic, cumbersome, multi-layered, decentralized, and dizzying undertakings—hundreds of thousands of polling precincts, tens of millions of ballots, tens of thousands of poll workers, well over 100 million voters, millions of words of voter instructions and guidelines in guidebooks and statute books, not to mention each individual's unique interaction with this widely dispersed, typically underfunded and understaffed civic leviathan.

Election 2020 was vastly more complicated than any election that preceded it in the modern era, almost incomprehensibly so. The COVID pandemic has warped our sense of time so it may be easy to forget but most of Election 2020 was stalked by a deadly virus for which we had no vaccine protection. Well-founded fears about spreading the virus haunted preparations for and implementation of primaries starting in mid-March. To understand elections is to understand they are planned months in advance. In ways the public usually doesn't realize, election officials quietly and meticulously devote months and sometimes nearly a year to design and print ballots and build and maintain a successful election's human and mechanistic infrastructure: voter databases, large county-based processing and tabulating machines, precinct-based voting machines and tabulators, precinct locations, and poll worker recruitment and training. These labors constitute the least glamorous and gruntiest of civic grunt work.

Those who do it usually, almost without question, seek no higher office or greater political glory. They are civil servants in the truest sense of the word. They function to ensure a peaceful, error-free, and trouble-free election. When they do this work well, the election passes without notice, except for outcomes that certify winners and losers, thereby propelling governing to its next phase. There is never

a headline on the Wednesday morning after a successfully administered election that "Election Officials Succeeded!" Many thousands
of Americans are volunteer poll workers and many have done this
work for decades. A good number rise to positions of authority and
supervise, again as volunteers, polling precincts or clusters of precincts. There are elected officials who oversee local elections and
state elections. They are vastly outnumbered by civil servants who do
this thankless and laborious work year-round with the fervent hope
that elections come and go with minimal discord, delay, and doubt.

We have now come to doubt the phrase *public service*. Where election administration is concerned, this is worse than a cynical indul-
gence, it is patently false and destructive. Election administration,
at its best, epitomizes local control, local supervision, local cooperation, and local collaboration. You vote in your neighborhood. You
are assisted by your neighbors. Your neighbors record your vote and
send it along to another group from another neighboring community and on through a chain of neighbors who count and establish
how your city voted. This process is among the least alienating,
most intimate, and most collective experiences of our increasingly
alienated, distant, and atomized lives. Elections ought to remind us
of the title of a wildly popular TV drama: *This Is Us*.

But the fact that those running elections are trustworthy, while
a key element, isn't the only reason that voters should trust our elections. There are also several layers of checks and balances that
ensure that only eligible voters can get registered, and that each can
cast only one ballot, and that secret ballot will be counted, transparently and accurately. The public servants who administer elections
rely upon established procedures to demonstrate to all voters the
value of each individual ballot. There are occasional, episodic incidents of attempted fraud, but thanks to these procedures, they are
almost always detected and prosecuted.

First, voter lists are constantly being checked against other data
to verify accuracy. Thanks to innovations like online voter

registration, and better "motor voter" registration at motor vehicles agencies, when a voter first gets on the voter lists, they do so after personally presenting themselves at their DMV, and presenting documentation indicating their status in the state, and their residence. Online voter registration in most states is checked against the motor vehicles data to confirm it matches. Election officials send regular mail to most voters, and when that mail gets returned as undeliverable, they use that information to update the voter lists.

In the last decade, one of the most important tools for voter list accuracy and integrity has been invented and deployed—the Electronic Registration Information Center, or as it's known, "ERIC." David Becker led the effort to create ERIC while at the Pew Charitable Trusts. ERIC is a sophisticated data center that states choose to join (it is not mandatory), and which the states run (each state sits on the board of directors), and which the states pay to maintain (they split the roughly $1 million annual budget). States in ERIC share data from their voter lists and motor vehicle agencies, using high-level security to protect the integrity of the data. In return, they receive information on when any voter with a record in their state has moved to a different address in their state, moved to another state, or died. In addition, the states have access to data indicating whether their voters might have double-voted in another state during the same election. This information has led to a revolution in election security and integrity.

Since ERIC's inception in 2012, with seven states (led by four Republican election officials and three Democratic election officials), it has grown to over thirty states in 2022, representing around two-thirds of all eligible voters in the United States. These states range from blue Connecticut, Illinois, and Oregon, to red Alabama, South Carolina, and Texas. In less than ten years, ERIC has been responsible for identifying over 25 million voters who had either moved from their address on file or died, enabling those states to update their voter lists consistent with federal law. Over half a million voters who had died since they last voted were identified by ERIC during that time. And while ERIC has confirmed that double-voting is rare, with only a few dozen likely cases of fraud nationwide in a major election, it has helped identify those rarities.

And that's just a sampling of the checks and balances in place before a voter even gets a ballot. When a voter requests a mail ballot, whether online or on paper, voter identity on that request is checked against the voter list to make sure all the information matches. In states where all voters receive a mail ballot (like California, Colorado, Oregon, Utah, and Washington), the regular mail contact gives election officials significant feedback on whether any voters have moved. In every state, regardless of whether a voter has specifically requested a mail ballot or was sent one automatically with other voters in the state, the voter list reflects that they've received a mail ballot, and if they show up to vote in person, protections are in place to ensure they can only cast one ballot. Each voter who receives a mail ballot must either surrender that ballot before receiving an in-person ballot to cast, or is required to cast a provisional ballot, which is held separately and only counted if the voter's mail ballot is canceled or isn't returned.

The counting process is similarly filled with redundancies and transparency to ensure its integrity. Each tabulator has multiple redundant memory devices, and each is checked to make sure they match. Each also usually prints a hard copy of the tallies in each machine, so those also can be checked and double-checked against the other media on which the counts are stored and can be presented and observed by representatives of the parties and the candidates, even at the precinct level. Every place the count is stored, whether on paper or digitally, is checked and double-checked at the precinct, county, and state level, with multiple observers.

And, as demonstrated more fully below, we have more audits confirming the ballot counts than ever before, and that process is also observed fully by representatives of the parties and the candidates.

Our nation has been doing elections for a long time, and we've learned many lessons along the way. We know how to run elections with integrity, and we do that better than we ever have before. We trust our neighbors and fellow citizens, and that trust is verified through rigorous, repetitive, and transparent procedures.

TEST RUNS AND FORESHADOWING— THE 2020 PRIMARIES

Election 2020 tested all these systems and brutally so. Almost everything was thrown into some manner of unpredictability and borderline chaos. Well-laid plans for primaries had to be scrubbed or altered. Seventeen states as well as Puerto Rico and Guam changed the dates of their primaries. Fears of voting in person led to increased interest and demand in voting early or voting by mail. Those changes were made on the fly in many states after primaries were delayed so new procedures could be created.

Historically, poll workers in America have tended to be older Americans who have the time and willingness to log long days at polling precincts. Ask yourself if you can remember the median age of poll workers at your local precinct. Mid-thirties? Mid-forties? Mid-fifties even? Most likely not. Poll workers, in general, are in their late fifties or older. Which age quintile was most susceptible to the worst of COVID-19? Poll workers were withdrawing in droves, understandably choosing their health over (again . . . try to remember the anxious days of March, April, and May in 2020) COVID infection, hospitalization, and possibly death. Election officials had, almost overnight, a new and unexpected problem: how to replace legions of poll workers. That meant setting up recruitment and training drives—all virtually and all under intense time pressures. Thousands upon thousands of Americans who had never worked polling places before stepped bravely into the civic breach. They answered a quiet call of democracy and served. They learned the rules quickly and took up posts in precincts, some of which had to be moved or combined with others due to a shortage of poll workers, budget limitations, or health protocols. All this stressed primary election systems.

In addition, one of the first protective measures we all took in the pandemic was "social distancing." Not knowing more about the virus, how communicable it was, and who might be infected, we needed to find spaces where we could conduct our daily business without being in close proximity with one another. Elections were not immune from this challenge. Many polling places we'd relied upon in the past could not be configured to allow for adequate spacing between citizens. Election officials, often with very little time, had to replace these smaller sites and find larger sites that could accommodate crowds while permitting spacing. Other factors— some political, some legal—created borderline chaos.

Michigan held its primary March 10, the day after the first of three massive economic shocks tied to the pandemic. On March 9, the Dow lost more than 2,000 points, the S&P fell by 7.6 percent, and global oil prices fell 20 percent while Chevron and ExxonMobil lost 15 percent of corporate value. March 9 became known as #BlackMonday and that moniker trended dolefully on Twitter. Looking back, the week was our first window into pandemic disruptions and the Michigan primary was the last big election untouched by COVID contortions. Lockdowns had not yet come. (If you can remember, most of us didn't even know what "lockdown" meant.) President Trump had yet to declare a limited travel ban, Tom Hanks had yet to announce a positive test, and the National Basketball Association had yet to suspend its regular season. All of that would happen the next day, March 11.

In this tense atmosphere, Michigan held its primary with only minor revisions. Democratic turnout was 1,587,679 votes, more than 300,000 voters higher than 2016 (1,205,522) and nearly two-and-a-half times larger than the 2008 turnout of 601,219. Again, the numbers illustrated intense Democratic interest in the presidential contest. The following day, March 11, Biden for the first time canceled events and moved them to virtual encounters. He had been scheduled to attend fundraisers and a rally in Chicago on March 13 and a rally in Miami on March 16. Biden also announced the formation of a special health committee to provide "expert advice regarding steps the campaign should take to minimize health risks for the candidate, staff, and supporters." Trump's Coronavirus Task Force held its first White House briefing on March 16, issuing guidelines limiting gatherings to ten or fewer people and recommending the closure of bars, restaurants, and gyms in areas of high virus transmission. "With several weeks of focused action, we can turn the corner and turn it quickly—a lot of progress has been made," Trump said from the podium at a packed White House Briefing Room. In the meantime, Biden's campaign announced it was "decamping in Philadelphia at headquarters until further notice." Trump had not made adjustments to his campaign travel, though he would eventually.

Arizona held its primary as originally scheduled on March 17, just as the nation was really beginning to shut down. Health protocols were just beginning to be understood and implemented so the primary, in general, proceeded as originally planned. The day before, the Dow Jones Industrial Average, NASDAQ Composite, and S&P 500 fell by 12 to 13 percent with the Dow eclipsing its record losses of March 12 and circuit breakers halting trading for the third time in a week (March 8, 12, and 16). Asia-Pacific and European markets closed March 16, global oil prices fell 10 percent, and the Federal Reserve Bank of New York announced a $500 billion repurchase to buffer losses and increase liquidity. The pandemic had triggered a global economic cataclysm.

But Arizona had a major advantage. Arizona is one of the states that had pioneered easy and secure mail voting, decades ago. This was a reform largely championed by Republicans in the state, who used mail voting to great effect, particularly with older, property-owning voters who were disproportionately predisposed to prefer voting by mail. In recent years, well over 75 percent of all Arizona voters voted by mail in every election, and were very familiar with this method. When the pandemic hit, Arizona's election system was better prepared than most. During the March 17 primary, days after worldwide economic chaos, Arizona Democrats voted in this atmosphere of gloom and uncertainty. Turnout was 536,506 votes, more than 70,000 higher than the comparatively larkish 2016 primary. Again, the Arizona results were a signal of strong Democratic interest and participation, auguring what was to come in November.

In Wisconsin, it was unclear until almost primary day, April 7, whether the vote would be held at all. Democratic governor Tom Evers unilaterally attempted to shift the primary to a universal mail-in election. On April 2, just five days before the primary, a U.S. district court judge refused to postpone the vote but did extend allowable absentee votes postmarked by April 13. Republicans challenged the ruling to the U.S. Supreme Court and on April 6 it overruled and said legal absentee ballots had to be postmarked by April 7, but could be received as late as April 13. In a dizzying prelude to the primary, Evers on April 6 also called a special session of the legislature to delay the primary. The GOP legislature again refused to budge. Evers, again on April 6, then signed an executive order pushing the primary to June 9. The Wisconsin State Supreme Court ruled Evers lacked authority. Evers appealed the U.S. Supreme Court, which ruled against him and ordered he had no authority, absent consent of the legislature, to move the primary date.

Amid all this chaos, legal jousting, and political tussling, the primary was held on April 7. Unsurprisingly, voters were a bit confused but suffered through long lines, last-minute closures of some polling places, and a postal system that struggled to meet a wave of mail-in ballots. Most notably, due to the challenges and changing circumstances, and difficulty finding poll workers and suitable locations,

Milwaukee saw the number of in-person polling places reduced to five, down from their normal number of over 180.

Overall, 1.55 million Wisconsin voters participated. That was 34 percent of eligible voters, higher than the 31 percent primary turnout average over the previous forty years. Democratic turnout was 925,065 votes, a shade below the 2016 turnout of 1,007,600 votes in a primary conducted with no pandemic and no legal dogfights. The high 2020 turnout foreshadowed strong Democratic interest in the general election. As the *Washington Post* observed: "Democrats are so mobilized in the Trump era—either for Democrats or against Trump—that they are showing up in unexpectedly high numbers, even under Wisconsin's difficult pandemic circumstances." It was determined many months later that health and safety protocols worked and the primary was not, as some feared it would become, a super-spreader event.

Pennsylvania held its primary on June 2, having moved it from April 28 to improve access, minimize health risks, and prepare for a surge in early and mail-in voting. In 2019, Pennsylvania's Republican legislature and Democratic governor Tom Wolfe approved a sweeping election reform law that increased the use of early voting, either in-person or via mail-in ballots. This new law was a compromise, led by the Republican majority in the legislature, that wanted to eliminate "straight-ticket" voting that was perceived to give Democrats an advantage to achieve victories up and down the ballot. In exchange, Democrats got something they wanted—no-excuse mail and early balloting, collectively called "vote-by-mail," as those casting a ballot early in person are still considered to be casting a "mail ballot"—for any Pennsylvania voter, something that the commonwealth hadn't before permitted in its over-250-year history.

As a result, every county had to adapt to an expected, but manageable, shift toward early and mail voting. The pandemic accelerated this shift far beyond that which was previously contemplated. In many jurisdictions, the primary brought a tenfold increase in vote-by-mail—sometimes higher. Many townships and counties were simply unprepared and had to resort to hand counting these mail ballots, a time-consuming and laborious process. As in other states, the pandemic required the consolidation of some polling precincts and the moving or closing of others.

Even so, the primary proceeded with only minor glitches. Turnout was 1,595,508 votes, relatively high considering the nominating contest had long since ended. Bernie Sanders had suspended his campaign April 8 and endorsed Joe Biden on April 14. By contrast, the 2016 Pennsylvania Democratic primary turnout was 1,681,427 votes. That contest was held April 26 when the nomination battle between Clinton and Sanders was in full swing. Again, the 2020 Democratic primary turnout indicated sustained party energy and interest in the coming general election. It should have been, if you will pardon us, a sleepy primary. It was not. Democrats acted as if the primary was a warm-up for the general election. Strictly from a turnout perspective, it was.

"Elections in America are very much like an iceberg," Bob Harvie, the commissioner from Bucks County, Pennsylvania, told us. "Americans, you know, see the very top of it. You know, those who chose to vote, they go in, they, you know, they go home, they see the results the next day or that night or whatever. And that's what they see. They don't see all the work that goes on ahead of time. They don't see the months and months of preparation. They don't see the hours and hours of work afterward, all of it done by just, you know, citizens from their community. They're not partisan. It's just everyday people who are just doing what they need to do to make this country run."

Georgia canceled its March 24 presidential primary and moved it first to May 19 and then to June 9. More than 200,000 votes had been cast for the March 24 primary via mail-in ballots before it was officially canceled. Those votes were counted in the June 9 primary. "All of a sudden COVID hits us by the middle of March," Georgia secretary of state Brad Raffensperger told us. "That upset every election worker. How are you going to run an election with COVID? Well, obviously, more voters would want to vote absentee in our system."

Turnout was 1,086,729 votes, the highest ever for a Democratic presidential primary in Georgia. By comparison, turnout in 2016 was 765,366 votes. Georgia witnessed a 42 percent increase in turnout from one Democratic presidential primary to the next. That is a statistical shift of staggering proportions, one that illustrates a surge in interest and population and should have, under any rational set of political calculations, signaled to Republicans statewide that 2020 would be a different election cycle, one where Democratic turnout of unprecedented volume was not only likely but assured. We raise this point because no one who cast doubt on Georgia's general election process raised questions about the conduct of the primary. It's worth noting the primary was marred in some Atlanta precincts by long lines, confusion over polling locations, and inadequate poll worker training. The election in November, by comparison, was conducted much more smoothly, with virtually no lines, despite taking place during the pandemic. In 2020, what was plainly apparent from June 9 forward was sky-high Democratic interest in and energy about the coming general election.

The Big Truth in Georgia was that Republicans missed the obvious signs—not of fraud but of Democratic mobilization. They also disparaged voting by mail, no one more vocally than Trump. "President Trump, what he did is he really discouraged people to vote absentee," Raffensperger said. "When you start creating doubts in the voter's mind, then what do they do? They step out, they step back. At the end of the day, it really hurt his chances." In Georgia and elsewhere, blaming election administrators for political malpractice became a convenient and venal Trumpian dodge.

COVID, GEORGE FLOYD, AND PRE-2020 ANGST

Again, you cannot separate the political atmosphere around the pandemic and primary elections from the larger conversation about election administration during the general election. The pandemic deepened fault lines about the role of government, individual liberties, the balance of commerce, and public safety. It even swerved into silly areas such as whether the U.S. Constitution prevented mask mandates. We understand a silly fault line is still a fault line and in 2020 each pandemic-fueled fault line can be seen in retrospect as related to or aligned with skepticism, hostility, or stubborn opposition to—fill in the blank: government leaders, health experts, scientists, fact-checkers, judges, and anyone else associated with discussion or implementation of restrictions perceived to be pointless, annoying, quasi-legal, or all three.

We also understand that 2020 was not defined only by COVID. The murder of George Floyd in Minneapolis provoked another national trauma that, somewhat like the COVID pandemic, took many forms and affected millions of Americans differently. Lines were drawn there, too, about what is or isn't a legal, lawful protest and what is rioting or looting. Some Americans saw large peaceful protests across the land occasionally marred by violence or looting. Other Americans saw protests setting the stage for lawlessness or attempting to disguise or apologize for it. Long before November's general election, America was at a boil with nasty debates over what the pandemic meant to civil liberties, what George Floyd meant to the idea of justice, what America meant as an experiment.

No one can credibly separate the tumult of the pandemic and George Floyd from the psychic forces roiling beneath the 2020 election. America was in a place of disrupted pain, a place of economic, social, and workaday uncertainty. It was a time of unmooring and disorientation. Voters saw the election as something bigger, something that would or could provide a response to troubled times. The election took on galactic importance. The stakes felt primal, running deep into our marrow—much higher than the by-now cliched rhetoric of "the most important election of our lives." In many quarters on both sides of the political spectrum, it felt possibly like the most important election since the Great Depression, since before the Civil War, the most important, possibly, ever.

We have all lived painfully for nearly two years in the reality of a country that seems incapable of understanding itself, talking to itself, or comprehending antecedents of its own acidic alienation. We keep pointing to statistics, procedures, evidence, laws, and reason when we discuss Election 2020. They fall short, woefully short. And they don't fall short only at the feet of fanatics. They fail before otherwise reasonable people who just sense in their gut that something went wrong. That they don't know what it is may be their own fault, but we try to understand them. Many of these people have donated to Trump or others who have vowed to fight "election fraud," but have done nothing more than pocket their money and send more solicitation emails. Don't believe us, believe one of America's wealthiest election deniers, Patrick Byrne, former CEO of Overtsock.com. Byrne has spent millions of his own money fighting to overturn the 2020 election. He wrote a book about it. In it, he tells Americans who donated to Trump's election fraud efforts they have been fleeced.

And yet, those who doubt the election result and may have even been, in Byrne's words, fleeced in the process nevertheless adhere to the notion that the election was deeply flawed. These voters, many of them Trump loyalists of varying degrees of intensity, will have much to say about America's future. We do not judge or presume that most of them are less than decent, law-abiding, patriotic Americans. Their rights are no less precious than ours. The Big Truth is we must solve the question of what 2020 was together or we will turn even more aggressively against one another. Elections are foundational. They are, as we have said, a civic altar.

THE 2020 ELECTION WAS
DIFFERENT, BUT NOT THAT DIFFERENT

Let us start with things about 2020 that could look unusual or could provoke curiosity.

First, the 2020 election had blazingly high turnout. Democratic primaries offered signs of this. Even so, turnout was off the charts. This is not suspicious. But it is unusual. Let's look at the numbers. The total number of votes cast in the 2020 general election was 159,738,337. It was the largest number of votes cast in any election in American history and constituted the largest voter turnout in any national election (by percentage of voting eligible population, also known as VEP) since before 1900. And let us hasten to remember, in 1900, many women and Black men could not vote. In other words, it was the highest turnout ever seen, by every measure, since the United States instituted universal suffrage of adult citizens.

Midterm elections lack the magnetism of a presidential contest and therefore produce lower turnout—but the 2018 midterm (which we will get to in a minute) has special relevance to 2020. But first, a primer on recent midterm election turnout. The historic 1994 midterm, where Republicans won control of the House of Representatives for the first time in forty years, had a turnout of 41 percent of the VEP. The 2010 midterm that saw Republicans regain control of the House after losing it in 2006 (with a gain of a historic sixty-three seats) also produced a turnout of 41 percent. The next midterm in 2014, where Republicans regained control of the U.S. Senate, registered 37 percent. Here is the interesting part about 2018. It produced the highest modern-era turnout for a midterm election—50 percent of the VEP cast ballots and Democrats regained control of the House. At that time, no one, not even Trump, questioned turnout in 2018 or alleged fraud—though it was a statistically significant increase over previous midterm elections.

SOME PEOPLE DIDN'T VOTE
FOR ANY PRESIDENTIAL CANDIDATE

It is normal for there to be a slight "undervote" in the presidential race. Some people in every election choose not to vote in every race, and while it's usually rare in a presidential election to opt out of voting for president, it happens, to a small degree. But in 2020, an unusually high number of Americans chose not to vote for anyone for president. More than 1 million Americans—1,330,433—despite all the underlying interest and white-hot coverage, bailed out on the presidential question. That's one out of every 120 ballots nationwide where the voter chose not to vote for president.

This may have been decisive in two battleground states. Biden's margin of victory in Arizona was 10,457. In Arizona, 33,531 voters did not cast a vote in the presidential contest. In Georgia, Biden's margin of victory was 11,779. In Georgia, 23,199 voters did not cast a vote in the presidential contest. If Trump had captured a third of the non-vote in Arizona and half of it in Georgia, he would have won both states. While the totals of non-presidential votes in Pennsylvania, Nevada, Michigan, and Wisconsin were smaller than Biden's margin of victory, some Republicans believe it is possible Trump could have won two states (Arizona and Georgia) with more persuasion, more outreach. "We had twenty-three thousand Georgians who skipped the presidential ballot," Georgia Republican secretary of state Brad Raffensperger, a veteran of numerous elections, told us. "And yet they voted down ballot, all of their races, and then the Republican congressional races. Republican congressmen [in Georgia] actually got thirty-three thousand more votes than President Trump. I've been down ballot in every election. You never got as many votes as your governor or someone higher up on the ballot. It was just a situation that doesn't happen normally."

THE ELECTION LOOKED CLOSE. WAS IT?

The election seemed somewhat close to some. For ardent Trump supporters it may have looked unsettlingly close. But somewhat close is not close and should not be cause for concern or delegitimization of an election.

At a couple of levels, the election was a wipeout. Biden collected, officially, 81,283,098 votes to Trump's 74,222,958, a margin of 7,060,140 votes and a percentage split of 51.3 percent to 46.8 percent. That's not close.

But, as we all know, presidential elections are not decided by the popular vote (see Hillary Clinton, Al Gore, Grover Cleveland, Samuel Tilden, and Andrew Jackson). We elect presidents via the Electoral College and the votes assigned to each state based upon its representation in the U.S. House and U.S. Senate. As we all know, the modern threshold is 270 electoral votes, by whatever combination can be achieved. A convenient way to think about a presidential election in terms of the Electoral College is the World Series in terms of runs scored. The winner of the World Series is not the team that scores the most runs across the games played. Rather, it is the team that wins the most individual games by whatever run total is required in each game. The same holds true for presidential elections within the Electoral College. What matters is the game played, if you will, in all contested states and the District of Columbia.

With that as a background, let us peer into the closeness of the 2020 election from an electoral vote perspective. Biden won three states by a combined 42,921 votes. They were Arizona (Biden margin 10,457), Georgia (Biden margin 11,779), and Wisconsin (Biden margin 20,682). If Trump had won those three states—meaning a shift of less than 43,000 votes cast across a sea of some 158 million cast—the electoral vote total would have been 269 for Biden and 269 for Trump. Under rules established by the Constitution and consistent with previous elections in which an Electoral College majority was not obtained, a contingent election would have been held in the House of Representatives. In such an election, the majority within each state delegation determines for whom to cast that state's one allocated vote. Since more states in the new House of Representatives sworn in following the 2020 election were controlled by Republicans, Trump would have likely been elected to a second term. Moreover, if Trump had won the single electoral vote in Nebraska's Second Congressional District (a contest he lost by 22,091 votes), he would have won the presidency outright had he also won Arizona, Georgia, and Wisconsin—the tally being 270 to 268. For Trump supporters, that looked tantalizingly close. The sense of so-close-you-can-taste-it victory was intensified by the expectation, set in motion by polling data throughout October, that Biden was poised for some manner of popular vote/Electoral College rout. Trump defied expectations again!

To acknowledge the election results in Arizona, Georgia, and Wisconsin were close is not the same as saying they were worryingly close or so close that if recounts were held (which in many cases they were) results would have been any different. Here is what we mean. According to the election data group Fair Vote, between 2000 and 2019 there were 5,778 statewide general elections. In thirty-one of those elections recounts were conducted, for a recount percentage of 0.54 percent. Of those thirty-one recounts, sixteen were deemed to have been consequential, meaning the margin of victory was 0.15 percent or less. Of those sixteen consequential recounts (again out of 5,778 statewide general elections) only three were reversed. Those three were the 2008 U.S. race between Minnesota Republican senator Norm Coleman and eventual winner Democrat Al Franken; the Vermont state auditor race in 2006; and the Washington governor's race in 2004. In the Minnesota race, the vote swing was 440; in Vermont it was 349; and in Washington it was 390. Margins of victory in Georgia, Arizona, and Wisconsin were nowhere near this close—not by any statistical or historical measure. This is a testament to the increased reliability of our election systems. In the world of elections and recounts, a margin of over 10,000 votes is essentially a landslide.

These were certainly not numbers familiar to Trump supporters on Election Night. Equally alarming for them, possibly, was the way early returns played out—even though media coverage before the election consistently preached patience and highlighted the possibility of an early Trump lead built on in-person voting that might fade as mail-in ballots in some states were counted. Whether Trump supporters heeded or even heard those advisories is unclear. What was evident to Trump supporters on Election Night was that the president appeared to be out-performing polling data and racking up impressive wins, chiefly in Florida, Ohio, and Iowa. To acknowledge the sense of surprise among Trump supporters when election results began to stall and then turn against him is not to excuse Trump's indefensible declaration early on November 4 that he won and the election had been stolen. We excuse none of the baseless, incendiary, and purposefully inciteful language Trump used up to and after the January 6 riot. We simply acknowledge how this might have all looked in living rooms across the country. For those households deeply devoted to Trump where his repeated fantasies about a rigged or stolen election—one hopelessly tainted by mail-in ballots—were not only accepted but embraced as gospel truth, the night may have been confirmation something unjust was afoot.

In truth, what was afoot—as many in Trump's inner circle confided in the election's aftermath—was poor voter mobilization in key states, misspent campaign resources, and misguided overconfidence. What was also afoot was precisely what had been predicted over and over—Trump voters cast a higher percentage of ballots on Election Day and those ballots were counted first, showing an early Trump surge. Mail-in ballots were counted later, and in key states like Michigan, Pennsylvania, and Wisconsin this was because Republicans demanded it—thereby making it appear Biden's ability to catch up and pass Trump was somehow occurring *after* the election. This was a misunderstanding, one Trump maliciously manipulated. No fraud. No theft. No rigging.

The 2020 election was the widest margin of any election in the twenty-first century where Barack Obama was not a candidate. In 2000, George W. Bush won the election, despite losing the popular vote, by a margin of only 537 votes in one state—Florida—meaning that if less than 300 votes had switched, Al Gore would have become president. In 2004, Bush won reelection by only one state in the electoral college—Ohio, by less than 120,000 votes. If only 60,000 voters in that one state had voted for John Kerry instead, he would have been president. In 2016, we all recall Trump lost the popular vote by nearly 3 million votes and won the three decisive states in the Electoral College—Michigan, Pennsylvania, and Wisconsin—by a combined total of less than 78,000 votes.

The 2020 election, in contrast, had the widest popular vote margin of those four elections, and it was the only election of the non-Obama elections in this century that was decided by a margin of more than one state in the Electoral College, where the margins in all the states exceeded 10,000 votes, and where the winner also prevailed in the popular vote.

SUBURBS, EXURBS, AND THE DENSITY DYNAMIC

Something really important is happening in American politics. Suburbs are changing demographically. That is changing voting patterns and, naturally, producing results that don't fit previous patterns. While Trump and his allies erroneously claimed voter fraud in major cities like Detroit, Milwaukee, and Philadelphia, he ignored one very inconvenient fact. He actually reduced his margin of defeat in those cities, compared to 2016. In other words, even with the hysterics around mail voting, drop boxes, and minority voters, Trump exceeded expectations in many large urban areas.

But cities are not where Election 2020 was decided. Biden grew his vote in rural areas compared to Clinton, and Trump grew his vote in cities compared to 2016. According to an analysis of Census data by journalist Reid Wilson, Biden won 91 of America's 100 most populous counties. Trump won 95 of 100 of the nation's least-populated counties. The key could be found in suburbs and exurbs. Cities didn't propel Biden to victory. In state after state, shifts in suburban and exurban patterns proved decisive. These trends were visible in states Trump won and states he lost. Trump gained some 375,000 new votes in Los Angeles County. He gained almost 200,000 in Florida's Miami-Dade County (home of Miami) and more than 100,000 in Harris County (home of Houston). Trump also made sizable gains among Hispanic voters in Texas's Rio Grande Valley, a shift that allowed him to win Texas more comfortably than pre-election polls predicted. In fact, twenty-one of the counties where Trump's vote increased the most over 2016 were in Texas.

Those patterns were present in all the hotly contested states. Biden's dominant pattern was found in suburbs close to urban centers and counties on the perimeter of those suburbs—which demographers classify as exurbs. Trump won the suburbs in 2016. He lost them in 2020. This continued a trend first apparent in the 2018 midterms, when Democrats outperformed Republicans. A Bloomberg City Lab analysis highlighted this effect in Georgia. It found that nine of ten counties that "swung the most towards Biden were either an exurb or a middle suburb." It cited Forsyth County. "A fast-growing area on the northern edge of the Atlanta metro, more or less equidistant to downtown and the more rural communities of the Blue Ridge Mountains, the county is solidly red. But Republicans' margin of victory narrowed by 14 percentage points between 2016 and 2020." As early as 2012, technologist and historian Dave Troy identified the linkage between population density and predictive political outcomes, pegging the inflection point from Republican to

Democratic leanings at 800 people per square mile. In 2020, analysis suggested that demarcation line may have shifted to 700 people per square mile. Most red counties have densities fewer than 500 per square mile. Most purple counties have densities between 400 and 1,500 per square mile. Blue counties have densities above 1,500 per square mile. This was true in Georgia and elsewhere.

Pennsylvania—Biden out-performed Clinton by more than 100,000 votes in the Philadelphia suburban counties of Montgomery, Chester, Delaware, and Bucks.

Michigan—Biden out-performed Clinton by 31,000 votes in Kent County and by more than 94,000 votes in Oakland, Washtenaw, Macomb, and Ottawa Counties.

Wisconsin—Biden won more than 35,000 votes than Clinton in Dane County, home of Madison, and out-performed her by 7,500 in heavily Republican Waukesha County.

What matters in the context of 2020 is that patterns of voting noticed in one state were observable in other states—whether it was hotly contested or not. As we have noted, turnout was higher in battleground states. But the underlying patterns were observed across the country in terms of suburbs and exurbs, with density strongly predictive of partisan vote patterns.

EARLY AND MAIL VOTING: THE REALITY

What also possibly looked amiss to Republican voters in general, and Trump loyalists specifically, was the role early voting and mail-in voting played in the 2020 result. In some states, this was a genuinely new dynamic. Change is always disconcerting, and in the frenzied atmosphere of the 2020 election, it became explosive. Voters were simply not accustomed to so many changes in so many different places. And let's address one aspect of this up front. In the aftermath of the 2020 election, there have been calls in some corners for a return to voting and counting on Election Day, meaning most people vote on Election Day and all votes are counted that day or early next morning and that's it. This is gauzy nostalgia for a time that has never existed. We have for generations had some form of early or absentee voting. We have spent days counting votes after presidential elections. Yes, elections have been called by networks or wire services and candidates have conceded, but the actual counting and certification of final, determinative results— the ones that codify the allocation of electoral votes—has always taken days if not weeks. This was true in 2016 when Trump won. In fact, results were slowed somewhat when Green Party candidate Jill Stein sought, as was her legal right, recounts in Wisconsin, Pennsylvania, and Michigan. (Clinton had already conceded and did not endorse these efforts, which yielded recounts that confirmed Trump's victory.) Let's dispense with the mythology that America has always voted and counted on Election Day. That has never, ever been true.

But there was a big surge in casting a ballot by mail or in-person via early voting. Just because it was early or by mail doesn't mean it was suspect or devious. And millions of Americans embraced early voting in 2020, either in person or through mail-in ballots. This was somewhat of an increase, but in recent decades we have seen an ever-increasing number of ballots cast early, or by mail. This process comes with safeguards and redundancies to track and confirm ballots—in fact, there were electronic means for voters to confirm receipt of their ballots that were inconceivable even a decade ago. The level of visibility and verifiability through electronic tracking and paper ballot confirmation was without precedent in our history. Early voting in person was unquestionably as secure as it ever has been. Voting by mail was more trackable and verifiable than ever as well. And good thing because we, as a nation, voted early as never before, likely due to the pandemic.

According to the United States Election Project, over 100 million voters cast their ballots via mail or early in-person voting, compared to over 57 million in 2016 (then a historic high that Trump, as the victor, never questioned). The surge likely reflected issues of safety and convenience. We should stress, a ballot is a ballot whether it is filled out in person on Election Day, in person days before, or at home and postmarked on or before Election Day (as is required to be legally counted). There is nothing about the timing of a vote cast that increases or decreases its reliability. Each is equally reliable and valid. So, yes, voting early was way up in 2020. Overall, 43 percent of all ballots cast in 2020 were sent by mail and 26 percent were cast in person before Election Day (early in-person). In 2016, by comparison, 21 percent of votes were cast by mail and 19 percent early in-person.

More voting by mail and voting early in-person benefited both Biden and Trump. Yes, Biden won more votes among those who chose to vote early. But Trump also received millions of early votes through the mail and early in-person turnout. How else did his popular vote total increase by more than 11 million over 2016, a historic outcome for a sitting president? Trump could not have come as close as he did and shock the pundits and pollsters without the thrust of millions of early votes. It cannot be that those votes are legitimate and the early votes for Biden are not. It stands to reason that the methods to gather, process, count, and report early vote totals for Trump were as valid, verifiable, and sound as those for Biden (never mind all the confirming, reconfirming, and double reconfirming recounts conducted in places like Georgia and Arizona).

To label mail-in votes inherently defective is also to declare Trump's vote total invalid or suspect. This neither he nor his ardent supporters do. Only Biden early votes can draw suspicion. This makes no practical, mathematical, or procedural sense. Again, we go back to Trump's victory in 2016, the 2018 midterm, and the 2020 primaries—all places to uncover or highlight significant defects. None existed in those elections and none existed in the 2020 general election. It is illogical and dishonest to assert that the same system and methods that yielded those non-contested results suddenly spewed forth a corrupted, skewed, rigged, or stolen election. Here's something else to consider. Voters aged sixty-five and older, a key Trump constituency, cast mail ballots at a higher rate than voters younger than sixty-five.

That mail-in ballots skewed more heavily to Biden is due to one reason and one reason only—that Trump himself caused his supporters, and his supporters only, to doubt this secure, effective method of voting. His voters, misled by his rhetoric, opted out of this key voting option, defying earlier trends, which showed mail voting to slightly benefit Republican candidates in past elections.

5

MISDIRECTION

NO one likes to be taken for a fool and no one likes to be told they've been taken for a fool. There are those who peddle The Big Lie who make money from it. There are those who use it to gain a momentary political advantage. Gaining wealth or power from subverting democracy and demeaning the Constitution is awful. Calling it patriotism bastardizes the word and insults those who truly love American democracy.

These grifters occupy a narrow albeit influential range of the debate about the 2020 election. Many of them have written books on this subject. At various times, we will quote from them—not because we believe their varied arguments against Election 2020 are valid, but because none of the books actually agree on what happened. This strikes us as a kind of proof of concept of a con. Agreeing on what the con is makes it harder for many people to profit from it. By calling the con many things, lots of people can get in on the hustle. One book, by Patrick Byrne, contends "industrial scale vote flipping" stole the election from Trump. Another book, by Peter Navarro, says, flatly, that no vote flipping happened at all, but that the real culprit was "ballot box stuffing." Another book, by Mollie Hemingway, dismisses both of those so-called explanations while contending the election wasn't stolen so much as it was "rigged" by hostile media coverage, social media censorship, and Democrats who bent the rules. This tapestry of conflicting accounts conveniently keeps The Big Lie alive and tries to hide the fact that money has been made and appears certain to be made as long as that lie persists.

We therefore have genuine concern and compassion for the millions of Americans over whom purveyors of these contradictory and self-canceling claims of a fraudulent election hold sway. Honestly, if the election had been stolen, don't you think there would be a single explanation? There are not multiple ways a bank is robbed. There are not multiple ways someone is murdered or burglarized. There is one crime with one trail of evidence. That there is in the space of purported 2020 election fraud so many conflicting claims demonstrates that fiction is afoot, and for those beguiled by it we offer another explanation, one based on verifiable information, the truth. We believe most of the millions of Americans who express doubt about the 2020 election love America, cherish democracy, and believe in the rule of law. We don't believe they have ill intent or seditious motives. They may feel alienated from cultural and demographic trends, they may have felt at some level left behind by the digital economy, and they may feel a kinship with Trump and fellow Trump supporters that, all other things being equal, makes them wonder what actually happened.

It is to this wide and important swath of America we hope to speak. We especially seek to reach those who have donated money on behalf of "election integrity" or Stop the Steal appeals. First, we note that money has not been used for either purpose by Trump. Hundreds of millions of dollars were raised in November and December of 2020. Patrick Byrne, a Trump supporter and the former CEO of Overstock.com, claims in his book *The Deep Rig* that money raised to "Stop the Steal" was never used for that purpose.

All available public financial records verify this fact. Let us quote
Byrne:

> So I say to whatever Republican loyalists around the country
> coughed up those hundreds of millions, in donations of $10 and
> $20 . . . You were fleeced. It was a big joke: rank-and-file Republi-
> cans gave a pot of hundreds of millions of dollars to Republican
> Bigshots to unscramble what had happened on November 3, and
> from where I sat, nothing went to any activity related to doing so.
> It was all being stashed by people at the top, licking their chops.

Byrne described that fundraising haul as a swindle. "They were
sitting on the money," Byrne also wrote. "I never saw a penny of it
being spent in any way to 'stop the steal.'" Records show Trump
spent none of the funds he raised after Election 2020 to pay for
recounts—as was his right. The national Republican Party and state
parties footed most of the bills for post-election litigation. Trump
spent little of what he raised. Other Republicans, seeing the same
gold mine, began to mimic this tactic.

One of the great ironies of this tactic is that Trump effectively got
his fellow Republicans, and the party as a whole, to reject the integrity of an election in which they exceeded expectations in nearly
every single close race, with the exception of the presidency. Republicans won virtually every single congressional race rated a "toss-up"
by the *Cook Political Report*, and expanded their margins in state legislatures. In fact, reviews of the ballots in key swing states like Georgia and Arizona confirmed that many voters voted Republican on the
entire ballot—with the exception of the presidential race, where
many voted for Biden or left the race blank. This is a truth that many
suspected, but that Trump and his inner circle refused to allow
themselves to believe—that Trump was actually the weakest Republican candidate on the ballot, underperforming other Republicans.

Perhaps Trump knew that he had lost, and that his fantasy that Democrats had rigged an election against him while almost handing the House of Representatives to Republicans made absolutely zero sense. He did not pursue efforts to confirm and challenge the results in swing states. Most obviously, as discussed below, the Trump campaign had an absolute legal right to full, statewide recounts in the states of Michigan, Pennsylvania, and Wisconsin—all states Trump falsely claimed he won but for fraud, even though Wisconsin was decided by roughly the same margin as 2016, Pennsylvania was decided by a margin roughly twice that of Trump's win in 2016 (over 84,000 votes), and Michigan was decided by a margin well over ten times that of Trump's win in 2016 (over 154,000 votes). He would have had to pay for these statewide recounts—roughly $20 million for all three, which would have occurred prior to the meeting of the Electoral College in December 2020. Candidate Jill Stein did the same in 2016, and Trump had raised hundreds of millions of dollars in the aftermath of the election, specifically for the fights against the alleged fraud. But when he had the opportunity to confirm the results, from recounts of all the paper ballots in these three states, which would have revealed any problems with the vote-counting machines, he chose to keep those deposits in the bank.

"Across the board really hardworking, good, honorable Americans have been totally betrayed to and lied to by him," Liz Cheney told us. "And you see it in the fundraising, by the way. All this stuff of where he's asking people to continue to contribute money, you know, based upon a total fantasy. His lies represent such an existential threat that, you know, that makes it incumbent upon those of us who are Republicans to say, 'No. What he's saying is not true.'"

Holding on to these millions makes this look like a very long con. Every long con relies upon a promise—"LOSE WEIGHT" or "GET RICH QUICK"—followed by an essential misdirection. In a simple con, the misdirection might be a thin person who was formerly overweight, or someone who was formerly struggling financially living large. A simple con of this sort might get its target to buy a product they wouldn't otherwise purchase. But a longer, more complex grift requires more comprehensive misdirection, enabling it to keep the mark on the hook longer, constantly sending money.

Think of the corrupt religious revivalist, who constantly promises the end of the world, and even predicts a date certain for the event, all the while raising money from his believers, so they can attain salvation. When the world continues to exist after his predictions, he inevitably finds that he misinterpreted the communication from God, and gives his followers a new date, in the future, of course, all the while continuing to fleece his flock.

Like the promises of Armageddon, The Big Lie required constant efforts at misdirection. But Trump was experienced with such misdirection, having elevated it to an art form over many decades. His identity has been defined by the outward appearance of wealth. And whenever possible, he has exaggerated and even lied about that wealth, to bolster his image. Every time the grifters have had an opportunity to prove the alleged fraud, and every time they failed, they promised that another "big reveal" was just around the corner. Seemingly without end, MyPillow CEO Mike Lindell has another "most important class action lawsuit in world history" to heckle an election repeatedly scrutinized, verified, and certified.

Trump is a master at taking a small suspicion and building it into a grand conspiracy. He is also skilled at using simple imagery to sell big ideas or gaudy lies. "There is something deeply American about him," Raskin said of Trump. "In that there is one American archetype of someone who is an absolute fraud and charlatan who is able to pull the wool over the eyes of millions and millions of people. We cannot deny that figures like that have arisen periodically in our history. There is no doubt there is a cultural niche for him. He also has a sense of irresponsibility and abandon that leads him to roll roughshod over every conceivable norm and tradition of the country. He's brazen. He's ungovernable." Trump's pattern matters. Let us go back a few years, before Trump was president. For years, he was one of the primary purveyors of the "birther" lie, asserting without evidence that President Obama was born outside of the United States, in Kenya, and therefore was not eligible to be president. He repeatedly promised evidence to support his allegations, even on particular dates, and each time failed to deliver any such evidence. These are the basic tools of the con.

Trump's con didn't begin after the 2020 election, or even during the most recent campaign. In early August 2016, as Russia was actually attempting to interfere with our elections and sow distrust about the integrity of our voting process, Trump said the 2016 election would be "rigged," either intentionally or inadvertently. This aided our adversaries by injecting doubts into American democratic processes. After he unexpectedly won the election by legitimately winning a majority of votes in states that comprise a majority of the Electoral College, he continued to fan the flames of doubt. Having been defeated in the popular vote by 2.9 million votes (the largest popular vote defeat for a presidential winner in history) and even before the certified electoral votes were delivered to the National Archives, Trump began to rail against fraud in states like California. There was no evidence of these claims, recklessly made even before some states certified official vote counts.

Trump went so far as to suggest that a report put out by the Pew Charitable Trusts was evidence for his claim. The report he apparently cited—"Inaccurate, Costly, and Inefficient"—was a comprehensive assessment of the state of the voter lists in the nation, written five years earlier, which demonstrated that it was difficult for voter lists to keep up with the mobility of American voters, resulting in voter records with bad addresses, but made no findings with regard to voter fraud at all.

That Pew Charitable Trusts report, cited by Trump, was actually authored by David Becker, an expert on the issue of voter list accuracy and the rarity of voter fraud. But Trump continued to spread falsehoods about the popular vote and fraud, even after he duly took office as the winner of the electoral vote, earning him four "Pinocchios" from the *Washington Post*.

In fact, voter fraud—the act of someone casting a ballot that shouldn't be cast, as in the case of an ineligible person voting, or someone voting more than once—is exceedingly rare. Academics, right-leaning institutions like the Heritage Foundation, Republican election officials, and the Department of Justice during the George W. Bush administration have failed to find evidence of widespread voter fraud. Voter fraud is rare, and not a serious threat to American elections because in those rare instances when it occurs, it is detected and prosecuted.

But fact-based refutations did not stop Trump's efforts. Instead, he created a Presidential Advisory Commission on Election Integrity, led by Vice President Mike Pence and one of the most noted purveyors of the myth of widespread voter fraud, former Kansas secretary of state Kris Kobach. Even though Trump empowered and funded the commission, the highly incentivized Trump allies who comprised it had to disband the commission after a few months, having found zero evidence suggesting any significant fraud, generating only controversy and embarrassment.

The next few years were filled with attempts at misdirection and controversy in other areas, but as we entered the end of 2019 and the beginning of the 2020 presidential campaign, the efforts at electoral misdirection began to take center stage again, particularly after the COVID-19 pandemic began to wreak havoc on the election process, during the primaries.

In particular, as it became clear that the pandemic would require social distancing and other efforts to minimize the spread of the virus, many suggested that voting by mail would be the solution to all our electoral problems. While that was likely an overstatement, mail balloting would prove to be an important part of the way voters and election officials navigated the voting process during a global pandemic, and was a key element in how election officials success-fully managed record turnout in 2020. So, of course, mail voting became the first of many targets for Trump's misdirection machine as the campaign between Trump and Biden began to take shape.

SECURE MAIL VOTING

Mail voting has been a part of American elections since at least the Civil War. Millions of our military and overseas citizens have relied upon it to make their voices heard, and their right to use the postal service to deliver their ballots is protected by federal law. States have allowed absent voters to cast their ballots by mail, and for decades, states representing the entire political spectrum have allowed any eligible voter to vote by mail ballot.

Mail voting has been widespread and popular for many years. At least thirty-four states and the District of Columbia allowed any voter to cast a ballot by mail in 2020, and these states range from those controlled by Democrats, like California and Washington, to those controlled by Republicans, like Arizona and Utah. In the 2016 election, nationally, about one in four ballots was cast by mail. Twenty-one states saw more than 20 percent of their voters return mail ballots. Of those twenty-one states, fourteen were won by President Trump in 2016, including Florida, Iowa, Michigan, and Ohio. In that election and ones before it, Republicans liked vote-by-mail, often preferred it, and felt it was entirely secure. Trump certainly didn't raise concerns about overwhelmingly high mail ballot returns in states he won in 2016, such as Arizona (73 percent mail ballots), Iowa (41 percent), Montana (64 percent), or Utah (69 percent). Of the thirty-five electoral jurisdictions that allowed widespread mail voting heading into the 2020 election, twenty of them had cast their electoral votes for President Trump in 2016.

In fact, prior to Trump's poisoning of his voters' minds with regard to this particular method of voting, the evidence is pretty clear that mail voting was much more widely used by voters who were older, who owned property, and who were more likely to be white than the overall population. In other words, the voters who tended to vote by mail were disproportionately inclined to favor Republican candidates. States like Arizona, Florida, and Utah had moved toward more mail voting, led by Republicans who likely believed more mail voting would benefit their party. Entire Republican campaigns were built around encouraging their voters to cast their ballots by mail, as early as possible, enabling them to concentrate their get-out-the-vote efforts on the remaining few Republican voters who preferred to vote in person.

And it's clear why Republicans believed in and relied on the security of mail voting prior to Trump's delegitimization of the process. There are multiple checks on ballot security inherent in mail voting. In most states, including Florida, Georgia, Ohio, and Wisconsin, a voter must specifically request a mail ballot. That request is vetted by election officials against the voter registration database, to confirm the voter's eligibility, and that the information received on the mail ballot request matches the information on file. Even in the minority of states where ballots were sent to all active registered voters, including Colorado, Oregon, Utah, and Washington, the voter lists are constantly checked against the postal service, motor vehicle department records, and other data to ensure that the information is accurate.

Mail ballots are coded on the exterior envelopes to enable election officials to verify that only official ballots are used, and that they know exactly who has received a mail ballot. When a mail ballot is sent out, the voter's record in the elections database is updated to indicate that they've been sent a mail ballot. Thus, a voter who has received a mail ballot will be flagged if they attempt to vote in person, requiring them to either surrender their mail ballot or cast a provisional ballot, which will only be counted if their mail ballot is not returned by the deadline.

Once a mail ballot is received by election officials, it undergoes additional verification, usually by matching the signature on the outer envelope to the signature on file in the voter's record. Sometimes, additional verification like a Social Security or driver's license number, or a copy of an ID, is required. Only after all of these verification measures have been met is a mail ballot processed for tabulation. Georgia famously checked the 2020 mail ballots in the state multiple times, using staff trained by the Georgia Bureau of Investigation, and audited the results of those signature matches, confirming the security of the process.

There are additional, broader verification benefits of mail voting. By spreading out voting over more days, and via more methods (including in-person early voting), it increases the chance that a malfunction, a cyberattack (such as on the voter database, changing voter information), or a wide-scale attempt at voter fraud (such as a double-voting scheme) will be detected, and detected early. If voter files had been tampered with, or if someone was attempting to vote multiple mail ballots, early and mail voting serve as an early warning system, enabling election officials to detect and fix the problem before it infects the electoral process.

The move to mail voting was likely to benefit Republican voters (because they were more familiar with it) while enhancing election security and creating more options for voters understandably worried about health and safety during the 2020 election. Nevertheless, despite the potential for campaign advantage, even before the major candidates were formally nominated at their conventions, Trump and his allies began to spread disinformation about the security of mail voting. As early as the primaries, Trump tried to misdirect American voters, falsely insinuating that mail voting was somehow new and nefarious, and dissuading them from one of their main choices on how to vote.

The problem with this strategy? Only his supporters believed him. For the majority of Americans who opposed Trump, and knew that mail voting was secure and convenient, and wanted to ensure that they could vote in safety during a pandemic, their inclination to vote by mail was only increased. Indeed, many voters might have first decided to cast their ballot by mail precisely *because* Trump seemed to hate that method of voting so much. And as all sophisticated, modern campaigns will tell you, the more of "your" voters who vote by mail, the more efficient your campaign becomes, as you can "bank" more votes early, and concentrate your efforts in the last days of the campaign on only those voters who haven't voted yet. Modern campaigns use text messages to regularly remind voters who have to vote how and where they can. Voting by mail allows voters and campaigns to track who has and who has not cast ballots. These are now basic tools of successful campaigns, digital incarnations of old-fashioned methods such as using phone banks to call voters or door-knockers to encourage them to vote in person.

But Trump's strategy had another, more insidious effect. It was a salt-the-earth strategy, seeding in the minds of Trump voters the idea that the election could be or would be rigged. Never mind that he won in both 2016 and 2020 in states with extensive mail voting; never mind that Republican election officials and legislators supported the procedure; never mind that he and his campaign failed to raise challenges to the mail voting process in many states he complained about; never mind that Trump himself, and his family, chose to cast mail ballots—the misdirection about mail voting played a leading role in Trump's long con of the American people. Despite all these efforts, in the main, Trump's slander of mail voting failed to sufficiently damage the nation's faith in their democracy. So Trump and his increasingly shrill echo chamber shifted to an ever-growing list of election prevarications.

"Every president, frankly, has recognized and understood that our elections are not perfect, but they are the most effective and important democratic system that's ever existed," Liz Cheney told us. "There is a system in place to challenge it. And the president's obligation and responsibility is to ensure that the laws are faithfully executed, to defend the other branches of government, and fundamentally to defend our electoral system. And when you have a president whose language so consistently tears down our election system and feeds into the idea that somehow America's democratic process is disgraceful and so fundamentally broken, that is very dangerous."

BALLOT DUMPS/SPIKES

Starting with his bizarre speech in the early morning hours after Election Night, and continuing in the days after the election, Trump began to spread another lie—that there were inexplicable "ballot dumps" that occurred primarily in Democratic areas, overwhelmingly for Biden, that must indicate widespread fraud in those jurisdictions. This claim was similar to many of the other false claims in that there was a shred of truth to it, but Trump and his allies spun these small truths into a fantastical image of fraud when, in fact, there was none and the underlying small truth could be reasonably explained.

Here is the small truth: in many jurisdictions, there were large numbers of ballots reported in batches at various times, and that, in many of these places, those ballots tended to trend Democratic. There are multiple expected reasons for this. In fact, given the voting dynamic that Trump himself had created, had it not happened, there would have been genuine cause for suspicion or doubt.

First, voters should understand that ballots are counted in batches. They are not reported out one at a time. They are counted in groups, as they are collected, stored, and tabulated. These batches vary in size, from a few dozen to hundreds. Larger, urban counties, with more voters in them, tend to have more batches, with more ballots per batch. The tabulations of each batch are recorded and stored through multiple redundant means, and checked and double checked. And each batch is kept together, intact, so it can be audited and/or recounted and checked against the recorded tabulations.

Second, there were several key states—Michigan, Pennsylvania, and Wisconsin—where the legislatures refused to allow election officials to begin pre-processing mail ballots before Election Day. In all three, larger than normal numbers of mail ballots were requested and returned, due largely to the pandemic. Importantly, existing election laws did not allow election officials in those states to begin the process of verifying the identity and other information on mail ballots, and prepare them for rapid tabulation, until Election Day itself. This was not a best practice—other states with somewhat more experience with mail ballots, like Florida and Ohio, allowed for pre-processing of these ballots weeks before Election Day, to ensure integrity, and to allow voters to correct any errors or exclusions on their ballot envelopes.

Pre-processing has another important benefit, one that plays out on Election Night and the morning after. Pre-processing allows for reported vote total results as quickly as possible. Without pre-processing, it takes longer to tabulate mail ballots because they must be properly inspected and verified first, which ensures integrity (though other states do that integrity check earlier), but may delay getting results. But Trump and other critics of Election 2020 used the perceived time it took to tabulate results to sow doubt when, in fact, their political allies demanded the slower process and then criticized it as somehow flawed or suspicious.

As the public record clearly shows, election officials from both parties in Michigan, Pennsylvania, and Wisconsin pleaded with their legislatures, each of which refused to act adequately to allow for the quick processing and counting of the expected influx of mail ballots due to the pandemic. Only in Michigan was there even a minor accommodation—some counties could begin pre-processing mail ballots the day before Election Day—but this was insufficient time to overcome the problem. Why didn't the Republican-dominated legislatures in these states make this minor modification to the law, even if it was only temporary during the pandemic, when beseeched by election officials of their own party? Was it because they didn't want to undermine the false claims being made by the presidential candidate of their party?

This phenomenon was predictable, and in fact, predicted. President Trump had, to his detriment, poisoned his voters' minds about voting by mail so they, of course, chose to vote in person. Election Day and other in-person ballots are among the first to be reported, since the verification of voters occurs once, at the polls, before the voters receive their ballot, after which the ballots are placed in a scanner ready for rapid reporting of the tabulation as soon as the polls are closed. Mail ballots, however, are usually validated twice, once when the voter requests a ballot, and once when the ballot is returned, and that process takes time before the ballot can be tabulated, as described above. If the process for validating and counting mail ballots cannot begin until Election Day, or Election Night, those ballots will be among the last to be counted. And when they skew overwhelmingly Democratic, because the Republican presidential candidate has repeatedly told his voters not to vote by mail, this creates a dynamic where much of the late-reported vote favors the Democratic candidate. This was discussed even months before the election, and even given a name—the Blue Wave.

Many, including David Becker, prepared the media and the American public for the so-called Blue Wave. Major Garrett also reported extensively on this emerging reality of slower-than-typical election results. The bottom line: there was no way to avoid results coming in the way they did in 2020, not because of anything Democrats or Biden did, but solely because Republican legislators in key states refused to prepare for the challenge of processing an influx of mail-in ballots, which they knew was coming. States with better, preexisting laws that allowed for pre-processing of mail ballots— even states Trump won, like Florida and Ohio, saw the same disproportionate Democratic tilt in mail ballots as did other states. But they avoided strong Blue Wave effects because they were able to report batches of pre-processed mail ballots very quickly, along with in-person ballots, shortly after the polls closed.

Nevertheless, Trump and his allies attempted to use faulty analysis about these "ballot dumps" or "ballot spikes" to con his supporters into believing that something untoward was being done, even though what he was talking about was the normal process of verifying and counting ballots.

Indeed, at various times in the days and weeks after the election, Trump and his allies had demanded that states "stop the count," including famously in the early morning hours of November 4th, while at the same time he complained that some jurisdictions had "stopped counting" in the middle of the night, allegedly to allow for fraud to take place. They couldn't get their story straight—had states stopped counting, or must the ongoing count urgently be stopped? The simple fact is that ballots were continually being counted in the days after the election, in every single state—from Texas to California, from Montana to Alabama—just as they always were during every presidential election. While states and counties may have given their workers brief periods of rest, and change shifts for workers to continue the count, at no point was the count stopped, nor should it have been. The process of unofficially counting the ballots, to be audited and certified as official, has always taken weeks.

But simple and eternal facts like these would not stop further efforts at misdirection.

THE PRESENCE OF BIPARTISAN OBSERVERS

In the days after the election, Trump and his operatives in the states where he was clearly losing, or where ballots were still being tabulated (mostly those mail ballots that couldn't be processed until Election Day), began to spread unfounded rumors that observers from their campaign were being excluded from watching the counting of ballots. That the Trump campaign knew this allegation to be false did not dissuade it from this course of action.

In general, every state allows duly-qualified observers from the campaigns and the parties to observe the polling places and ballot-counting. Election officials understand this transparency is an important part of promoting an understanding of the integrity of election processes. Well-trained observers can also be valuable in spotting potential problems (long lines, etc.) and communicating with election officials. There is one unbreakable rule of election observation: an observer does not interfere with the process of election officials or voters under any circumstances. This is true whether you're a Democrat or Republican, whether it's a presidential election or a special election for dogcatcher, whether you're in Arizona or Angola. If an observer sees a problem, he or she is trained to contact the relevant authority, usually the election official in the jurisdiction, and allow that official to fix it.

On Election Day 2020, and in the counting that proceeded afterward, there was a veritable army of observers (or poll watchers, as they're sometimes called), in every state. By law, they had full access to watch the process of casting and/or counting ballots, but they could not interfere. In many places, it was required that observers register with election officials beforehand, or be nominated by a campaign or a political party—to guarantee that election officials and poll workers knew the observers were properly authorized and trained. The Trump campaign and the Republican Party in particular, along with the Biden campaign and the Democratic Party, had recruited watchers to confirm the integrity of the count. Both teams focused on battleground states, such as Michigan, Pennsylvania, and Wisconsin.

Nevertheless, Trump almost immediately, in the days after the election, claimed that his observers were being excluded from vote-counting centers. His campaign led his supporters to erroneously believe that his representatives were being prevented from observing counting being conducted in the TCF Center in Detroit and the Pennsylvania Convention Center in Philadelphia, for instance, which couldn't have been further from the truth. Each site, and others like them, where mail ballots were being verified and counted, had dozens if not hundreds of poll watchers from both parties. Even when mobs of Trump supporters converged on the TCF Center, requiring workers to cover the windows to allow the vote counters the ability to count the ballots as prescribed by law, there were literally hundreds of Republican observers inside the arena, watching the counting.

Allowing observers to watch vote-casting and counting is a best practice, allowed in every state. It promotes transparency and confidence. And indeed, every state allowed observers from both parties and campaigns to observe and report any problems. But misdirection and the long con requires that the losing candidate manufacture the appearance of malfeasance, and so the grift continued.

THE INTEGRITY OF THE VOTING MACHINES

Shortly after it became clear that Trump was losing in nearly every close battleground state, he and his team of deniers shifted to a particularly desperate bit of misdirection. As transparent and secure counting of the ballots was ongoing in nearly every state (not just the ones where the margin was close), and before the vote counts were official, Trump and his surrogates began to claim that the voting machines were programmed to switch votes from Trump to Biden. He would have his supporters believe that was the only way to explain his defeat. This myth had marquee billing in Byrne's book *The Deep Rig*, and continued election disinformation in 2021 and 2022 from My Pillow CEO Mike Lindell.

Putting aside the obvious contributing factors to Trump's defeat—his eye-of-the-needle narrow victory in 2016 (with a popular vote loss of nearly 3 million votes), his historic unpopularity in the polls, his party's big losses in the 2018 midterms, and deep questions about his handling of the pandemic—this claim was particularly off-the-wall. As his campaign knew, vote-counting technology is federally certified, and subject to pre- and post-election logic and accuracy tests, observable by representatives of the parties and the candidates. Furthermore, election cybersecurity and confidence measures had been significantly beefed up since Trump's narrow victory and Russian attempts to interfere with the 2016 election. This increased security was achieved in cooperation with states across the country. It was coordinated by Trump's own team at the Department of Homeland Security and its Cybersecurity and Infrastructure Security Agency.

The progress in just four years, led by the states, was significant. In 2016, about 75 to 80 percent of all voters cast their vote on auditable, reviewable paper ballots, which can be checked and double-checked to confirm the count was accurate. Several large battleground states, including Georgia, North Carolina, Pennsylvania, and South Carolina (all won by Trump in 2016), had a significant percentage of their ballots cast only digitally in 2016, without a paper ballot that the voter could review. There is absolutely zero evidence that there was any compromise of those ballots (even after recounts and audits), but the ability to transparently demonstrate the integrity of the election was limited in those states in 2016.

But between 2016 and 2020, more states moved to auditable, verifiable paper ballots. Georgia, North Carolina, Pennsylvania, and other states like South Carolina and Virginia ensured that all of their jurisdictions provided paper ballots for voters. In states like Georgia, North Carolina, Pennsylvania, and South Carolina, this was accomplished thanks to support or an outright mandate from the Republican-led legislatures in those states. This resulted in nearly 95 percent of all ballots in the 2020 election being of the auditable, verifiable paper variety. Indeed, every ballot (with the exception of a very small number of ballots cast by voters with disabilities on special devices) in every single battleground state was on paper. In Arizona, Colorado, Florida, Georgia, Michigan, Minnesota, Nevada, New Hampshire, New Mexico, North Carolina, Ohio, Pennsylvania, Virginia, Wisconsin, and thirty other states, all ballots were paper. This was a significant improvement over 2016 and resulted in the largest number of auditable paper ballots being cast in American history.

Additionally, more states than ever before conducted robust audits of these ballots, confirming that voting technology reached the accurate outcome. Here is how that process works: During a post-election audit, a random, statistically significant sampling of ballots is reviewed by hand, under transparent observation by the public and representatives of the parties, and the counts of those ballots are compared to the counts that the technology yielded. If those counts match the electronic counts, voters can be sure the machine tallies reached the accurate outcome. The practice of auditing paper ballots has steadily grown over the last decade.

In 2020, forty-three states and the District of Columbia conducted audits, independently confirming accurate results. This included the first real audits conducted in states like Pennsylvania and North Carolina (since they didn't have paper ballots statewide previously), and statistically robust audits in Michigan. Perhaps most notably, Georgia conducted the highest-level audit that can be done—a full hand count of all the paper ballots statewide. Georgia counted all the ballots once unofficially, then counted every single presidential ballot *again,* by hand in front of observers from both parties, before certifying the vote. Finally, at the Trump campaign's request, the state re-re-counted all the ballots one more time. These three counts of the presidential ballots agreed that the outcome was correct.

Consequently, with more confidence than we have had in any previous election, we know the technology worked as intended. Pre-election testing and post-election auditing confirmed the results. This should have stopped the Trump assault on fundamental truths about America's democratic processes, but of course, it did not.

While these insinuations began earlier, the low point of the parade of malignant falsehoods came during a press conference at the Republican National Committee on November 19. There, Rudy Giuliani and Sidney Powell laid out a fevered dream of conspiracies, involving, among others, former Venezuelan dictator Hugo Chavez, Dominion Voting Systems (a company they falsely alleged had ties to Venezuela), a secret European computer server, and an orbiting satellite, all of which allegedly changed millions of Trump votes to Biden votes. Powell, using the language of Nordic folklore (borrowed hilariously from the movie *Clash of the Titans*), vowed to unleash the legal equivalent of a Kraken—to right the supposed wicked wrongs of Election 2020. As hair dye streamed down the sweating brow of Giuliani, the spectacle exceeded parody.

But these false claims cannot be discussed without acknowledging that, to some degree, left-leaning activists had planted the seeds for these claims years before. In 2004, the CEO of Diebold, a company that, among other things, produced electronic voting machines for states like Ohio, had foolishly made a partisan statement in favor of then-president Bush, which became a focal point after Bush's somewhat-narrow margin of victory of more than 100,000 votes in that state. Despite the lack of any evidence of malfunction or malfeasance, and the presence of bipartisan election boards in every Ohio county, several Democrats disappointed by Massachusetts senator John Kerry's defeat raised frivolous claims of election fraud, culminating in a failed objection to Ohio's electoral votes during the

2005 joint session of Congress. Unlike Trump in 2020, Kerry did not support the objection, and had conceded defeat to President Bush months before.

This so-called "hacktivism" continued on the left for several years, with mixed results. On the one hand, many computer scientists and others who raised the alarms about non-auditable electronic voting deserve credit for moving states without them toward paper ballots and audits, which allowed for unprecedented verifiability in 2020. On the other hand, there were zealots who brought unsuccessful lawsuits in places like Georgia, North Carolina, and Pennsylvania, raising largely unfounded doubts about the paper ballot voting systems those states had recently purchased that allowed for secure and transparent elections.

While not one of these lawsuits succeeded in forcing a jurisdiction to abandon the paper ballot systems, each elicited misleading testimony falsely conflating the risk of cyberattack, which might be present on any electronic device, to the ongoing likelihood of a "hacked" election. As we have said, this imagined risk is greatly if not entirely neutralized by effective audits and other election security protections that render such an attack exceedingly unlikely and prone to almost certain detection.

Deceptively, the Trump campaign, looking in any direction for anything that might provide a shred of credibility, seized on this testimony to prop up their frivolous claims. In the aftermath of the 2020 election, they used testimony from "experts" who likely opposed Trump to prop up their assertion that the voting systems were attacked. Peter Navarro, Trump's White House trade adviser, took it upon himself after the election to concoct all manner of allegations about voter fraud and a stolen election, writing a book called *In Trump Time*. In it, Navarro writes:

Ever since election day, Powell had repeatedly gone on television to make extravagant claims about election fraud. The problem with Powell's claims was not so much the statements themselves but her abject refusal to provide even a scintilla of evidence that they were true—much less provide the infamous "Kraken" that Powell claimed would crack the case wide open.

We pause here to note Navarro applauds Powell's election disinformation. As he wrote, Navarro did not take exception to "the statements themselves." He just wanted some shreds to back it up. We continue to quote Navarro:

> Let me be crystal clear for the historical record: Damn Dame Powell did incalculable harm to the battle against election fraud with her zaniness. Through guilt by association, she enabled the anti-Trump media to tar us all with her Gone To Crazy Town brush. Let the history books, then, assign Sidney Katherine Powell to an appropriate dust bin. She more than earned it.

To the great detriment of our country, these falsehoods about Election 2020—thinly buttressed by alarms raised earlier on the extreme left—were not mere zaniness. They became widgets in a frightening machine to overturn the election. The most chilling example of this is the revelation of the draft Trump executive order (mentioned earlier) that sought to enlist the Departments of Defense and Homeland Security to seize voting machines—presumably as an excuse to keep Trump indefinitely and unconstitutionally in power.

The executive order heavily relied upon the claims made by those on the left raising flawed doubts about voting machines in previous elections. Oddly, it quoted paragraphs of dicta from a Georgia court case that actually denied the remedies sought by the plaintiffs. Here is one of the great ironies of Trump's brand of election 2020 denialism: his attempted coup found a thin veil of credibility from hyperbolic theories manufactured by his opponents. It is also a caution to anyone across the political spectrum who may inflate concerns about election integrity for their own political gain—such claims cannot be contained to benefit only one's political allies, and are just as likely to be used to delegitimize valid electoral victories benefiting your own political positions.

We will not outline the entire voting machine hacking delusion in this book, as promoted by the Trump forces, as it is so divorced from reality that to rebut all the contentions would be to validate it more than it deserves. It appears clear that even the Trump campaign knew that these allegations were false before the RNC press conference, a fact that will serve them poorly in the ongoing defamation litigation against members of the campaign by Dominion Voting Systems. But in addition to the fact that Chavez has been dead for years, that Dominion is based in Colorado with no connection to Venezuela, and that there is no secret server or satellite, it's important to note why this conspiracy isn't credible, and in fact, is impossible.

First, as we mentioned above, the results in nearly every state, and in particular in the battleground states, were independently reviewed and confirmed. The results were not dependent upon a single machine count, but rather multiple counts using different devices and methods prior to certification. Those counts were certified because they were confirmed independently, and repeatedly checked and double-checked. Anyone who says otherwise is, quite simply, lying.

Second, the devices that count ballots are not connected to the internet. They are tested both before and after elections for malware. And this is all done with observation from members of the public. While no technology is unhackable and impervious to malware, and voting machines are no exception, the lack of connectivity makes it very difficult to infect voting machines in large numbers. It's not impossible to infect a single machine, physically, with something like a USB drive, but it is also extremely difficult to do this undetected, given the high level of physical security surrounding these machines, including locked rooms, limited access, logs of those who have access, and post-election audits that would likely detect any interference.

Finally, and perhaps most importantly, our system of elections is highly decentralized. A federal general election is not a single election happening on a single day. It's about 10,000 elections going on in 10,000 different jurisdictions using different technology and procedures, on a series of days culminating on Election Day. It is close to impossible to infect a nationwide election with a technological attack, and change the outcome of an election. It would require a conspiracy of thousands of election officials and others all over the country, without any of them revealing the existence of this extensive conspiracy.

And it would require nearly perfect prognostication about where the election is closest. For such a successful conspiracy to be pulled off, the conspirators have to flip votes in the closest states—if California or Texas were to flip, that would raise a lot of questions. And even then, you need to try to flip the fewest number of votes—if your preferred candidate wins by too much in a state expected to be close, that raises further scrutiny and vastly increases the chances an audit will detect the malfeasance. So someone trying to defraud a national election would need to correctly predict the closest states, and flip the fewest number of votes to change the outcome in that state. And this would need to be planned months in advance with a conspiracy of thousands of trained operatives. Imagine how difficult that is—in the summer of 2016, how many predicted that Michigan, Pennsylvania, and Wisconsin would be the key states, with the narrowest margins, delivering the election to Trump in 2016; and in the summer of 2020, how many predicted that Arizona and Georgia would be the swing states in the 2020 election, with Trump winning Florida by the widest margin of any presidential candidate since 2004?

In short, it is close to impossible to flip a national election to make it appear as if the loser actually won. What's more, if anyone was foolish enough to attempt it, it wouldn't work, and the perpetrators would almost certainly get caught.

There is ample reason to believe the Trump campaign knew all this when it made these wild claims. The campaign had an internal memo dismissing the voting machine hacking theory prior to the Giuliani/Powell press conference, and the campaign declined to request statewide recounts in the key states of Michigan, Pennsylvania, and Wisconsin, although it was entitled to under state law. The campaign requested a recount of only two Democratic-leaning counties in Wisconsin—Dane and Milwaukee—neither of which uses Dominion systems in their elections. Those recounts confirmed the original tabulation. The statewide audit and recount of paper ballots in Georgia (which does use Dominion systems statewide) also confirmed Trump's loss there.

Despite every fact confirming Trump's loss, and the impossibility of each attempt at misdirection, the con continued as the grifters kept dangling disinformation before their marks.

PHILANTHROPY'S ROLE IN ENSURING A SAFE ELECTION

As the pandemic raged through the spring and summer of 2020, some primaries descended into chaos as election officials sought to find appropriate places and ways for voters to cast a ballot and struggled to find enough poll workers to staff those locations. Election officials needed new polling sites that accommodated social distancing. They needed to print more paper ballots and purchase new ballot scanners to meet the increased demand for mail balloting. They needed to buy plexiglass, masks, hand sanitizer, cleaning supplies, and single-use pens. And as an unprecedented number of voters were scrambling to understand how to navigate the voting process in the middle of a global pandemic, election officials needed to provide more voter information and education than ever before. None of these additional expenses could have been anticipated even a year earlier, and election officials needed additional resources.

There was some relief from Congress in April 2020. Washington appropriated $400 million as part of the CARES Act to assist the states with election expenses related to the pandemic. But this was only a small fraction of the total needed by election officials, amounting to less than $2 per eligible voter for the rest of the primary and general election period. Though election administrators and others begged Congress and their state legislatures for more funding, their needs remained unaddressed, putting voters—and the workers who administer elections—potentially at risk.

In late August 2020, it was clear that the government was not going to provide adequate resources to ensure that 160 million American voters and a million election workers would be safe during the general election. Into this void, philanthropy stepped in—specifically, Mark Zuckerberg, founder of Facebook, and his wife, Priscilla Chan.

In late August 2020, David Becker was contacted by a representative of Zuckerberg and Chan. They asked what was needed to ensure a safe election, and specifically what election officials needed that they didn't have. Becker told them that election officials needed help educating the unprecedented numbers of voters expected to participate in November about how to navigate the voting process. Becker was hearing from election officials in many states—red and blue, large and small—that they were concerned that there were going to be many first-time voters, and many voters who were scared about contracting COVID during the voting process. In addition, there were significant changes in the voting process—many of which were instituted well before the pandemic, such as new voting machines in Georgia—and many voting options, like mail voting, that voters were considering using for the very first time.

Pennsylvania was a case in point. Well before 2020, major voting procedure changes had been planned in the state, largely under the direction of the Republican-majority legislature and bipartisan election officials. In major counties like Philadelphia and Allegheny (home of Pittsburgh), new voting machines would be used for the first time in a major election, producing an auditable paper ballot. Voters in Philadelphia, for instance, hadn't voted on a paper ballot in their polling places in generations. In addition, in 2019, the legislature had allowed for no-excuse mail voting throughout the state for the first time ever. Finally, there had been litigation to clarify the rules around mail voting, requiring voters to seal their mail ballots in an inner "secrecy" envelope, and requiring election officials to reject mail ballots that weren't properly sealed. For the vast majority of voters in Pennsylvania who had never voted by mail, this could be very confusing.

Zuckerberg and Chan responded quickly, providing approximately $65 million in grants to Becker's 501c(3), the Center for Election Innovation & Research (CEIR), to regrant to states for non-partisan voter education—how to cast a ballot safely, how to request a mail ballot, where to return ballots, where in-person voting sites were located, and how to volunteer to be a poll worker. In early September 2020, CEIR contacted state election officials in every state, inviting them to apply for these grants. Twenty-four states applied, submitting budgets and plans for spending the funds for voter education, in a strictly nonpartisan fashion. One state, Louisiana, withdrew its application after submitting, and the other twenty-three states received grants they requested. CEIR was able to get these states their needed funds within about a month from the initial notice of the availability of the grants.

Another nonprofit, the Center for Tech and Civic Life (CTCL), also received funds to regrant election officials. These funds were allocated to county and local election officials, thousands of jurisdictions across the country, who are the ones primarily responsible for the casting and counting of ballots. While the CEIR grants went to state officials for voter education only, the CTCL grants were available to local election officials to ensure their voters and workers could remain safe, and that the ballots would be counted as quickly and accurately as possible—to purchase cleaning and sanitizing supplies, more voting scanners to process mail ballots, and so on. CEIR and CTCL did not coordinate their grant awarding.

These grants were all made out in the open, and very publicly. As early as September, media were reporting about the availability of these grants, and the intense need for more resources. Not only was the public broadly aware of these grants well over a month before the election, it is clear that the Trump campaign and its supporters were specifically aware of these grants, well before Election Day. In fact, seeking to deny election officials the funds they desperately needed to facilitate a successful election, Trump and his allies brought lawsuits seeking to prevent use of the philanthropic donations in Wisconsin, Michigan, Pennsylvania, Texas, Iowa, and South Carolina, losing them all.

Nevertheless, despite courts repeatedly upholding philanthropy's role in supporting the election, and despite finding zero evidence suggesting that any of the funds were spent improperly or in a partisan way, the grifters persist in suggesting that the funding itself was somehow nefarious. That these claims are often tinged with anti-Semitic tropes is without doubt, as the con artists throw out the names "Zuckerberg" and "Soros" as often as possible, evoking the threat of "globalist" puppet masters influencing our elections. That George Soros had nothing to do with the grants is irrelevant, as is the fact that these grants were open and transparent and legal—it completes the picture and inflames those targeted, keeping them angry and donating.

To put a final stamp on the transparency of these grants, David Becker and CEIR released a full accounting of the grant spending in March 2021, before many of the recent attacks on the philanthropies that assisted elections. A full list of the states that applied for and received grants, along with the full amount of each grant, was released publicly. States won by Biden, such as Georgia, Maryland, and Washington, received grants, along with states won by Trump, such as Kentucky, Missouri, and Ohio.

But this hasn't stopped the election deniers from creating a culture of sore-loserism. In state after state, they have pushed bans on private funding in future elections. Make no mistake—philanthropic funding of elections should never be Plan A. It was only necessary in 2020 due to Congress's failure to adequately shore up our election system in the face of a global pandemic. Private funding will likely never be needed again, but if legislators wanted to truly make such funding obsolete, rather than banning the efforts of philanthropists, they might want to consider doing what is necessary to ensure that election offices receive adequate public funding in the future. But instead of dealing with the problem, some legislators continue to fuel the grift.

BALLOT "HARVESTING"

But those continuing the grift were not done shifting their meritless claims, over 500 days after the election. In 2022, election deniers and Trump allies began selling tickets to a "documentary" claiming thousands of ballot "mules" delivered ballots to drop boxes to steal the election from Trump. These claims, like so many before, ricocheted in right-wing media circles, making noise and drawing attention. Predictably, they were as false as their abandoned "fraud" forebears.

First, ballot "harvesting," as the election deniers call it, is not nearly as suspicious as the election losers would have us believe. It is, quite simply, the act of delivering someone's ballot to a secure drop box or mailbox. Usually, this is done by a family member, or a care worker, and importantly, the ballot is delivered after it has been voted and sealed into an outer envelope. The ballot is still secret, and the voter is still fully verified when the ballot is returned.

Assistance with delivering ballots is legal in 31 states, and not at all unusual. Some states regulate who can deliver ballots (family and care workers) and how many ballots can be delivered. There is zero evidence the practice packs a partisan advantage. Here again, deniers cite laws they knew existed before the election, did not challenge in advance, and now retroactively blame for straight-up defeat.

The filmmakers showed a small amount of alleged video evidence of someone returning multiple ballots, but these videos actually prove that the ballots were returned lawfully. In Georgia, for instance, the secretary of state investigated a claim offered by the Trump backers and determined the man "caught" on video was merely returning ballots for himself and his family, legal and proper under Georgia (and many other states') law.

Second, the hysterical claims made about "mules" are fueled by sloppy methodology and confirmation bias. As the Associated Press reported, the filmmakers bought cell phone location data, without independent verification of its accuracy, to try to see if the same phone pinged near a drop box several times in a month. By their own admission, this cell phone location data is not particularly accurate—at best it can pinpoint within several meters. Since ballot drop boxes are typically in locations with heavy foot traffic— government offices, libraries, schools, shopping centers—this vague data proves literally nothing. As Jen Fifield, a reporter from Votebeat, noted, "Say you go to the library once a week in the weeks leading up to the election and there happens to be a ballot drop box there. You're now one of 2,000 'ballot trafficking mules.'"

Finally, and perhaps most importantly, there's absolutely zero evidence that any of the ballots returned by the so-called mules were illegal or improper. The group that organized this research, True the Vote, made that clear when founder, Catherine Engelbrecht, testified before a Wisconsin legislative committee: "I want to make very clear that we're not suggesting that the ballots that were cast were illegal ballots."

In sum, ballot delivery by trusted individuals has been done for years, in red and blue states. Data that election deniers have recklessly foisted into this debate does not and cannot show if there were ballot "mules." What's more, the term "mules" is meant to conjure imagery of cartels and organized crime, suggesting ballots are similar to elicit drugs. Deniers are consistent. They denigrate democracy at every turn. And everyone from the Georgia secretary of state to the founder of the group that conducted the research confirms no evidence of illegal ballots. But other than that, please continue to donate to the election denial cause!

All over the country, agitators against "Zuckerbucks," "ballot mules," and the *next* conspiracy-of-the-day theory make profit-seeking claims they will not and cannot make in court—where, inevitably, they would have to withstand scrutiny of evidence and procedure. This, in our mind, reveals the essence of the grift—fundamental contempt for the foundation of every pluralistic society: rule of law.

CONTEMPT FOR THE RULE OF LAW

Throughout this entire chapter, you've seen how, time and again, each claim raised by the election deniers was rejected by anyone who subjected it to even the slightest scrutiny. In turn, election officials of both parties, courts at every level—state and local, trial, appellate, and Supreme—and even Trump's own attorney general, Department of Justice, Department of Homeland Security, Federal Bureau of Investigation, Department of Defense, and even the Trump campaign itself, all found the claims made by the losing candidate to be completely without evidentiary support. Trump's allies, paid to find voter fraud sufficient to alter the outcome, have come up completely empty in every state—Arizona, Michigan, Wisconsin, and everyplace else. Two years after the election, that remains the case.

Nevertheless, they persist. On every conspiracy platform and channel they can find, they continue to lie to the supporters of the former president, all the while lining their pockets at the expense of those same supporters. The losses in court don't seem to phase them, and while they promise new, blockbuster lawsuits to be brought any day now, they never quite seem to find their way to court to actually produce the evidence they claim they have. Like a deadbeat debtor, the check is in the mail, it's coming tomorrow, always tomorrow.

In past elections, both candidates and parties trusted in the rule of law. If they won or lost lawsuits, they respected those judgments, and exhausted their remedies through appeal, sometimes taking their grievances all the way to the highest court. Perhaps this was best demonstrated in Florida 2000, when both parties litigated numerous cases through the Florida state and federal court systems, both sides winning some and losing some, with the clock ticking in a truly close election decided by only 537 votes. But when the highest court in the land ruled on December 12, 2000, that the recount must be stopped, effectively and finally rendering Bush the winner of Florida's electoral votes, and the presidential election, Vice President Gore respected the ruling of the court. There is little doubt that he disagreed with the Court's ruling, and a majority of Americans polled believed the ruling was political, not legally based. But there was no further appeal possible, and to continue the fight would have done lasting damage to the rule of law and American democracy.

Gore, knowing that, did not call every reporter he knew to criticize the justices of the Court. He did not call a press conference to lambaste the Republican appointees who voted for George W. Bush. He did not call a rally on the Mall to protest the perceived injustice on January 6, 2001. He did not encourage or demand that the Department of Defense, or Department of Justice, or FBI, investigate alleged fraud or seize the butterfly ballots from Palm Beach County. He did not raise money from his supporters to "Stop the

Steal." He had his days in court, presented evidence, and when he had run out of time, and made every claim he could, he did what anyone with a deep-seated love for our nation and his fellow citizens would do. On December 13, 2000, Gore conceded the presidency to Bush and wished him well.

In the years that followed, Gore did not seek to undermine President Bush. He committed himself to serving America and the global community. He did not even choose to run against Bush in the next election, even though there is little doubt that he continued to have sincere policy disagreements with the Bush administration. In short, he was a patriot, who put country over party and over self.

Contrast that with the loser of the 2020 presidential election. Losing the popular vote by the second largest margin of any presidential candidate in this century, and the largest margin of any sitting president running for reelection since Jimmy Carter in 1980, Trump sought to undermine the very foundation of democracy and the rule of law. Despite being admonished in harsh judgments written by federal judges he appointed, Trump kept deceiving his supporters on social media and through credulous fringe cable networks. Rather than commit himself to the welfare of his fellow citizens and the preservation of democracy, Trump lashed out and sought attention. Rather than build a legacy of statesmanship for himself, he resorted to more scams and get-rich-quick schemes. Rather than help his party build a lasting majority, he promoted intraparty squabbles and enforced election-denying litmus tests. When the history of the Trump era is written, it will be this indulgent phase, this selfish and groundless attack on democracy and the rule of law, that will indelibly tarnish and diminish that which remains of Trump's legacy and any of his arguable achievements.

THE VICTIMS OF THE LONG CON

The voices of denunciation likely to be heard loudest years hence will not be ours. We predict they will be the voices of those victimized by The Big Lie, Americans who believed a president wouldn't deceive them and whip them into a frenzy on falsehoods. These Americans have borne witness to the con, and become some of its most pitiable casualties. They may come to see what they could not before—that Trump lied to them and the nation, that the election wasn't stolen, and that they committed crimes against noble American traditions. Their depth of regret, bordering on grief, could be palpable.

There are so many victims of this grotesque grift. Some invaded the Capitol to save the country from what they now see as the phantom danger of a stolen election. The true theft, they came to understand, was perpetrated by Trump, a president who stole their faith in the law, incited them to violent trespass, and jabbered on while their lives crumbled.

Prosecutors brought many cases in 2021 and 2022. As of this writing, 816 individuals have been charged with a variety of misdemeanors and felonies. Of those, 251 have entered guilty pleas.

Two were convicted in jury trials. Many defendants were held awaiting adjudication, a harrowing experience for those unfamiliar with the privations of jail time. Many defendants lost their jobs, others saw their health deteriorate, while still others saw their marriages collapse. The direct victims of The Big Lie—chiefly U.S. Capitol Police and D.C. Metropolitan Police—will suffer for the rest of their lives. They confronted insanity and rage, and in so doing part of our national soul.

Collateral damage fell across the country. All of us are changed, less confident about what unites us, more uncertain about the strength of our institutions and norms. But other damage was done. Lives were ruined. Lives of Trump supporters were fed into the woodchipper of The Big Lie, scattered to an indifferent, egoistic wind.

To read the letters of Capitol riot defendants is to enter a world of deep regret, confusion, and sorrow. Several penned letters from their jail cells, pleading for mercy while invoking the language of redemption.

Robert Scott Palmer pled guilty to assaulting, resisting, and impeding officers using a dangerous weapon. He was sentenced to sixty-three months in prison, which, as of this writing, was the longest of any rioter charged. Palmer's legal team said the following in court papers:

> Mr. Palmer went to the Capitol at the behest of the former president. Like many others who participated in the Capitol riot, Mr. Palmer blindly followed the many figures who falsely but persistently claimed that the election had been stolen from the president. Those voices, including the voice of the then-president himself, had convinced persons such as Mr. Palmer that the election was fraudulent and that they must take action to stop the transition of the presidency. It is relevant to consider that the riot almost surely would not have occurred but for the financing and organization that was conducted by persons unconnected to Mr. Palmer who will likely never be held responsible for their relevant conduct.

In his letter to the presiding judge, Palmer wrote, in small, sometimes pinched cursive, the following:

> A lot if not most of the defendants I have been incarcerated with would object to me saying that we were rioting. To be quite honest your honor if asked about it when it first happened in January I would have been counted in that group. I have over the course of close to a year come to a different conclusion. Since then I realize that well-meaning Trump supporters were lied to by those that at

the time had great power meaning the sitting president, as well as those acting on his behalf. They kept spitting out the false narrative about a stolen election and how it was "our duty" to stand up to tyranny. Little did I realize that they were the tyrannical ones desperate to hold on to power at any cost even by creating the chaos they knew would happen with such rhetoric. For listening to them your honor let me offer please and I can only hope and pray it is accepted by the honorable court my most sincere apologies.

Palmer apologizes first to all police officers attacked by "the angry mob." "They are the real heroes of the day. The emotional as well as physical scars that some will carry for the remainder of their lives is a great tragedy and I wish with every fiber of my being that I could change it but I am powerless to."

He then apologizes to lawmakers inside the Capitol "who were carrying out their constitutionally bound duties to certify what now turns out to be the legitimate will of the American people. That is one of the greatest and proudest traditions of our country the peaceful transition of power and I am truly ashamed that I was part of a group that tried to circumvent that transition."

Palmer's letter was by no means an outlier. It is, in its own way, pitiable and profound. It hurts Palmer that so much had to go wrong for him to reconnect himself to American traditions—ones Trump so carelessly debased.

Boyd Camper pled guilty to misdemeanor illegal parading, demonstrating, and picketing in the Capitol. He was sentenced to sixty days. "I felt kind of duped," Camper told the court, adding he came to Washington because "President Trump invited us there." About the fraud claims spewed by Trump, Camper said he "was in this state of disbelief." That has lifted. Camper now sees the election as valid.

James Bonet pled guilty to misdemeanor illegally entering the Capitol. He was sentenced to ninety days. His lawyer told the court:

"It's our president who was inciting these people to do this," arguing Bonet and others were listening to the "highest ranking official in the country."

Zachary Wilson pled guilty to illegal parading, demonstrating, and picketing. He was sentenced to two years' probation. At sentencing, he told the court: "I was caught up in President Trump telling everybody the election was stolen. He had everyone enraged."

Leonard Gruppo also pled guilty to misdemeanor parading, demonstrating, and picketing. He was sentenced to two years' probation and a $3,000 fine. Gruppo's attorney informed the court he was a Special Forces medical sergeant. Gruppo wrote a six-page, single-spaced letter to his presiding judge, complete with photographs showing his method of entry inside the Capitol.

> I am truly sorry for my actions. I should have known better but somehow that day, I didn't. I have already paid a terrible price for this, and I believe I *should* pay a significant price for what I did. I am not trying to avoid punishment. I only ask that what I have already suffered be considered as part of any further sentence. My fellow countrymen have already beaten me up quite badly. I don't have much left. I've sold as much as I could to make ends meet; property, belongings, as much as I could. I have downsized to a small, 2 bedroom apartment. I have a little left but not much. Why did I go up to the terrace? Why did I enter the Capitol building? I don't have a good answer. I've gone over it a thousand times and I'm still not sure why I didn't recognize what was happening and take alternative action. There were some factors influencing me that day which cannot be discounted. We were told "everyone is going to the Capitol" and "be peaceful." There were easily over half a million people there all pushing toward the building, and I was caught up in that. There was someone with a bullhorn urging everyone to keep moving forward. The entire experience was surreal. I trusted the President and that was a big mistake.

Gruppo's letter described his actions that day, none of which the court determined to be violent. It continued:

Clearly, this was a life-altering mistake and I take full responsibility for my actions, but I am not an evil person. I am not a conspirator, insurrectionist, or anarchist. I went to the rally to support the sitting President of the United States of America. The rally moved to the Capitol, and I went with it. I am a lifelong patriotic American who loves my country and would die for my country. I am deeply saddened by what happened that day and the tremendous pain it has caused so many. I wish I could take that day back.

Gruppo then offered this lengthy apology:

I want to apologize to my countrymen for the part I played and the terrible pain this has caused our nation. I am very sorry the Capitol police were put in a situation where they had to choose between protecting Congress and protecting the public and the angst that has caused them in the aftermath of all this, leading some to commit suicide. That is horrible and I am deeply sorrowful over that. I am very sorry for my part in any disruption to congressional proceedings that day. It was never my intent to do so. Nevertheless, I realize I did unintentionally contribute to that, by prolonging the disruption of our democratic process, and I am truly sorry. I am also sorry for any fear and anxiety that my presence caused to our congress men and women. I apologize to President Biden, President Trump, Vice President Harris, Vice President Pence, Speaker Pelosi, and our other congressional leaders, for the trouble I have caused and any doubt my participation in the events of that day cast on the results of the election. I am sorry. Once Congress certified the election, I immediately accepted the results and urge anyone who has not, to do so.

Gruppo then turned without hesitation to the fate that awaits:

There is little else I can say or do to show my regret. I'm sorry. I have been sorry. If I am to be made an example and held up as a deterrent for others, let me assure anyone paying attention please don't do what I did or anything like that, or you will suffer greatly, and your life will be ruined. Follow the rules. Follow the laws. Love one another. I say this as I desperately cling to the remnants of what was until recently, an exceptionally productive and useful life, a life I hope the court will deem worth salvaging. Nevertheless, I will accept whatever additional punishment I am given without complaint. I promise I will never communicate about this to the media or the public, directly or through a surrogate, so long as I live. When this is behind me, I will be a better citizen than I have ever been, and a better neighbor, son, brother, father, and husband, until the end of my days. You will never hear my name again. I beg for mercy from this court.

January 6th defendant Dustin Thompson was found guilty and sentenced related to several charges stemming from his invasion of the capitol, including stealing a coat rack. In his defense, his attorney, Samuel Shamansky, did not deny that his client stormed the Capitol—"he most certainly did," he conceded—but asked the question "why."

It is hard to imagine a more striking example than the President of the United States directly instructing an individual to engage in the precise conduct for which he is later indicted. . . . Mr. Trump and his conspirators engaged in a concerted effort to deceive the public, including Defendant, into believing that American democracy was at stake if Congress was permitted to certify the election results. . . .

Thompson himself testified in his defense, stating "Besides being ordered by the President to go to the Capitol, I don't know what I was thinking. . . . I was caught up in the moment. . . . If the President is giving you almost an order to do something, I felt obligated to do that." Even the federal judge, while noting Thompson's culpability, noted that "The insurgency, and it was in effect that, is very troubling. . . . I think our democracy is in trouble because unfortunately we have charlatans, like the former President, in my view, who don't care about democracy and only care about power."

By this time, it may be obvious but requires observing that those who wrote to the court as defendants in the Capitol riot demonstrated, no matter how belatedly, contrition, accountability, and courage far exceeding that of the ignominious figure who spurred them toward criminality.

The grift continues, despite its obvious nature. As of this writing, in spring of 2022, an odd assortment of Trump train straphangers— those along for the ride and taking others for a ride—were still crisscrossing the country, peddling distortions and division. Promising, now nearly two years after the 2020 election, that despite the fact that they've failed to produce a shred of evidence raising questions about the outcome, despite losing every court case, despite refusing to subject their conspiracy theories to court scrutiny and cross-examination, that salvation is just around the corner. That soon, just you wait, the big lawsuit is coming. That any day now, the states are going to decertify their electoral votes. That just around the corner, Biden will be removed as the Kraken reinstalls Trump to his rightful place on the throne. And just like every big grift, the promises go unfulfilled, while the grifters' pockets get filled.

6

THE CONSPIRACY
AND THE CONSEQUENCES

COUP is a terrible word. We don't use it lightly. We don't speak of coups in this country because we've never seen a successful one (Aaron Burr in 1806 and some business tycoons in 1933 gave it a go). Actual coups happen elsewhere. A coup arises from a sick political system, writhing in its last agonies before slipping into an authoritarian coma of suppression and stillness.

We didn't see a coup in 2020. But we must be honest with ourselves about what we did see and, more importantly, what has been revealed since the riot at the U.S. Capitol on January 6, 2021. When the history of this noxious era is written, federal judges who ruled on post-riot litigation will be credited with helping us all see through the haze—sharpening our view through the unflinching lens of the Constitution.

"I sort of think about it as though we, all of us, on January 6th, we all looked into the abyss," Liz Cheney told us. "And responsible public servants and responsible elected officials have a duty to pull the country back from that. And Donald Trump instead is trying to drive us into the abyss for his own gain and his own purposes."

Cheney said she spent months trying to put Trump's actions in another historical context.

"I've tried to think about how to provide people with an example of how dangerous his actions were. And one way to think about it, because we have become numb to Trump in so many ways, is to imagine if (President) Dwight Eisenhower had mobilized an angry mob and sent them to march on the Supreme Court during the Brown versus Board of Education argument and sat by and watched while they attacked and did nothing. That is inconceivable. It is inconceivable that he would have done that. But that's essentially what Trump did to prevent the counting of electoral votes."

As you'll see throughout this chapter, the efforts to install a defeated candidate in the White House concentrated primarily on six states—Arizona, Georgia, Michigan, Nevada, Pennsylvania, and Wisconsin. In each of these states, all ballots were cast on paper, and the confirmed and certified margin of victory was greater than 10,000 votes. In two of these states, Michigan and Pennsylvania, the margin of victory exceeded 80,000 votes. As we consider the actions taken in the attempted coup, recognize that while cloaking themselves under the auspices of "democracy," they were challenging the clear will of the people in these states, while never raising challenges or concerns about other states, like North Carolina, where Trump was certified the victor by a margin of less than 75,000 votes, closer than in either Michigan or Pennsylvania.

SEEING IS BELIEVING

We all know what we saw. We can't unsee it, as much as some of us might want to. The Capitol was stormed and desecrated. Police officers were beaten and bludgeoned. Blood was spilled. A protester hoping to break through the etched glass of the oaken door leading to the floor of the U.S. House of Representatives was shot and

killed. Ashli Babbitt was not a martyr. She was a vandal attempting a criminal act of trespass to disrupt the lawful functioning of
government. For a time, Babbitt became an object of some import,
even to Trump. We know who shot her. We know why. We know
no criminal charges were brought against U.S. Capitol Police Lt.
Michael Byrd because he was protecting lawmakers inside the
chamber, seeking cover from the menacing mob. Babbitt's death
slowed the onslaught. The tide receded when confronted with
actual force, force meted out in defense of something we had taken
for granted since Appomattox, government functioning without the
grisly harassment of rebellion.

What we have learned since is that Babbitt was not the tip of the
spear. She was collateral damage in a far more coordinated, cynical,
and anti-constitutional assault. What we have come to see—only
gradually and through the methodical unearthing of emails, draft
legal briefs, draft executive orders, depositions, and interviews—is
a weeks-long campaign carried out from the White House and in
coordination with the Trump reelection campaign to dismantle the
peaceful transfer of power at every turn.

On March 28, 2022, U.S. District Judge David Carter, a Marine
veteran of Vietnam and Bronze Star recipient for valor in the 1968
Battle of Khe Sanh, issued a ruling in a dispute between the January
6 Committee and Trump lawyer John Eastman (which will receive
closer scrutiny in the pages ahead) over access to documents. At
issue was whether Trump acted corruptly and broke the law with
Eastman's assistance. If so, the lawyer-client privilege Eastman was
asserting to shield documents from the January 6 Committee would
be pierced. Inside the forty-four page ruling was this shattering
declaration:

> Based on the evidence, the Court finds it more likely than not that
> President Trump corruptly attempted to obstruct the Joint Session
> of Congress on January 6, 2021.

Carter, an appointee of President Bill Clinton who has won praise from litigants on all manner of legal disputes before him, ruled against Eastman and for the Committee's request, concluding as follows:

> Dr. Eastman and President Trump launched a campaign to over-turn a democratic election, an action unprecedented in American history. Their campaign was not confined to the ivory tower—it was a coup in search of a legal theory. The plan spurred violent attacks on the seat of our nation's government, led to the death of several law enforcement officers, and deepened public distrust in our political process.

More than a year after the attack on the Capitol, the public is still searching for accountability. The case cannot provide it. The Court is tasked only with deciding a dispute over a handful of emails. This is not a criminal prosecution; this is not even a civil liability suit. At most, this case IS a warning about the dangers of "legal theories" gone wrong, the powerful abusing public plat-forms, and desperation to win at all costs. If Eastman and Trump's plan had worked, it would have permanently ended the peaceful transition of power, undermining American democracy and the Constitution. If the country does not commit to investigating and pursuing accountability for those responsible, we fear January 6 will repeat itself.

The outlines started at least as early as November 4, while votes were still being counted and results had not been deter-mined in Arizona, Nevada, Georgia, North Carolina, Pennsylva-nia, Michigan, and Wisconsin. Former Trump energy secretary Rick Perry texted White House Chief of Staff Mark Meadows the following:

> HERE'S an AGGRESSIVE STRATEGY. Why can't the states of GA and NC PENN and other R controlled state houses declare this is

BS (where conflicts and election not called that night) and just send their own electors to vote and have it go to SCOTUS.

The January 6 Committee also obtained a text to Meadows from Donald Trump Jr. on November 5, that echoes much of Perry's text. It suggested multiple layers of Republican election resistance could ensure a second Trump term. "We have multiple paths. We control them all." Trump Jr.'s text also read in part: "We have operational control Total Leverage. Moral High Ground POTUS must start 2nd term now."

"It is an arresting piece of proof that people in the Trump entourage at the highest levels were planning to refuse the election outcome and to use means of political control to overturn the result," Raskin told us, referring to Trump Jr.'s text message.

As court records in litigation of Trump's civil liability for the January 6 riot show, he "began to sow seeds of doubt about the validity of the November 2020 election in the weeks leading up to election day. . . . On election day, [he] claimed victory before all the votes were counted. He tweeted that 'they are trying to STEAL the Election. We will never let them do it'" (Amit Mehta ruling, February 2022). In the awful days between Election Day and January 6, mirroring Trump, feeding his narcissism became, within some circles, a sycophantic obsession. With it came an anti-constitutional casualness akin to circus clowns juggling Mason jars of nitroglycerine. On November 5, Alabama representative Mo Brooks tweeted doubts about "an honest election." On November 6, Donald Trump Jr. said the campaign had uncovered evidence of fraud the media was ignoring. And so it would go. It is unclear if Perry's text was the first suggested path to overturn the election, but it widened the aperture on how early the sickening coup saga began. Perry would not loom large later, but the sentiment began to percolate and found voice in later lawsuits, Trump outreach to state lawmakers and officials, the drafting of fraudulent electoral votes, and, ultimately, to the manufacturing of preposterous (even within the White House) executive orders and lawsuits. All this dangerous energy crackled through Trump's tweets and resentful "Stop the Steal" rhetoric, stoking among his supporters combustible emotions of anger, fear, and panic. That fed internet chatter, some public, some in less-trafficked furrows of the dark web, about violence, revenge, and rebellion. Dress rehearsals to January 6 were conducted in Washington, D.C., on November 14 and December 12, where police officers were beaten and protesters arrested. As court records show, "The President was aware of those rallies, as he tweeted about them, and would have known about the violence that accompanied them."

We must pause this narrative to note that, in March 2022, Trump withdrew his endorsement of Rep. Brooks in Alabama's Republican primary for U.S. Senate. Brooks was insufficiently loyal to The Big Lie. Trump accused him of going "woke" by saying GOP voters should move on from 2020 and focus on 2022 and thereafter. Remember, Brooks appeared at the January 6 rally in body armor (concealed beneath his yellow hunter's jacket and camouflage baseball cap) and urged the assembled to head to the Capitol. "Today is the day American patriots start taking down names and kicking ass," Brooks said. After Trump pulled his endorsement, Brooks dropped this explosive revelation—that Trump hounded him for months after Biden took office to cancel the election and reinstall Trump. Brooks released a statement that read in part: "President Trump asked me to rescind the 2020 elections, immediately remove Joe Biden from the White House, immediately put President Trump back in the White House, and hold a special election for the presidency. I've repeatedly advised President Trump that January 6 was the final election contest verdict and neither the U.S. Constitution nor the U.S. Code permit what President Trump asks. Period." When denialist wings of the GOP war over purity tests—instead of dumping denialism entirely—reason has turned to rot. In January 2021, the truest believers showed how rot can turn to riot.

But there is substantial evidence Trump himself was conclusively informed the election was lawful, and was not stolen. Former Trump White House Chief of Staff Mick Mulvaney told us the 2020 election was valid and many in the White House at the time knew it. He told us people Trump trusted had surveyed allegations raised early on in states like Arizona, Wisconsin, and Georgia and reported back, in relatively short order, that Trump lost fair and square. Ultimately, though, Trump refused to accept these conclusions and began to surround himself with the most ardent election deniers and entertain their most extreme legal strategies.

"When you are taking your legal advice from My Pillow guy, what do you expect?" Mulvaney said, referring to Lindell.

Mulvaney also told us Trump was intolerant of any Chief of Staff that tried to control access to him either in person or by phone. "He would be furious. He had to be in control." Meadows could not, Mulvaney said, have kept Powell, Giuliani, Byrne, Navarro, Lindell, Flynn, and Lin Wood out of the Oval Office. He could only "balance" their appearance with other voices more grounded in federal law, the Constitution, and presidential power. Whatever else Meadows did or did not do, it appears he was among the voices of balance regularly in meetings over harsh election tactics along with White House Counsel Pat Cippolone.

Nevertheless, within the Trump White House, much of the effort was clumsy and disorganized. The White House Counsel's office was in a state of near-constant revolt. There were other rivalries and disagreements—about how far and how long to challenge election results, how to handle the transition, and, because it was still raging, how to deal with the pandemic. Some election subversion efforts went further than others. But none appears to have been discouraged. This led, as court records show, to a conspiracy Trump participated in to preserve his presidency. Trump and his misguided followers inside and outside the White House, it is now clear, were willing to use any desperate tactic, any harebrained scheme, any scabrous legal argument, to keep Trump in power.

The machinations even involved the wife of a Supreme Court justice, in a significant role. In late March 2022, reporting by CBS News's Robert Costa and the *Washington Post*'s Bob Woodward revealed that Virginia Thomas, long a vocal and visible figure in the Beltway conservative movement, exchanged at least twenty-nine text messages with White House Chief of Staff Mark Meadows, urging him to use all available White House resources to overturn Biden's election. The sequence of the texts closely follows Trump rhetoric about taking election challenges to the Supreme Court, where her husband was a sitting justice.

On November 10, after the Associated Press and top network and cable news declared Biden the winner, Mrs. Thomas texted Meadows: "Help This Great President and stand firm, Mark!!! You are the leader, with him, who is standing for America's constitutional governance at the precipice. The majority knows Biden and the Left is attempting the greatest Heist of our History." Thomas has acknowledged attending the January 6 "Stop the Steal" rally, though she said she left before Trump spoke, a contention for which there is no confirmation. Thomas urged Meadows to make Powell the face of legal challenges to Biden's election. She also sent Meadows a conspiracy theory video about watermarked ballots (a QAnon meme at the time suggested that such watermarks were Trump's secret method to track mail ballot fraud). On November 5, Thomas texted Meadows a passage then circulating on right-wing web channels. It read in part: "Biden crime family & ballot fraud co-conspirators (elected officials, bureaucrats, social media censorship mongers, fake stream media reporters, etc.) are being arrested & detained for ballot fraud now & over coming days & will be living in barges off GITMO to face military tribunals for sedition." GITMO is a reference to the U.S. military prison at Guantanamo Bay, Cuba, for terrorists captured during the war on terror and awaiting trial. There were no arrests and no media detention barges—off Cuba or anywhere else.

The text messages came as a shock, even to those familiar with the depths of conspiratorial actions. Justice Thomas and his wife have always asserted that her advocacy and his work on the bench were separable and, indeed, separate. But Virginia Thomas's text messages to Meadows, then entrenched in efforts to overturn the election, raised startling questions about Justice Thomas's independence from his wife's advocacy. Even longtime defenders of Justice Thomas were given pause by the implications of Virginia Thomas's actions and Justice Thomas's subsequent actions on the bench: he was the only justice to side with Trump's legal challenge to the January 6 Committee's demand for White House records related to the Capitol riot. To put it bluntly, Justice Thomas was the only Supreme Court justice to rule against public disclosure of information that would have implicated his spouse in efforts to subvert the election. As the *Post* later wrote: "It now appears Justice Thomas voted against disclosing information about an effort his wife was directly engaged in. It's also plausible (though not yet established) that he voted against disclosing his wife's contacts with the White House— whether knowingly or not."

Mulvaney told us he found Virginia Thomas's text messages to Meadows "problematic" and that Meadows had every opportunity to redirect them and not engage. "All you have to do is say I am up to my neck in things at the White House and I don't have time for this," Mulvaney said. "Every Chief of Staff has that power. But to engage? To write back?"

We did not see a successful coup. We saw an attempted coup. The evidence, which took real shape in January 2022 and grew more visible as the year went on, could be found in the spoken and written words of those who worked on Trump's behalf. Of course, some could not bring themselves to call this a coup. It was sometimes described as the opposite, as an attempt to restore constitutional

order. For a time, Trump apologists said he never wanted to overturn the election. He merely wanted to investigate alleged improprieties. Trump was the ultimate debunker of this myth—saying in a
statement in late January that he wanted Pence to "overturn" the
election. That was followed days later by a spokeswoman who said
Trump would not relent until "there was a different outcome." This
was Trump and acolytes saying the quiet part out loud, erasing all
doubt about intent.

Even so, Trump's lawyers tried in court to shield him from liability, specifically civil liability for harms inflicted on members of Congress and U.S. Capitol police during the riot. Trump's lawyers argued
that nothing Trump said about the 2020 election should make him
subject to civil charges because they were part of his official acts as
president and therefore protected. This blanket protection was
sought for all speeches and tweets undermining the election result
up to and including his January 6 speech at the "Save America"
rally. In February 2022, D.C. Circuit Court judge Amit Mehta, in a
112-page ruling allowing lawsuits against Trump, the Proud Boys,
and the Oath Keepers to proceed, said the following:

> The President, the Proud Boys, the Oath Keepers, and others "pur-
> sued the same goal" [a requirement under federal law] to disrupt
> Congress from completing the Electoral College certification on
> January 6th. That President Trump held this goal is, at least, plau-
> sible based on his words and actions. He repeatedly tweeted false
> claims of election fraud and corruption, contacted state and local
> officials to overturn elections results, and urged the Vice President
> to send Electoral ballots back for recertification. The President
> communicated directly with supporters, inviting them to Wash-
> ington, D.C., to a rally on January 6th, the day of the Certification,
> telling them it would be "wild." He directly participated in the
> rally's planning, and his campaign funded the rally with millions
> of dollars. At the rally itself, the President gave a rousing speech in

which he repeated the false narrative of a stolen election. The crowd responded by chanting and screaming, "Storm the Capitol," "Invade the Capitol," "Take the Capitol right now," and "Fight for Trump." Still, the President ended his speech by telling the crowd that "we fight like hell and if you don't fight like hell, you're not going to have a country anymore." Almost immediately after these words, he called on rally-goers to march to the Capitol to give "pride and boldness" to reluctant lawmakers to "take back our country." Importantly, it was the President and his campaign's idea to send thousands to the Capitol while the certification was underway. It was not a planned part of the rally. In fact, the permit expressly stated that it did "not authorize a march from the Ellipse." From these alleged facts, it is at least plausible to infer that, when he called on rally-goers to march to the Capitol, the President did so with the goal of disrupting lawmakers' efforts to certify the Electoral College votes. The Oath Keepers, the Proud Boys, and others who forced their way into the Capitol building plainly shared that unlawful goal. Second, it is also plausible that the President was aware of the essential nature and general scope of the conspiracy. He knew the respective roles of the conspirators: his was to encourage the use of force, intimidation, or threats to thwart the Certification from proceeding, and organized groups such as the Proud Boys and the Oath Keepers would carry out the required acts.

Over and over Trump and others said the election was unlawful, despite dozens of court rulings unanimously verifying the outcome of the election, and only the mob could restore lawfulness. This tactic should not surprise. Those who seize power through non-judicial means often cloak their usurping maneuvers in the tranquilizing language of order, legality, and high moral purpose. Our nation will decide, over time, if Trump's attempted coup was more comic than tragic, more idiotic than insidious, more foolish than frightening. More than anything, we would argue it was unjust, un-American, and anti-constitutional. America in early 2022 was awash in post-2020 White House sewage: revelations of attempts to seize voting machines in rural Michigan; moves to undermine Wisconsin results before they were even certified; the creation of fraudulent electoral vote slates; draft memos, lawsuits, and executive orders to overturn (in some cases militarily) the election; White House call logs with suspicious gaps; White House documents torn apart and taped back together while others were—as if to vivify the sewage metaphor—plunged down West Wing toilets. There is no comparable set of offenses against the law and spirit of America. As Judge Mehta said in allowing civil suits against Trump to proceed: "To deny a President immunity from civil damages is no small step. The court well understands the gravity of its decision. But the alleged facts of this case are without precedent."

And yet, some of the energy behind the attempted coup has not subsided. Trump has tried to glorify the ignominious, praising the Capitol riot at a rally in Arizona on January 15, 2022, and dangling pardons to convicted Capitol rioters (presuming he was reelected in 2024) at a rally in Texas on January 29, 2022. Trump made election denialism the centerpiece of his 2022 rallies, foreshadowing how it would become a litmus test for a Trump midterm endorsement. Early in 2022, Trump also began to fixate on races to elect local election officials. From Mar-a-Lago in mid-January, Trump recorded a brief video for Pennsylvania Republicans, describing his interest in local election professionals. "We have to be a lot sharper next time when it comes to counting the votes," Trump said. "Sometimes the vote counter is more important than the candidate." There is no gray area here, no room for multiple interpretations or alternative facts. Trump said vote counting supersedes casting votes. Everything he and his supporters attempted to achieve to deny Biden the presidency is consistent with this diseased definition of democracy.

All available evidence in 2022 showed Trump was not shamed. He was emboldened. Talk of pardons of rioters and incendiary language about mass protests against prosecutors investigating potential Trump financial or election wrongdoing—also spoken in late January—served to confirm the worst fears of those who voted to convict Trump at his second impeachment trial. Those lawmakers, Republican and Democrat, warned that if Trump was not convicted and prevented from running for future office, he would further degrade the rule of law by acting as his own vigilante or by trying to inspire violence on his behalf. Nothing about Trump's language or conduct in 2022 suggested that will ever change. The variable, the one upon which the Republican Party and possibly the nation may well turn, is the degree to which Trump supporters and self-identified Republicans would be willing to adhere to abnormality.

Some Republicans in Washington began to distance themselves. In early February 2022, fault lines emerged. On February 4, former vice president Mike Pence addressed the Federalist Society, hive of originalist constitutional interpretation and advocacy, to rebuke Trump.

> Our founders were deeply suspicious of consolidated power in the nation's capital and were rightly concerned with foreign interference if presidential elections were decided in the capital. . . . But there are those in our party who believe that as the presiding officer over the joint session of Congress, that I possessed unilateral authority to reject electoral college votes. And I heard this week that President Trump said I had the right to "overturn the election." But President Trump is wrong. I had no right to overturn the election. The presidency belongs to the American people and the American people alone. And, frankly, there is no idea more un-American than the notion that any one person could choose the American president. Under the Constitution, I had no right to

change the outcome of our election. And Kamala Harris will have no right to overturn the election when we beat them in 2024.

Pence had said much of this before in speeches at the Ronald Reagan Presidential Library and in New Hampshire. What was different, this time, was Pence's specific answer to Trump that he had the power to overturn the election. Pence told us he added the lines—"President Trump is wrong. I had no right to overturn the election."—because Trump accused him of failing to do something he could have done. Pence also told us he stayed out of the fray for months after the Capitol riot but emerged to defend himself and the Constitution. He had done so in those earlier speeches, but the clear repudiation of Trump, he told us, only came in response to Trump's provocation. In a mid-February 2022 speech to the Stanford University Republican Club, Pence called January 6 "a tragic day" and said that rioters were "wrong" and should be "held accountable." "We did our duty that day," Pence told the young conservatives at Stanford. "I kept my oath and moved our nation forward that day."

The Federalist Society speech, though, made instant national headlines. Pence is a political animal and so he bracketed his rejoinder with carefully considered language—noting the founders' fear of foreign intrigue (one of the greatest worries on their minds when America began) while adding a bit of partisan sniping about 2024, both of which are normal parts of political discourse in our country. Pence stated the obvious. But in times such as these the obvious has been obscured, clear truths distorted by disinformation, hucksterism, and greed. A leading exponent of all three, former White House senior strategist (fired in 2017) Steve Bannon called Pence a "stone-cold coward." Bannon figured prominently in efforts to overturn the election, as we shall soon review.

Other GOP schisms appeared that very same day. The Republican National Committee censured Reps. Liz Cheney of Wyoming and Adam Kinzinger of Illinois for joining the House Select Committee investigating January 6. The censure resolution accused both of "participating in a Democrat-led persecution of ordinary citizens engaged in legitimate political discourse." The censure was far less meaningful than the words therein. (Cheney and Kinzinger went about their business undeterred.) But the national GOP had now gone on record to sanitize the Capitol riot as "legitimate political discourse." The RNC hastily released a statement after the censure vote, saying it was referring to subpoenas issued to Republicans who did not storm the Capitol. But the RNC wrote the censure resolution. The RNC had every opportunity to denounce mob violence and vandalism at the Capitol while simultaneously taking issue with the scope of the select committee's investigation and chose not to. In its zeal to censure Cheney and Kinzinger, the RNC sanctioned thuggery, just as it sanctioned the unscrupulous election denialism (Giuliani, Powell, and too many others) that fed it. Noteworthy as well is Trump's legal claim that he bore no responsibility for January 6 because the violence and vandalism grew out of "the independent and intervening acts of third-party rioters." Rioters he had incited with lies.

The RNC's conduct, of course, prompted questions. On February 9, 2022, McConnell, the Republican leader in the Senate, did as Pence had—stated the obvious. "We were all here. We saw what happened. It was a violent insurrection for the purpose of trying to prevent the peaceful transfer of power after a legitimately certified election from one administration to another." Even so, Sen. Josh Hawley, a Missouri Republican who led efforts before and after the riot to overturn the election, said the RNC resolution "reflects the view of most Republican voters." On February 13, 2022, Kinzinger addressed the intraparty rift on CBS's *Face the Nation*: "I have lost faith in some of the courage of my colleagues. I thought that every person, when they swore an oath, they had some version of a red line they would never cross. This is a moment we have to choose."

Trump lashed out at Pence and McConnell, predictably and monotonously. But polling in early 2022 showed Trump was not as powerful among rank-and-file Republicans as he once had been, with detectable albeit low-wattage anxiety about another Trump run in 2024. Those close to the former president were equally divided on his plans, roughly half certain he would run and the other equally convinced he would not. As 2022 progressed, the tension around Trump's decision about 2024 seemed to grow less consequential against the feral idea of election denialism. With or without Trump, a national party that believed, despite all evidence to the contrary, that Election 2020 was a fraud and therefore embraced unnecessary and harmful changes to voting procedures and possibly voting outcomes represented a genuine threat to democracy. For the nation and the future of democracy, the question appeared to have less and less to do with Trump and more to do with a national party's basic relationship with the Constitution, and the concept of self-governance.

In any era, when stating the obvious becomes synonymous with political bravery, truth and courage are simultaneously diminished. The question for America, therefore, turned not so much on what happened on January 6, 2021, but what forces conspired to bring rioters to a boil and our nation to the brink. This examination proved a fitful exercise for Republicans, forcing upon them that most devilish of political choices—power or principle. Benjamin Franklin's words, recalled by Maryland Democratic representative Jamie Raskin in his 2021 impeachment summation, seemed more vividly prescient one year later: "I have observed that wrong is always growing more wrong until there is no bearing it anymore. And that right, however opposed, comes right at last."

AUDITS IN NEVERLAND

Still, Trump remained a huge roadshow draw, packing in crowds of at least 10,000 in Arizona and Texas. At both, warm-up speakers competed to slather over The Big Lie. Tauntingly, Trump chose Arizona for his first 2022 rally and spent most of it denouncing election results there. One would think Trump would avoid Arizona since even an incompetent, handpicked pro-Trump "auditor's" report on the Maricopa County election confirmed what all previous evidence had already established—Biden won Arizona by over 10,000 votes. The auditors had no experience with election procedures and admitted as much as they went along. They didn't know how to put together an audit and made no effort to secure the chain-of-custody of ballots or double-check their results.

The inspection fell way behind schedule, went way over budget, and provoked more ridicule than results. The auditors searched for nonexistent bamboo ballots from China. They futilely searched for ballots allegedly mismarked with Sharpie pens—but only by pro-Biden voters. They also were on the hunt for mathematical tabulations that would prove votes were flipped (Trump to Biden). They came up empty. The Florida company in charge of the process, Cyber Ninjas, operated in secrecy and denied access to its funding sources or methods of vote tabulation. Its final report found nothing substantive to question the validity of the election, even though Trump promised over and over that it would. The Ninjas raised minor technical points, most of them more telling as proof of the Ninjas' incompetence and misunderstandings about election processes. But as motivated and well funded as they were, they could produce no evidence of widespread fraud or concerns about the election results. In early January 2022, Cyber Ninjas folded, unable to pay its debts or demonstrate any competency in voter evaluation.

To be clear, the most aggressive staging of a Trump-inspired inspection of votes in Arizona's most populous county yielded nothing to confirm dark Trumpian doubts, nothing to validate corruption conspiracies. Farmers in the West would call it a dry hole. Yet Trump denialism raged on. "We had a tremendous victory in Arizona," Trump thundered at his rally. "It was taken away. We had a rigged election and the proof is all over the place. We have a lot of proof." The Ninjas, by their own admission, found no proof.

Nevertheless, the Arizona spectacle spawned other, similar efforts in Wisconsin, and attempted "forensic audits"—a term that has no actual meaning in election circles—in other states Trump lost. Every examination of the 2020 election failed to unearth evidence of significant fraud or malfeasance. In every case, the results were confirmed.

What was Trump's purpose? The answers suggested themselves in actions taken to delegitimize the 2020 election and, when those failed, subsequent efforts to replace or disempower nonpartisan election professionals. These moves were designed first to extend Trump's presidency. Secondly, they appear aimed at the way votes are counted in future elections—inserting partisans into the counting process to achieve more favorable pro-Trump outcomes. These efforts were in full view in 2022.

THE BAGMEN

Every big con needs its bagmen, and the attempted coup had a rogues' gallery. Some wore MAGA hats and carried Gadsden flags. Some wore suits or possessed law degrees and, in some cases, worked inside the White House. As of this writing, the prospect of criminal charges and convictions for election-related crimes appears uncertain. But in January and February 2022, federal and state investigations ramped up on several fronts including the Capitol riot, the manufacture of fraudulent slates of electoral votes, the attempted conscription of local officials in Michigan to seize election equipment, and what might have been a coordinated effort to threaten and intimidate election workers. The investigations were unfamiliar. America had never seen a multi-pronged effort to bludgeon a presidential election.

Many of the participants appeared to fear no reputational harm. As noted, Patrick Byrne wrote an unapologetic account of his efforts with Powell, Flynn, and Kerik. Others, like White

House trade adviser Peter Navarro wrote a book, half of which was devoted to efforts to overturn the election, and then gave extensive, confessional TV interviews about the scheme. In November of 2021, Bannon was charged with contempt of Congress for refusing to comply with a subpoena from the House Select Committee investigating January 6. On December 14, 2021, the House voted to hold former White House Chief of Staff Mark Meadows, himself a member of the House of Representatives for seven years, in criminal contempt. It was the first time a former member had been so charged.

Initially, Meadows cooperated with the panel, handing over some 9,000 pages of documents. He then reversed course and refused to fully comply with the committee's subpoena. Trump's super PAC Save America donated $1 million to the Conservative Partnership Institute, a conservative nonprofit where Meadows served as a senior partner, shortly after the House Select Committee was established. During House debate on the contempt charge, text messages obtained from Meadows were read to indicate how deeply involved Meadows was in attempts to overturn the election. One text to Meadows described him as being the "tip of the spear."

Another text to Meadows, sent by strong Trump supporter Sen. Mike Lee (R-Utah), on Jan. 3rd, said "Everything changes, of course, if the swing states submit competing slates of electors pursuant to state law." Some Republicans in several key states took steps to submit their own, uncertified slates of electors, outside the boundaries of state law.

Lee sent many texts to Meadows Jan. 4 that read like a warning and a deepening sense of misgiving about the persistent scheming—without Constitutional legitimacy—to overturn the election.

"I know only that this will end badly for the president unless we have the Constitution on our side," Lee wrote. "And unless these states submit new slates of Trump electors pursuant to state law, we do not. . . . We simply have no authority to reject a state's certified electoral votes in the absence of dueling slates, with the Trump slate coming from a state legislative determination."

No state legislature went through that process, meaning the entire charade should have died and been buried before Jan. 6. As we all know it was not, to what should be (but alas is not) the undying shame of the perpetrators.

The list of bagmen was extensive. Giuliani, derided by some in the Trump universe as addled and mostly intoxicated during election subversion efforts, tried his best to recede from public view. He had his law license suspended in New York for violating codes of conduct by submitting knowingly false allegations of election fraud. Giuliani and Powell both face a defamation suit from Dominion Voting Systems, accusing them of intentionally lying about vote manipulation within Dominion election machines. In an early pleading in that lawsuit, Powell's lawyer told the court that Powell believed "no reasonable person" should have taken her accusations seriously—that they were political, not legal, and certainly not based on established or researched facts. In his book *In Trump Time*, Navarro wrote: "That Powell's ultimate defense against a slap-suit [sic] lawsuit filed to shut her up was that the stuff she had said was so crazy that nobody would ever believe her was in and of itself zany." Dominion alleges it filed its lawsuit to protect its lawful business against defamation that could harm its profits and employees and needed to seek redress.

The list goes on and on. My Pillow CEO Mike Lindell met with Trump repeatedly after Election Day, suggesting he had proof of massive fraud. That continued well into 2021 when Lindell hosted a three-day symposium in mid-August 2021 in Sioux Falls, South Dakota, where he promised to reveal reams of evidence, specifically packet captures (network data intercepted by hackers) that would prove China "switched" votes from Trump to elect Biden. Lindell, we should note, is also a defendant in the Dominion suit against Powell and Giuliani. On the second day, the livestream showed Lindell onstage as part of a late afternoon session. When news broke that a federal judge ruled the Dominion lawsuit could proceed, Lindell was seen getting up from his seat and, according to *Business Insider* coverage, "rushing off stage abruptly, disappearing behind a dark curtain." The talkathon produced nothing. Rob Graham, a cyber expert who attended the symposium, tweeted on day two: "He gave us experts NOTHING today, except random garbage that wastes our time. All day Mike Lindell has been on stage saying cyber experts are happily working on packet captures. We are not. We haven't been given the packet captures we were promised."

Amazingly, in early 2022, Lindell went further out on the fringy limb, saying he had enough proof of election fraud to jail almost all of America. "We have all the pieces of the puzzle. We have enough evidence to put everyone in prison for life, three hundred and some million people. We have that back all the way to November and December. Evil is revealing itself. Evil is popping up like pocket gophers. It's everywhere." There is a disturbing pattern worth noting. Lindell said hundreds of millions of Americans should be arrested. As we highlighted earlier, former House Speaker Newt Gingrich said members of the House Select Committee on January 6 could be arrested if Republicans win back majority control of the House. Trump, as noted earlier, said mass protests—bigger than the Capitol riot—should be waged against "vicious, racist" prosecutors (all of whom happen to be African American) investigating him. Before leaving the White House, Trump seriously considered using the military to seize ballot boxes. These are applications of police and military powers never before discussed openly in American society. And those who speak this language of police-state brutality appear to share one thing in common—a servile affection for strongmen and the one-dimensional politics of autocracy, precisely what our revolution, Constitution, and Bill of Rights were erected to oppose.

Former New York Police Commissioner Bernard Kerik also surfaced in an effort to contest the election. He grappled with the House Select Committee on January 6 over testimony and purported evidence of fraud. In early 2022, Kerik had supplied some documents, while refusing to produce others. He was part of Bannon's so-called War Room at the Willard Hotel near the White House, epicenter of pre–January 6 planning. One of the documents Kerik produced confirmed that the harassment of election officials in states where Trump lost was a key element of the campaign's post–election-defeat strategy, coordinated with officials at the highest levels.

Then there was Phil Waldron, a retired Army colonel who now owns a bar on the outskirts of Austin, Texas, and became a proponent of the China conspiracy gambit—an allegation that China infiltrated Dominion voting machines to change votes and elect Biden. Waldron, a psychological operations officer who served in Iraq, became part of former national security adviser Michael Flynn's orbit and worked with Byrne on the plan to seize ballots due to imagined foreign election interference. Part of that plan would allow the military (Byrne preferred the National Guard) to take control of ballots in six Democratically controlled counties. Thereafter, a supposed "audit" would occur (by whom it is entirely unclear) or the election would have been rerun under military supervision. Byrne wrote about this with dramatic flair in his book *The Deep Rig*, describing an Oval Office meeting December 18 with Trump, Flynn, Powell, himself, and others. Byrne said they crashed the White House uninvited.

Sidney [Powell] and Mike [Flynn] began walking the president through things from our perspective. In brief: there was a quick way to resolve this national crisis because he had power to act in ways he was not using. Under an executive order that he had signed in 2018 and another executive order that President Obama had signed in 2015, he could "find" that there was evidence of foreign interference with the election. Doing so, would give him authority to do *big* things, but we were going to ask him to do one *small* thing: direct a federal force (we suggested US Marshall (sic) Service + National Guard) to go to the six problematic counties in question and, on live-stream TV, re-count the paper ballots that were held as fail-safe backup. It would only take a few days. Even better would be if they imaged the hard drives and those images could be examined forensically. In either case, if there were no mischief found, then President Trump would concede. But if (as we suspected) evidence of tens or hundreds of thousands of improper votes was found in the six counties in question, then he would have a wide variety of options. He might have those six *states* re-counted on live-stream TV. Or he might have 50 states recounted on live-stream TV by federal forces . . . or he might skip that and have the National Guard re-run the elections in those six states.

The executive orders did not authorize such anti-democratic behavior, and the paper ballots, audits, and countless court cases confirmed that the voting technology worked correctly, the outcome was accurate, and the conspiracy theories spread by the election deniers were nothing more than a desperate attempt to avoid or delay the verdict of the American voters.

In court papers filed by Dominion, it was revealed that Byrne, in the summer of 2020, hired another player, Russell Ramsland Jr., co-founder of Allied Securities Operations Group, to help "reverse engineer" evidence to "mislead people into believing" the 2020 election was rigged. Waldron later teamed up with Ramsland to allege China, in cooperation with liberal philanthropist and activist George Soros, had hacked the election and flipped votes. When that gambit failed, Waldron produced a lengthy PowerPoint presentation about Trump declaring a state of emergency. That PowerPoint deck made it to White House Chief of Staff Mark Meadows. Waldron was aided and abetted throughout by Texas Republican representative Louie Gohmert, who would later vote against certification of electoral votes from Arizona and Pennsylvania. Gohmert also sued Pence in late December 2020, ordering a federal court to instruct Pence that he had unilateral authority to alter certified electoral votes. A Trump-appointed judge, Jeremy Kernodle of the Eastern District of Texas, dismissed the suit.

FAKE ELECTORS—THE REAL ELECTION FRAUD

The suit foreshadowed another scene in the drama played by law professor John Eastman, formerly dean of Chapman University School of Law in California. Eastman was the primary architect of the theory that Vice President Pence had the authority to ignore certified electoral votes and deny Biden the presidency. Eastman was also subpoenaed by the House Select Committee on January 6. The American Political Science Association took up disciplinary action against Eastman. But while Eastman may have been near the top of this scheme, he was far from alone.

Dozens of other Americans are implicated. In early 2022, state and federal fraud investigations were launched, involving fake electors and those who recruited and facilitated them. Several crimes might be implicated for those who knowingly signed fraudulent electoral vote certificates mailed to the National Archives as part of a conspiracy to deceive Congress, delay certification of the election results, and thwart the will of the people. In early 2022, it appeared that this was part of a coordinated effort run by Trump's reelection campaign (which left voice mails on the phones of phony electors) to sow confusion about slates of electors. This confusion would have purportedly empowered Pence to call a halt to the counting of electoral votes. Navarro outlined it in his book *In Trump Time.*

The political and legal beauty of the strategy was this: by law, both the House of Representatives and the Senate must spend up to two hours of debate per state on each requested challenge. For the six battleground states, that would add up to as much as twenty-four hours of nationally televised hearings across the two chambers of Congress. Through these televised proceedings, we would finally be able to short-circuit the crushing censorship of the anti-Trump media and take our case directly to the American people.

We should note that Navarro's interpretation of this "debate" is almost entirely factually wrong. It is almost certain that the debates in each house would be concurrent (a total of two hours for each state, total, meaning a maximum of twelve hours), and would not be televised. The spectacle the Trump team sought to create—to supplant the rule of law, rules of evidence, and consideration by the courts, presided over by judges that were predominantly of the same party as the losing presidential candidate—would almost certainly not take place even in their wildest dreams.

But the creation of the fraudulent slates of electors was not only a tactic to create delay and confusion. It was also a device to put Pence in a position to declare invalid electors valid and deny Biden the presidency. There is little question about the motive. What Navarro fails to understand is that even if members of Congress could have invented, by some illegal intervention of Pence's, a trace element of fraud as "proof," the Trump team would likely have had to provide that precise evidence (strong enough to withstand rebuttal) to the courts. That evidence was never found, let alone presented.

There were many versions of Eastman's memos. One ran six pages, another two pages, and another one page. The longer memo describes purported "illegal conduct by election officials." Nearly all the allegations arise from changes made to voting procedures due to the pandemic, ones announced well in advance (some dated to the primaries) and all of which had been either litigated or accepted as proper adaptations due to health concerns, a shortage of poll workers, or both. Nothing rose to the level of criminality. The longer memo also argued the Electoral Count Act of 1887 was "likely unconstitutional," a relatively novel theory since it had been guiding the ceremonial counting of slates of electoral votes since its adoption over 130 years ago. It also "war-gamed" several scenarios where electoral votes would be challenged on January 6, 2021. Four of the eight scenarios had Trump winning. "Bold, Certainly," the memo read. "But this election was stolen by a strategic Democrat plan to systematically flout existing election laws for partisan advantage; we're no longer playing by Queensbury Rules."

The one-page version of Eastman's memo, condensed for brevity for Trump and others, outlined the path to overriding the will of the people. It was produced in late December and starts by asserting "7 states have transmitted dual slates of electors to the President of the Senate." This was the opening line. And it was a lie. Seven states had not transmitted dual slates of certified electors. Not one had. Eastman knew this. So did everyone inside the Trump White House. What is clear now, but wasn't at the time, was the coordinated effort to produce fraudulent certificates of electors in those seven states. Each of these states (Arizona, Georgia, Michigan, Nevada, New Mexico, Pennsylvania, and Wisconsin) had already certified their electoral votes in accordance with state law and transmitted them to the National Archives by the appropriate deadline. The certificates carried the official seal and markings required for authentication. The counterfeit certificates did not. The fraudulent certificates looked nothing like the authentic certificates. But they looked almost identical to each other in language, formatting, and typeface. It was unclear in early 2022, when the fake electoral slates attracted the attention of federal and state authorities, if creating and submitting them for official purposes was a crime. But several investigations were launched. Criminal or not, the intent was to sow

doubt and provide a pretext for Pence to invalidate the legally certified electoral votes from at least six states. Read Eastman's words
from the one-page memo, all fodder for subsequent Trump harassment of Pence.

> VP Pence, presiding of the joint session, begins to open and count
> ballots, starting with Alabama. When he gets to Arizona, he
> announces that he has multiple slates of electors, and so is going
> to defer decision on that until finishing other States. This would
> be the first break with the procedure set out in the [Electoral
> Count] Act. At the end, he announces that because of the ongoing
> disputes in the 7 [sic] states, there are no electors that can be
> deemed validly appointed in those States. That means the total
> number of "electors appointed"—the language of the 12
> Amendment—is 454.

Eastman's assertion of nullification of electoral votes in seven
states (the original plan included New Mexico) meant that only
forty-three states had produced "validly appointed" electors. In no
case had a state sent dual electors or in any way suggested to the
National Archives or the U.S. Congress (House or Senate) that its
electoral votes were anything other than validly appointed. The
Eastman scenarios were, from the start, an affront to federal law,
state laws, and the Constitution, and more importantly, to the concept of American self-governance. Eastman's strategy continued as
follows:

> A "majority of the electors" appointed would therefore be 228 (454
> divided by two plus one). There are at this point 232 votes for Trump,
> 222 votes for Biden. Pence then gavels President Trump as re-elected.
> Howls, of course, from Democrats who now claim that 270 is
> required. So Pence says, fine. Pursuant to the 12th Amendment, no
> candidate has achieved the necessary majority. That sends the

matter to the House, where the "votes shall be taken by the states, the representation from each state having one vote." Republicans currently control 26 of the state delegations, the bare majority needed to win that vote. President Trump is re-elected there as well.

To be clear, the first step in this coordinated effort was to subvert state law in at least seven states, and the votes of every single voter in those states, regardless of who they voted for, by manufacturing fraudulent slates of electors. This subversion of state sovereignty was then heightened as a subversion of the Constitution by deceiving the Senate and the House into believing that states had produced that which they had not—dual slates of electors. One path to victory erased all votes from the supposedly contested states—Arizona, Georgia, Michigan, Nevada, Pennsylvania, and Wisconsin. The alternative sought to invalidate votes in all fifty states by ordering a contingent election in the House, where each state's multitude of voters is reduced to a single ballot cast by the majority party of its congressional delegation. Read it here in Eastman's sixth bullet point:

> The main thing here is that Pence should do this without asking permission—either from a vote of the joint session or from the Court. Let the other side challenge his actions in court. The fact is that the Constitution assigns this power to the Vice President as the ultimate arbiter. We take all of our actions with that in mind.

Pence did not have this power. No vice president has possessed this power. None ever imagined it existed. And one can only imagine what Eastman, Meadows, and even Trump himself would say if Vice President Biden had sought to exercise the same strategy in 2017, or Vice President Harris seeks to do the same in 2025. Even the assertion that one person could choose to defy the courts, defy the will of the American people, and defy the founding fathers is an affront to the Republic.

Pence knew his role was to preside over the legally submitted and certified slates of electors. He said so in a *Washington Post* op-ed on January 14, 2022:

> On January 6 an angry mob ransacked the Capitol, largely to get Congress and me, as president of the Senate, to use federal authority to overturn results of the presidential election that had been certified by all 50 states. Lives were lost and many were injured, but thanks to the selfless and courageous work of law enforcement, the Capitol was secured, and Congress was able to reconvene the very same day and complete its work under the Constitution and laws of the United States. Under the Constitution, elections are largely determined at the state level, not by Congress—a principle I upheld on January 6 without compromise. The only role of Congress with respect to the electoral college is to "open, present and record" votes submitted and certified by the states. No more, no less.

Pence was pressured to defile the Constitution, disenfranchise millions, and deny Biden the presidency. Pence was not the only person to stand in the breach. But his role was essential. For several fateful hours, as the Trump-inspired mob of maniacs roamed the Capitol and erected makeshift gallows outside to hang him, Pence remained inside the Capitol, surrounded by security, and began coordinating a federal response to repel them—since Trump would not. The pressure was more real than Pence has been willing to acknowledge and his op-ed did not mention Trump at all—continuing a pattern of post–January 6 minimization among almost all Republicans, even those who, like Pence, were among its most conspicuous victims.

The *Washington Post* reported a year later that Eastman accused Pence of causing the Capitol riot by refusing to override the legally submitted electoral votes. That *Post* reporting took on greater significance February 1, 2022, when Greg Jacob, chief counsel to Pence, testified for nearly nine hours before the House Select Committee on January 6. It was Jacob whom Eastman emailed the day after the Capitol assault to cast blame. Jacob had written to Eastman to say his "bullshit" legal advice had poisoned the White House, fed incendiary rhetoric at the January 6 rally, and provoked mob violence. Jacob said he, Pence, and the vice president's staff were under "siege" inside the Capitol. "The 'siege' is because *you* and your boss did not do what was necessary to allow this to be aired in a public way so that the American people can see for themselves what happened," Eastman wrote, according to the *Post*.

In October of 2021, Eastman tried to abandon his memo and his speech at the January 6 rally that preceded the storming of the Capitol. Eastman told the *National Review* that it would have been "crazy" for Pence to nullify electoral votes, because that approach was not legally "viable." Eastman tried to claim he didn't write all three memos. He also tried to back away from the memo's language that it was a "fact" that Pence (or any vice president) was the "ultimate arbiter" over the validity of electoral votes. Those exact words are in all versions of Eastman's memos and yet he told *National Review*, "I don't think that's true." Eastman said vice presidential authority was ambiguous. "It's certainly not been definitively resolved one way or the other," Eastman said. "There's historical foundation for the argument that the vice president is the final say and the argument that he is not. I think the argument that he is the final say is the weaker argument."

As Eastman told the Trump crowd at the January 6 rally: "All we are demanding of Vice President Pence is this afternoon at one o'clock he let the legislatures of the states look into this so that we get to the bottom of it and the American people know whether we have control of the direction of our government or not! We no longer live in a self-governing republic if we can't get the answer to this question." The Eastman memos point to an active effort—one given voice by him, Giuliani, Trump, and others on January 6—to extinguish our "self-governing republic."

However, there were those who would not stand idly as this was happening. There were twenty-seven state delegations under GOP control in the House in January 2021, not twenty-six, as the Trump campaign's memos suggested. The twenty-seventh state delegation led by Republicans had only one member—Rep. Liz Cheney, the at-large representative of Wyoming. She made clear she would have voted against seating Trump. In fact, in another state, the tie-breaking vote in Wisconsin's delegation would have been Rep. Mike Gallagher, who likely would have voted against seating Trump as well.

As we know, the Eastman memos served as the road map for Navarro and Bannon, both of whom enlisted, with Meadows's active support, more than a hundred House Republicans and eleven U.S. senators to seek a delay in the January 6 proceedings. Eastman worked with Bannon from a makeshift command post inside the Willard Hotel, one block east of the White House. The goal: to install Trump in the White House past the date when the Constitution required he leave by causing confusion in several states Trump lost. The GOP lawmakers had every reason to believe any move to send electors back to any states (or collection of states) would be met with legal challenges. The lawsuits would further slow the process, intensifying a sense of confusion and drift. But this was only part of the plot to abuse the power of the federal government to keep Trump in power.

WHY IS AN ENVIRONMENTAL LAWYER MESSING WITH THE ELECTION?

A vivid example can be found in the draft memo from Jeffrey Clark, an assistant attorney general for the Environmental and Natural Resources Division of the Justice Department. Clark had no experience in election law or Justice Department enforcement of election-related activities. But he insinuated himself into the election fraud conversation by letting Trump know he was a true believer and eager to investigate, instigate, and invalidate. So conspicuous and energetic was Clark's lobbying, he met with Trump and had several calls with him to discuss ways to overturn the election. Clark produced a memo on December 28 outlining an audacious plan to have the Justice Department urge Georgia (and eventually other swing states Trump lost) to convene a special legislative session to investigate and presumably invalidate the election results. Then, long after the federal deadline to certify and deliver electoral votes to Washington, a special session would impose its own slate of pro-Trump electors to replace the slate already certified. Clark sent the memo to Acting Attorney General Jeffrey Rosen and Acting Deputy Attorney General Richard Donoghue. The memo was contained in an email that read in part: "I think we should get it out as soon as possible. Personally, I see no valid downsides to sending out the letter. I put it together quickly and would want to do a formal cite check before sending but I don't think we should let unnecessary moss grow on this." The email and memo, revealed by the Senate Judiciary Committee, read in part:

> The Department of Justice is investigating various irregularities in the 2020 election for President of the United States. The Department will update you as we are able on investigatory progress, but at this time we have identified significant concerns that may have impacted the outcome of the election in multiple states, including the State of Georgia.

This was false. Attorney General William Barr had already concluded and publicly announced the Justice Department had found no evidence of fraud of sufficient or even near sufficient magnitude to change the outcome of the election. Courts in every contested state, including Georgia, where a Trump-appointed judge threw out the election challenge, found no evidence of significant concerns justifying overturning the certified results. Clark was recommending Justice Department leadership inform states investigations were ongoing and concerning when they were not. This was part of his audition to become acting attorney general, a position he discussed with Trump and, as testimony to the Senate Judiciary Committee would reveal, was part of a pressure campaign to intimidate Rosen and Donoghue. Clark discussed this memo with Trump and felt empowered to send it to Rosen and Donoghue. He later used his false representations about election fraud to curry Trump's favor and use it, as Senate Judiciary Committee testimony revealed, as a lever against Rosen and Donoghue, hoping pressure would force them to yield.

> The purpose of the special session the Department recommends would be for the General Assembly to (1) evaluate the irregularities in the 2020 election, including violations of Georgia election law judged against that body of law as it has been enacted by your State's Legislature (2) determine whether those violations show which candidate for President won the most legal votes in the November election, and (3) whether the election failed to make a proper and valid choice between the candidates, such that the General Assembly could take whatever action is necessary to ensure that one of the slates of Electors cast on December 14 will be accepted by Congress on January 6.

Several key points stand out, especially considering other maneuvers taken against the election in Georgia and other states. First, Georgia did not ask the federal government for advice on how to proceed in adjudicating controversies in the 2020 election. As Senate Judiciary Committee testimony would reveal, Trump repeatedly insisted the Justice Department investigate fraud allegations, even after Barr had determined they were irrelevant to the outcome. We should note here that Barr, on November 9, 2020, took the unusual step of authorizing federal prosecutors to investigate "if there are clear and apparently credible allegations of irregularities that, if true, could potentially impact the outcome of a federal election in an individual state." This was a sizable departure from Justice Department policy. Historically, the Justice Department had a policy of avoiding even the appearance of interference with an election. Barr was heavily criticized at the time, and the senior prosecutor for election crimes, Richard Pilger, resigned in protest.

Even after federal prosecutors investigated and found no evidence that would bring the outcome of the election into question, Clark, with Trump's blessing, was trying to get the new acting leaders at Justice to sign onto this heavy-handed intrusion into state election management. What's more, there was no claim in Georgia that violations of law had occurred or that voting rights had been compromised. By this time, the FBI and the Georgia Bureau of Investigation had already dismissed allegations of double vote counting and ballot shredding.

In fact, Georgia (like the other states) had, on its own and in accordance with its own practices, already confirmed the integrity of the election. The Clark memo would have had the Justice Department greenlight the legislature to commandeer this process with, it now appears clear, the purpose of empowering Republicans within that legislature to invalidate the election and impose a new result. This instruction can be found in the reference to the legislature taking "whatever action is necessary" to see that Congress accepts Georgia's electoral votes on January 6.

The memo also reveals something we have only recently come to understand as part of a coordinated external effort to overturn the election. The key section reads in part:

The Department believes that in Georgia and several other States, both a slate of electors supporting Joseph R. Biden Jr., and a separate slate of electors supporting Donald J. Trump, gathered on that day at the proper location to cast their ballots, and that both sets of those ballots have been transmitted to Washington, D.C., to be opened by Vice President Pence.

The memo discloses what the country would only come to learn about in early 2022—phony slates of electors (as discussed above). How did Clark know about this? Yes, there was media coverage of some pro-Trump Republicans attempting to meet in disputed states as "official" electors. But this was regarded at the time as political theater, meaningless to the lawful certification of electoral slates. As we can now clearly see, fraudulent electors were part of Eastman's gambit and Clark was in on it—though clearly Rosen and Donoghue were not.

In December, in a desperate last gambit, the Texas attorney general brought a case under the Supreme Court's "original jurisdiction," asking the high court to immediately hold a trial to throw out the electoral votes of the states of Pennsylvania, Georgia, Michigan, and Wisconsin. This effort was an unprecedented mugging of state sovereignty. In essence, states unhappy with the certified outcome of the election brought a lawsuit seeking to disenfranchise every voter in the states challenged because they didn't like the election rules that were in place well before the election in those states. On December 11, 2020, the Supreme Court dismissed the case, ruling "Texas has not demonstrated a judicially cognizable interest in the manner in which another state conducts its elections." The ruling was unsigned, though Justices Clarence Thomas and Samuel Alito said the Court should have heard the case. In response, Nebraska senator Ben Sasse, a Republican, said, "Since Election Night, a lot of people have been confusing voters by spinning Kenyan Birther-type, 'Chavez rigged the election from the grave' conspiracy theories, but every American who cares about the rule of law should take comfort that the Supreme Court—including all three of President Trump's picks—closed the book on the nonsense."

But it did not close the book. The White House, again at Clark's urging, seriously considered refiling the Texas case on behalf of the United States and all its voters.

The Supreme Court almost certainly would have dismissed the same suit filed on behalf of the United States, had Trump sent it forward. Texas was an instrument in Trump's attempt to subvert the election. It invented a nonexistent harm, that Texas electors were injured because Texas found fault with Pennsylvania's election procedures, contending they violated state law and the Constitution. No violations of state law or the U.S. Constitution were ever found. Yet, Texas, with Trump's enthusiastic support, sought to eradicate the expressed will of voters in Pennsylvania, Georgia, Michigan, and Wisconsin. It was never once clarified how everyone else elected on the ballots in those four states would have had their elections handled or decided. In fact, many supporters of the Texas suit ignored the vast implications of erasing general election results in four states—including their own election or those that created majorities in the state legislatures. As Pennsylvania told the Supreme Court:

> Texas waited until now to seek an injunction to nullify Pennsylvania's election results because all of the other political and litigation machinations of Petitioner's preferred presidential candidate have failed. The Trump campaign began with a series of meritless litigations. When that failed, it turned to state legislatures to overturn the clear election results. Upon that failure, Texas now turns to the Court to overturn the election results of more than 10 percent of the country. Texas literally seeks to decimate the electorate of the United States.

Rosen and Donoghue both dismissed Clark's memo on December 28, with Donoghue emailing Clark "there is no chance I would sign this letter or anything remotely like this." Later that same day, Clark, undeterred and emboldened by Trump, told Rosen and Donoghue that he wanted Rosen to convene a press conference to announce there was election corruption, and that Trump was considering changing leadership at the Justice Department. The next day, December 29, Molly Michael, Trump's personal assistant, emailed Rosen, Donoghue, and Acting Solicitor General Jeffrey Wall a draft lawsuit incorporating the Texas case as a cause of action with the United States as the plaintiff.

"Our country is deeply divided in a manner not seen in well over a century." So begins the draft lawsuit submitted for Trump's review. An email obtained by the House Select Committee from Kurt B. Olson, a lawyer who acted as special counsel to Texas attorney general Ken Paxton in the Texas suit, to Wall, reads as follows: "Last night, the President directed me to meet with AG Rosen [Acting Attorney General Jeff Rosen] today to discuss a similar action to be brought by the United States. I have not been able to reach him directly despite multiple calls/texts. This is an urgent matter."

The Trump lawsuit purported to solve the nation's "division" by asking the Supreme Court to "declare that the defendant states Pennsylvania, Georgia, Michigan, Wisconsin, Arizona, and Nevada administered the 2020 presidential election in violation of the Electors Clause and the Fourth Amendment of the U.S. Constitution." It further asked for a declaration that those electoral votes "cannot be counted" and prevent states from using their own election results to do so. Even more aggressively, it intended to ask the Supreme Court to authorize the states to "conduct a special election to appoint presidential electors," or, alternatively, "conduct an audit of their election results, supervised by a Court-appointed special master." This case was never submitted for Supreme Court review. Its existence, however, laid out, across more than fifty pages of legalistic language, a road map for a coup. It argued that the Supreme Court, as an instrument of the Constitution, could override a state's popular vote for president, countermand its procedures to determine electoral votes (all established well before the election), and order a special election or conduct its own audit with its own rules and supervision. It placed the federal government in control of a state election, provided the federal government assumed or asserted that state's election results were questionable—even if lower courts had already adjudicated allegations of fraud, mismanagement, or violations of state law.

Remember, this lawsuit, on behalf of the United States, was drafted after all manner of alleged controversies had already been settled in state and federal courts. Where recounts had been ordered, they had ratified earlier results. In Michigan, Pennsylvania, and Wisconsin, Trump had declined to request statewide recounts, even though he was entitled to them as a matter of state law. Allegations of fraud were either rejected for lacking evidence or withdrawn because . . . well, they lacked evidence. This proposed suit, clearly, was not about advancing the law but subverting it. The Trump White House gave serious consideration to a lawsuit that not only trashed the concept of federalism—respect for powers delegated to the states—but obliterated boundaries defining the limited role the federal government would play in local and state elections—even presidential elections. Lastly, the suit sought to impute on some states the power to invalidate elections on the ballot in other states—a massively unconstitutional, disruptive, and unnecessary intrusion.

On December 31, 2020, Trump summoned Rosen and Donoghue to the Oval Office for what was described by Rosen as a "contentious" meeting about why the Justice Department had yet to find election fraud. Trump told both he was being advised to fire them (a typical Trump intimidation tactic) and again raised the prospect of refiling the Texas suit. That same day, Clark again told Rosen he had spoken with Trump and again the president asked if he would take over for Rosen if Trump fired him. Clark told Rosen he was considering the move.

On January 1, 2021, Trump tweeted: "January 6th. See you in D.C." On January 2, Trump phoned Georgia secretary of state Brad Raffensperger to obtain access to Georgia ballots so enough votes could be found to produce victory. That same day, Clark, who had been seeking a briefing from the Director of National Intelligence on potential foreign vote hacking, revealed to Rosen and Donoghue that the briefing yielded no evidence of data tampering. He nevertheless pressed Rosen and Clark to authorize the letter calling for special sessions in six swing states. Clark also told Rosen he would reject Trump's desire to make him acting attorney general (replacing Rosen) if Rosen would just agree to sign the special session letter. Rosen refused. On January 3, Rosen and Donoghue met with Trump, White House Counsel Pat Cippolone, and other White House staff and lawyers. The meeting lasted nearly three hours and Trump, upon learning that mass resignations would occur among senior Justice Department lawyers if he installed Clark as acting attorney general, abandoned the Clark gambit and the idea of refiling the Texas suit on behalf of the United States.

Reviewing these and other efforts in which Trump continuously attempted to enlist the Justice Department in efforts to label the 2020 election "corrupt," the Senate Judiciary Committee concluded in part: "The Committee's investigation to date underscores how Trump's efforts to use DOJ to overturn the election results was part of his interrelated efforts to retain the presidency by any means necessary." Senate Judiciary Republicans found much more benign explanations in Trump's conduct. They concluded, in a separate report, that since Trump never fired Rosen or Donoghue, never refiled the Texas lawsuit, and never had the Georgia memo on special sessions sent, he was merely exploring options, taking advice, and acting as a protector of Americans who questioned the election outcome.

Whether that is true or not, Trump's legal and political arguments infected the country's beliefs about the 2020 election.

Doubts deepened because Trump repeatedly said the election was stolen, even after it was proven over and over—by courts, the Justice Department, the Department of Homeland Security, the FBI, the intelligence community, and the recounts and audits—Trump had fairly and legitimately lost. It was an echo chamber of grievance that would produce grievous results. The second line of the never-filed lawsuit on behalf of the United States reads: "More than 77 percent of Republican voters believe that 'widespread fraud' occurred in the 2020 general election while 97 percent of Democrats say there was not." What the public believes or does not believe about alleged or imagined fraud in any presidential election neither validates nor invalidates substantive legal issues surrounding that election. Having lost all substantive arguments about fraud, the draft lawsuit on behalf of the United States asked the Supreme Court to intervene "to ensure that the U.S. Constitution does not become simply a piece of parchment on display at the National Archives." In other words, to save the Constitution, one must destroy it.

EXCITED . . . INCITED . . . STORMED THE CAPITOL

All of this became part of the election-denying zeitgeist, with disastrous consequences on January 6. Elmer Stewart Rhodes, a former Army lieutenant with a Yale law degree, allegedly led a conspiracy to organize a small militia that would, in the words of the federal indictment charging him with seditious conspiracy, "oppose by force the lawful transfer of presidential power." Rhodes is the founder and leader of the Oath Keepers, which, according to the indictment, is "a large but loosely organized collection of individuals, some of whom are associated with militias." The Oath Keepers, in general, believe the federal government has been overtaken by "elites" who seek to strip Americans of their individual rights. According to the indictment.

Rhodes and certain co-conspirators, to include certain select regional leaders, planned to stop the lawful transfer of presidential power by January 20, 2021, which included multiple ways to deploy force. They coordinated travel across the country to enter Washington, D.C., equipped themselves with a variety of weapons, donned combat and tactical gear, and were prepared to answer Rhodes's call to take up arms at Rhodes's direction. Some co-conspirators also amassed firearms on the outskirts of Washington, D.C., distributed among "quick reaction force" (QRF) teams, and planned to use the firearms in support of their plot to stop the lawful transfer of presidential power.

Rhodes has pleaded not guilty to the charges.

Rhodes's words are telling. From the indictment:

On November 5, 2020—two days after the Presidential Election—Rhodes sent a message to an invitation-only, end-to-end encrypted group chat on the application Signal titled "Leadership intel sharing secured." In his message, Rhodes urged his followers to refuse to accept the election results and stated: "We aren't getting through this without a civil war. Too late for that. Prepare your mind, body, spirit."

On November 7, 2020—the date that President Trump was projected to have lost the Presidential Election—Rhodes wrote to the Leadership Intel Chat: "We must now do what the people of Serbia did when Milosevic stole the election. Refuse to accept it and march en masse on the nation's Capitol."

On December 11, 2020, Rhodes sent a message to an invitation-only Signal group chat titled "Dec 12 DC Security/Leadership." Rhodes stated that if President-elect Biden were to assume the presidency, "It will be a cloddy and desperate fight. We are going to have a fight. That can't be avoided."

On December 22, 2020, in an interview with a regional Oath Keepers leader, Rhodes stated that if President-Elect Biden were able to assume the presidency, "We will have to do a bloody, massively bloody revolution against them. That's what's going to have to happen." He urged President Trump to use military force to stop the lawful transfer of presidential power, describing January 6th, 2021, as "a hard constitutional deadline" to do so.

On December 23, 2020, Rhodes published another open letter to the Oath Keepers website. Rhodes explained, "tens of thousands of patriot Americans, both veterans and non-veterans, will already be in Washington, D.C., and many of us will have our mission-critical gear stowed nearby just outside D.C. Rhodes stated in the open letter that he and others may have to "take up arms in defense of our God-given liberty."

On December 25, 2020, Rhodes wrote "I think Congress will screw him [President Trump] over. The only chance we/he has is if we scare the shit out of them and convince them it will be torches and pitchforks time if they don't do the right thing. But I don't think they will listen."

On December 31, 2020, Rhodes wrote to the Leadership Intel Chat, "There is no standard political or legal way out of this."

Rhodes left his home in Granbury, Texas, on January 3 and headed for D.C. On the way, according to the indictment, he spent $6,000 on an "AR-platform rifle and firearms equipment, including sights, mounts, triggers, slings and additional firearms attachments." In Mississippi the next day, Rhodes spent another $4,500 on more firearms equipment. On the morning of January 6, Rhodes, according to the indictment, messaged the Leadership Signal Chat, "We will have several well-equipped QRFs outside D.C. And there are many, many others from other groups, who will be watching and waiting on the outside in case of worse case scenarios."

Rhodes entered the Capitol at about 1:30 p.m. and, according to the indictment, on the Leadership Intel Chat, "in response to a claim by an Oath Keepers affiliate that Antifa had breached the Capitol replied, 'Nope. I'm right here. These are Patriots.'" Rhodes then messaged Leadership Signal Chat, "Pence is doing nothing. As I predicted. All I see Trump doing is complaining. I see no intent by him to do anything. So the patriots are taking it into their own hands. They've had enough." A few moments later, Rhodes, according to the indictment, told Oath Keepers affiliates on the Leadership Intel Chat, "Hey, the founding generation stormed the governors [sic] mansion in MA [Massachusetts] and tarred and feathered his tax collectors. And they seized and dumped tea in the water. They didn't fire on them, but they street fought. That's where we are now. Next comes our 'Lexington.' It's coming."

The conspiracy succeeded, somewhat. The Capitol was invaded. Teams that Rhodes organized carried out their mission to enter the Capitol and disrupt the lawful transfer of presidential power, if only for a short time. Efforts were made to find Pelosi. Pence was threatened and had to take shelter, as did all members of the House and Senate. The QRF forces never materialized, but they could have and even more blood would have been shed. Even so, an armed assault on the U.S. Capitol was conspiratorially organized. Many participated. Weapons and ammunition were pre-positioned. Communications were established. The perpetrators penetrated the Capitol and sought to disrupt the proceedings. The indictment also alleged one team of Oath Keepers actively pursued House Speaker Nancy Pelosi but failed to locate her. There is a difference between violent efforts to halt the certification of electoral votes and lawsuits or other maneuvers to do the same. But the underlying spirit is precisely the same—decimate democracy. Trump and the Capitol rioters have that in common.

part three

7

WHAT HAS THIS WROUGHT?

THERE was a time when election officials, political reporters, political scientists, and historians worried if American democracy was dying from disinterest. Not dying so much as withering. Voter participation was mostly mediocre, borderline scandalous compared to other advanced democracies. The 2016 election, like most elections, saw only about 60 percent of eligible voters turning out, after a record-low turnout of less than 37 percent of all eligible voters in 2014. Analysts lamented that turnout in the 2016 election placed America thirtieth on a list of thirty-five nations with the Organization for Economic Cooperation and Development (OECD). "The headlines today are filled with talk about outside forces imperiling our democracy," Chip Bergh, CEO of Levi Strauss & Co., wrote in *Fortune* in September of 2018. "But, the truth is that the biggest threat we are facing is us. It's the apathy that keeps voters home in droves on Election Day, giving the U.S. one of the lowest voter turnout rates in the developed world."

Throughout the 1990s and early 2000s, academics noted with apprehension low turnout in local and state elections and even in midterm national elections where, routinely, participation hovered around

40 percent. Questions persisted about the longevity of democracy when a third of a population never bothered to vote at all and well over a half could only occasionally be bothered to. Lots of ink was spilled and papers written about a sort of dull lethargy around democracy—a take-it-or-leave-it ennui that seemed to sap democracy of its energy and vitality. Even David Becker wrote on this issue in early 2016, noting that "when a small minority of Americans is electing our officials and an even smaller proportion is nominating candidates through the primary process, accountability and democracy suffer."

How quaint these concerns now seem.

The questions now are not about participation or interest but trust and reliability. As noted, the 2018 midterms and 2020 presidential election saw record turnout. The same was true in the 2021 Virginia and New Jersey races for governor and other statewide offices. There is no shortage of interest and energy around voting. There is more interest now about registering to vote, methods to vote, the range of access to vote, and how votes are counted. That interest is not neutral. Turnout is affected by many factors, and campaign effects and polarization appear to be particularly strong elements affecting individual voters' decision to participate. And turnout can be volatile: in the last decade we've seen one of the lowest turnout federal elections (2014), the highest turnout midterm election (2018), and the highest turnout federal election overall (2020) in roughly a century.

In 2022, a debate raged over how these vital, interlocking parts of democracy function and who will oversee—meaning control—their use. The question for the nation is how to protect the mundane yet majestic machinery of democracy from abuse or manipulation. There is also heightened anxiety about protecting election workers from death threats, stalking, doxxing, and other mayhem. On one hand, we appear to care as never before about the cogs and gears of democracy. On the other hand, some of us want to take a sledgehammer to them by installing Election 2020 deniers in positions of election authority.

THE DANGERS OF DENIALISM

Let us be clear. This fight is occurring at the local and state level, where election denialism continues to fester. Those still influenced by Trump's stolen election absurdity (former Trump attorney general Bill Barr's words, not ours) have proven tenacious in their pursuit of power. In Colorado, Michigan, Pennsylvania, Wisconsin, Arizona, Nevada, Georgia, Texas, and elsewhere they have harassed election officials, sought to change local and state laws, ejected respected election officials, and, in many cases, peddled money-making lies for their own benefit.

As we write, Wisconsin Republicans in the legislature and some candidates are trying to sell a futile attempt to decertify the state's electoral votes as part of an impossible scheme to reinstall Trump in the White House. This was also touted by former state Supreme Court Justice Michael Gableman, who conducted a lengthy investigation of the 2020 election that Republicans and Democrats dismissed as ill-informed and illogical. Gableman denied Trump lost before receiving taxpayer funds from the GOP-led legislature to pursue his investigation. He subsequently attended election denial events in Arizona and South Dakota. Bernier, whom we quoted earlier, denounced Gableman's fixation with imaginary fraud. This particular argument is between Wisconsin Republicans who toyed with The Big Lie, giving it voice and the quasi-legitimacy of state investigations, and those who will stop at nothing to see Trump returned to the White House and so-called election criminals jailed. This is a fight at the far fringes of sanity, weakening the party and inspiring contempt among all but the most rabid. The Republican Party, according to legend, was born inside a schoolhouse in Ripon, Wisconsin, in 1854. It may die in Wisconsin, wrapped in the soiled laundry of The Big Lie.

"Republican elected officials have such an important obligation and duty," Cheney told us. "Because the unwillingness of so many Republican elected officials to tell the truth about what he's doing empowers him. And he has to be defeated. You can't just sort of stand on the sidelines as elected officials and say, 'Well, he's going to go away.' I don't see how you can convince yourself that fulfills your constitutional obligation. President Trump has gone to war with the rule of law. He's forfeited his right to participate in American political life, given his role in what happened on January 6th. There are too many people, among my colleagues, who are willing to excuse the behavior, look the other way. And their silence is complicity."

Democracy no longer suffers from a lack of participatory energy. It suffers from a lack of respect, allegiance, knowledge, humanity, and, most of all, trust. All of that and more will be tested in the 2022 midterm election and in the 2024 presidential election. America prides itself on being an energetic and ingenious country, a country that is flexible and creative under pressure and against long odds. All of that and more will be required in the next few years as we tame and, if possible, harness this newfound ferocity around the fundamentals of democracy.

This will not be easy work. Our national relationship to democracy has never been more uneven—possibly because the range of participation has never been broader. Diversity and inclusion are part of classical liberalism, the liberalism of Entitlement philosophers and theorists who inspired the founding fathers. Our democracy did not begin as an experiment in diversity. It began as an experiment in tightly regulated self-governance. We are now engaged in a great wave of diverse participation and shifting power dynamics where those long on the sidelines are now at the table (remember the political truism: if you are not at the table, you are on the menu). Who is in power and how they wield that power—from the presidency to local school boards—now feels central to our American experience.

We have not reached the promised land of complete pluralistic parity, but the look and intonations of power in America from city hall to Congress to the Supreme Court (historic breakthroughs in numbers of women and people of color elected) have shifted more in the first two decades of the twenty-first century than the previous two centuries combined. As we think about stresses to our democratic experiment, it would be dishonest and self-defeating to separate some of the angry questions about voting access from our history of racial estrangement and segregation. This book cannot solve this and will not begin to try. But we cannot describe fault lines in democracy without acknowledging this underlying source of pressure.

A comprehensive CNN poll on attitudes about democracy released in early February 2022 showed deep concern about our own collective future.

- Fifty-two percent said "American democracy is under attack."
- Forty-one percent said "American democracy is being tested but is not under attack."
- Six percent said "American democracy is in no danger."

Ninety-three percent of America agrees, in general, on precisely nothing. But more than nine in ten of us in early 2022 agreed the American democratic experiment was in danger. A majority agreed it was being assaulted. Republicans sensed danger more than Democrats and independents but not by as much as one might think. Sixty-six percent of Republicans said democracy was under attack, compared with 46 percent of Democrats and independents. Unquestionably, the sense that democracy is in serious jeopardy crosses party lines. Viewed through a racial lens, white Americans appear most alarmed, a manifestation, perhaps, of ebbing white democratic privilege. Sixty percent of white Americans believe democracy is under attack compared with 47 percent of African American voters, 31 percent of Latino voters, and 38 percent of all people of color. Anxiety is most pronounced among the old. Seventy-seven percent of Americans older than 65 believe democracy is under attack, compared with 31 percent of those eighteen to thirty-four (highlighting the generation gap over diversity and inclusion). Overall, 66 percent of Americans forty-five and older believe democracy is under attack compared to 35 percent younger than forty-five. Education is not a big divider. Fifty percent of those without a college degree believe democracy is under attack, compared to 55 percent with a college degree. Wealth matters, as it always has. Fifty-eight percent of those making more than $50,000 a year believe democracy is under attack, compared with 46 percent earning less.

Overall confidence in elections appears to be suffering and has suffered more as distortions and disinformation surrounding the 2020 election persisted. Only 44 percent of those surveyed said they were "very or somewhat confident" that elections now and in the future would "reflect the will of the people." That was down from 59 percent in a similar CNN survey in January 2021, mere days after the Capitol riot. In January 2021, more than a third of respondents (36 percent) said they were "very confident." That fell by more than half to 17 percent in early 2022. Of those who felt "just a little or not at all confident," most fell into the not confident at all category—29 percent in January 2021 and 33 percent in February 2022. Interestingly, in these survey questions, no one answered they did not have an opinion or lacked sufficient information to form an opinion. Whatever Americans think about democracy's present and future, they are paying attention and have ready opinions.

Some of those opinions, though, are even more worrisome. Half the country in February 2022 believed it was very likely (17 percent) or somewhat likely (33 percent) that "in the next few years some elected officials will successfully overturn the results of an election in the United States because their party did not win." Fifty percent of the country believed that. Forty-nine percent believed such anti-democratic maneuvering was "not too likely" (32 percent) or "not at all likely" (17 percent). Here is a clearer way to interpret this data, one that captures the sense of American anxiety about the future hijacking of an election: 82 percent of the country believes it possible a future election will be overturned by the losing side (17 percent likely plus 33 percent somewhat likely plus 32 percent not too likely). All of those categories are about possibilities, if not probabilities. Only "not at all likely" rules out anti-democratic antics. This is the crisis of confidence America must confront. This is what election denialism and subsequent changes growing out of that denialism have wrought. Democracy, at its core, promises three benefits to society: self-government, identification of rights, and respect/protection for those rights. In essence, that is what the Constitution provides and our system of checks and balances protects. All are threatened when we, as a nation, openly question whether our elections will be overturned in defiance of the will of the people.

Which brings us to the 2020 election. The CNN poll, which, we should note, is consistent with surveys conducted at different times and with different sample sizes, showed that 37 percent of America in February 2022 believed Biden "did not legitimately win enough votes to win the presidency," up from 32 percent in January 2021. Consistent and persistent debunking of election-denying conspiracy theories throughout 2021 did not shake the sense that Biden's victory was somehow suspect. There was some erosion, though, in certainty. In January 2021, among those who said Biden did not win legitimately, 73 percent said that opinion was based on "solid evidence" while 22 percent said it was based on "suspicion only." Those numbers in February 2022 shifted to 61 percent "solid evidence" and 39 percent "suspicion only." At the margins, this is progress. Denialism persists but its foundation is softer, more susceptible, we hope, to evidence and persuasion.

NEW RULES AND DEEPER DIVISIONS

But that is a long-term proposition. In the short term, laws have been changed as a result of these unfounded fears of fraud or illegitimacy surrounding the 2020 election. Those changes increase the risk of actions in 2022 and 2024 that could deepen questions about whether elections were conducted fairly, believably, and accurately. There was a rush in 2021 to tighten rules regarding access to voting early or voting by mail. These grew out of fears—fanned by pro-Trump partisans—that there was something intrinsically suspicious about these forms of voting. We have shown how voting by mail and early voting are neither pathways to fraud nor mechanisms that guarantee partisan advantage. Even so, laws were rewritten as if they were, and that will change the voting landscape, possibly producing unnecessary confusion, contention, and conflict. This is also what we have wrought.

In 2021, nineteen states approved thirty-four laws that can be fairly described as "restricting" access to voting. This, of course, is a somewhat spongy concept. Restrictive compared to what? For some, restrictive compared to changes made in 2020 for pandemic considerations (health, safety, access) may not be restrictive as much as corrective. We understand that point of view but would argue, as we already have, that these changes allowed for increased participation without sacrificing an iota of accuracy or verifiability. We would suggest that arguing for laws that reverse changes made in 2020 is more about discomfort with the election results than identifiable flaws in registration, voting, counting, or verification. We acknowledge there is no universal definition of "restrictive" voting laws, but we will list the categories of changes and let you decide. For our purposes, any change that materially limits the ability of voters to register and cast their votes the way they did in 2020 is restrictive. That's because the 2020 election wasn't fraudulent, as we have proven in numerous ways. If there was no fraud, no irregularities that would have come close to changing the outcome, again as we have shown, then what is the purpose of making registration and participation more difficult? It is hard to come up with a clearer explanation than trying to reduce the number and type of voters who participated in 2020—not because they cast ballots illegally but because they voted for a disfavored presidential candidate. (Remember, Republicans who have pressed for these restrictive changes won almost everywhere else down ballot in 2020).

How do we know? Georgia secretary of state Brad Raffensperger offered what, to him, was compelling evidence. Raffensperger occupies a unique space in the democracy debate. On the one hand, he is a conservative Republican, who supported Georgia's new voting law in 2021 that took a step backward from Georgia's recent history of accessible voting and gave the legislature new powers to potentially overrule or challenge local election officials. Conversely, Raffensperger faced death threats and repeated Trump broadsides for failing to overturn Trump's 2020 loss. Raffensperger contends Georgia, under his leadership, has balanced voter access with election security. Partisan Democrats don't always agree with that characterization, and Trumpian Republicans definitely don't see him that way.

Whatever you think of Raffensperger, this much is clear. After the 2018 Georgia gubernatorial election, where Democrat Stacey Abrams refused to concede and legal challenges to the results were rife (but ultimately withdrawn), Raffensperger came to Washington to ask national Republican heavyweights to help out. He went to the biggest think tanks. He went to the Republican National Committee and other committees dedicated to electing Republicans to the

House and Senate. He told them Democrats were making a stink in Georgia about election methods and that Republicans needed to invest in lawyers, researchers, and legislative efforts to increase voter integrity (as Republicans defined it). According to Raffensperger, in every meeting he got the same response. "No thanks. Not interested."

"I took office in January 2019," Raffensperger told us. "Immediately I had nine lawsuits from Stacey Abrams and liberal activist groups. We prevailed on most of those. But we went up and we met these conservative groups. We actually met with the RNC and said, 'Look what is happening here.' They said we don't have any money for these election issues." Raffensperger gave a more detailed account of this process in his book, *Integrity Counts*. Bottom line: Real election integrity didn't matter so much as feeding The Big Lie.

Republicans ought to think about this. The party infrastructure and its aligned think tanks jumped in with both feet to attack fellow Republicans (Raffensperger in Georgia and others in Nevada, Wisconsin, Pennsylvania, Arizona, and Michigan) when Trump lost. Mesmerized by the fraudulency of The Big Lie, many big-league Republicans, at least in terms of title and fundraising prowess, marched in lockstep. This has changed the way many Americans will register and vote in 2022 and 2024—with some changes possibly coming right before elections are conducted.

From 2021 through early 2022, many states passed laws that made it harder for eligible voters to cast a ballot and added to the potential for chaos and confusion during the counting and certification of votes. These states include Arizona, Florida, Georgia, Iowa, Texas, and many others. There have been far more bills proposed in more states that are not yet law.

These laws and bills are different and have different impacts. In some states, such as Georgia, where voter registration and access to early and mail voting was relatively easy, the new laws took a step backward. But in states like Texas, which was already one of the states that most restricted voter registration and mail or early voting, the new laws made things particularly difficult on eligible voters. In general, there were some common ways states gave credence to The Big Lie through unnecessary or restrictive legislation:

- Shortening the window to apply for mail ballots
- Shortening the deadline to deliver mail ballots
- Making it harder to get on an absentee voter list
- Eliminating or limiting sending mail ballot applications to voters
- Restricting assistance in returning a voter's mail ballot
- Limiting the number and location of drop boxes
- Banning provision of snacks or water for voters in line

These changes were, and are, unnecessary. Some are worse than others. Each ran counter to a powerful, verifiable truth: 2020 was the greatest triumph in the history of American democracy, with election officials under siege, dealing with record high turnout during a global pandemic, and somehow managing to deliver history's most transparent and accurate election. Early voting, mail voting, drop boxes, and easy and verified voter registration rules all contributed to this success.

Some proposed changes in service to The Big Lie would be comedic if not debilitating to the efficient and accurate administration of elections. In the aftermath of the 2020 election, Republican lawmakers in several states, including Arizona, Colorado, Missouri, New Hampshire, Washington, and West Virginia, introduced bills that would require election officials to hand-count all ballots, rather than to use faster, more accurate machines to initially count those ballots, followed by hand audits to confirm the counts.

These bills reflect a sad ignorance of the election process and the science around it. Hand counting of ballots takes much longer, and is impossible in most places in the U.S., given the complexity of the ballots and the deadlines for rapid counting. As the Associated Press reported:

> As one example, Cobb County, Georgia, performed a hand tally ordered by the state after the 2020 election. It took hundreds of people five days to count just the votes for president on roughly 397,000 ballots, said Janine Eveler, elections director for the county in metro Atlanta. She estimates it would have taken 100 days to count every race on each ballot using the same procedures.

After complaining that ballots took too long to count in some areas, those aligned with the Trump campaign were now setting up a process that would take even longer, well after constitutional and statutory deadlines requiring a certified result.

But delay isn't the only problem with such wrongheaded efforts. Hand counting also leads to less accurate results. Every piece of research analyzing the counting of ballots confirms what common sense tells us. Human beings are not effective at repetitively counting things over a long period of time. They get tired, they lose concentration. Machines are much better at accurately counting things like ballots quickly. Robust audits of the machines are necessary to confirm they worked as intended, and as noted above, auditing of voting machines was better than ever in 2020, with nearly all the states conducting audits of their technology. So Trump and his acolytes are urging counting to take longer and be less accurate. This is a perfect example of how these new laws, often passed under the pretext of "election integrity," carry a long-term danger—the gradual dismantling of election integrity.

An analysis of the March 1, 2022, Texas primary conducted by the Associated Press showed some of the risks of new laws restricting voter access. According to the AP, more than 27,000 mail ballots were tabbed for rejection under the new law. This was based on reports from 120 counties comprising most of the 3 million voters who cast primary ballots. The rejection rate in those counties was 17 percent, compared to 1 percent in 2020: more than one out of every six mail ballots cast. Identifying a ballot for rejection does not guarantee it will be discarded. But the new law raised more flags than before, proving, as was suggested before the primary, that many voters would be confused by new requirements, such as specifically listing a personal identification number for mail ballots that was the same as the one they used when they first registered to vote (which may have been decades previously).

On April 6, 2022, Texas officials released data from all 254 counties that found 24,636 mail ballots from the primary had been rejected, this out of 3,029,773 total ballots cast. The number of Democratic mail ballots cast was 110,967. Of these, 14,281 were rejected for a rejection rate of 12.9 percent. The number of Republican mail ballots cast was 87,980. Of these, 10,355 were rejected for a rejection rate of 11.8 percent. For comparison, in the Texas 2020 primary 982,362 mail ballots were cast and 8,304 were rejected, meaning the rejection rate that year was eight-tenths of a percent. We should make clear that voters in primary elections tend to be frequent voters in all states and therefore are experienced and generally more able to follow new rules and or instructions. Rejection rates of the kind seen in Texas in 2022 clearly demonstrate the needless culling of ballots from voters who were trying to participate.

This approach has nothing to do with improving election security or confirming eligible voting status. A voter with a valid ID is precisely that—a valid voter with confirmable ID. Tripping voters up to match when no match was previously required is just a disqualification trap masquerading as election security, a game of "gotcha" with your right to vote. Turnout in the Texas primary was higher than recent primaries—evidence of what we described at the beginning of this chapter, widespread interest and energy around voting. Defenders of the new Texas law said high turnout proved nothing was amiss, but they have no evidence to support this claim.

In fact, the Texas primary showed some of what we must fear— the corrosive influence of election denialism and its new spirit of suspicion and vengeance. Harris County is home to Houston, America's fourth largest city. Harris County was the focus of last-minute changes to voting in 2020, as Governor Abbott limited the number of drop boxes for voting by mail. Harris County has a population of more than 4.7 million and its combination of dense urban population, suburbs, and exurbs—where movement for jobs and better lifestyles is frequent—makes election administration a constant challenge. Harris County had a hard time during the March 1, 2022, primary. Some voting machines malfunctioned. In some precincts poll workers distributed incorrect ballots. And, as local and national coverage later revealed, an exhausted poll worker, nearing the end of a thirty-hour shift, mistakenly failed to include about 10,000 votes out of 360,000 cast in an unofficial tally. This error would have been discovered with or without the new law: extensive canvassing procedures during the review of the unofficial vote counts are designed to catch exactly this kind of error, and it would not have affected the official vote counts, which get certified days later. But in light of the error, the county's election administrator resigned a week later. Republicans sued, seeking a state takeover of Harris County election administration.

Harris County is a Democratic stronghold in Texas. Partisan interests in this matter cannot be ignored. Republicans said they were fighting fraud and corruption. Democrats said they were handling things as best they could with a new law (which confused even experienced voters), fewer poll workers, and in a climate of hostility that made election workers more nervous, haggard, and possibly less proficient. This quarreling epitomizes one of our greatest fears about the perverted potency of The Big Lie—it creates explosive fears, legal fights, and misunderstandings where they should not exist. Mistakes, as we have mentioned, happen in elections. There are remedies and safety nets. They work. But they can and will function poorly if laws keep getting changed, election workers are harassed, and election administrators fear for their lives and their jobs and face prison sentences if they make the smallest mistake. We are in a cycle of high-turnout elections. That is a very good thing, a healthy sign for our democracy. This is no time to erect needless barriers to voter participation or sow confusion and resentment over election conduct that may, because of human error or misunderstanding, create a momentary glitch that can and will be resolved because of redundancies already built into the system.

As we said at the beginning of this chapter, America's focus on democracy and its methods is acute. Consequently, 2021 also saw an effort to expand access to voting—also in reaction to The Big Lie. Roughly half the states fearful of election denialism acted to enhance voting protections in existing laws. One of the sad truths of the parallel movements in America to restrict and expand voting access is that our approach to democracy itself is diverging. Red states have trended in the restrictive direction, blue states in the expansive direction. This may intensify the sense of two political Americas where not only our party allegiance, ideology, and values conflict but the means by which we practice and interact with democracy is in conflict as well. The Constitution delegates great authority to the states in administering elections. Differing laws and approaches in all but clearly discriminatory cases do not violate the Constitution. But The Big Lie has led states to pull apart from one another more than ever, adding unhelpfully to our sense of national division and separateness.

States like California, Colorado, Connecticut, Delaware, Illinois, Maine, Maryland, Massachusetts, New Jersey, and New Mexico have made changes that expanded access to registration and voting, including some of the following:

- Expanding early voting
- Easing requirements for mail voting
- Expanding mail ballot drop box access and locations
- Modernizing voter registration
- Expanding access for disabled voters
- Easing voter ID requirements
- Restoring voting rights to former felons

We should note, some states did a bit of both by passing laws that added restrictions while also bringing more expansive policies. This hybrid approach melds the energies of The Big Lie, likely attempting to fix something that wasn't broken. What was most needed in the aftermath of 2020 was a calm survey of what worked best and a gradual revisiting of changes introduced somewhat hurriedly in some states in 2020 with an eye toward increasing voter confidence and security in future elections. The Big Lie cynically erased that opportunity, and only a very small number of states, like Kentucky, brought Democrats and Republicans together to learn from election professionals what worked best and what needed changing. It may cost us dearly if we don't take care with the tools of democracy—voter registration, casting ballots, counting ballots, certifying results—and the professionals who have risen to the task of protecting them and the election results they produce.

There are other troubling developments—ones that appeared in early 2022 that will only add to confusion and uncertainty about the trustworthiness of elections. Trump-backed figures have raised knowingly alarmist allegations about voter registration rolls, hoping to keep alive doubts about the 2020 election and weaponize misconceptions about voter registration to undermine confidence in future elections. The group is called the Voter Reference Foundation, an offshoot of a conservative nonprofit called Restoration Action. According to finance records, the funding of both can be traced to a super PAC that receives substantial financial backing from Richard Uihlein, one of the biggest donors in the Trumpist era of the Republican Party. The Voter Reference Foundation, or VoteRef as it is known, purports to analyze state voter registration rolls and seeks to highlight what it calls discrepancies or inconsistencies. Using methodologies that have been widely debunked, this "analysis" results in huge numbers of "false positives," as groups like these conflate names of individuals with others who have similar names in an effort to inflate the perception of fraud. Using shoddy data, flawed processes, and a predetermined outcome, groups like VoteRef want us to believe that "Juniors" and "Seniors," people who live at the same address, and people with common names, like "John Lee," "Maria Rodriguez," or "Sean O'Hara," are all committing massive voter fraud.

A common tactic of these groups is to suggest more people voted than were registered, which VoteRef has suggested happened nationally and in swing states. However, this is flat-out false. What these groups usually do to inflate their numbers, and justify their frivolous claims, is to equate "active voters"—voters who have likely voted recently and whose voter information is usually recently confirmed—with "inactive records"—records of voters who appear to have moved away from the jurisdiction. Registration rolls are a two-way process. Election officials maintain them and voters update their information, as necessary. This happens, as you might expect, at different times. Federal and state laws require election officials to maintain their voter lists. When they find a record is likely old, but haven't received confirmation from the voter, that record becomes "inactive." These records almost never reflect an actual voter (except in the rare case of an error, where a voter with an "inactive" record can confirm their residence and vote). "Inactive" records are not evidence of a failure to maintain accurate voter lists, but evidence of fidelity to accuracy. The presence of "inactive" records demonstrates a state is doing robust list maintenance. Anyone who adds the number of "inactive" records to the number of "active voters" is likely doing so to create the false impression of voter fraud.

This is no way to scrutinize or confirm an election. But to those disappointed in Trump's loss, and fed a constant stream of lies, it could sound like it might be. But also remember, voter lists are public. In every state, the voter lists are available well before the election, and they can be (and are) checked for validity. Most states allow voter challenges during voting, so that if there's a question of a voter's eligibility it can be resolved *before* they cast a ballot. These processes protect election integrity while also preventing sore losers from complaining about an election after they lost, when they could have raised challenges before the election took place. Or so one would think.

Also, recall that no such complaints about voter list inaccuracies came from Trump and his supporters in 2016, when he won the election. In 2016, for instance, only twelve states (and the District of Columbia) were using sophisticated data analysis from the Electronic Registration Information Center (ERIC) to keep their voter records up-to-date. By 2020, that number had almost doubled, to twenty-three states plus DC. Between 2012, when ERIC was created, and 2016, ERIC had helped states update 5.2 million voter records (usually due to a voter move). By 2022, that number had more than tripled, to 16.8 million voter records corrected and updated. Voter lists in America in 2020 were the most accurate they'd ever been to that point, and they've gotten even more accurate since, with now thirty-one states and DC in ERIC, updating over 25 million voter records that were previously out of date. Nevertheless, grifters continue their grift, even paying people to "canvass" neighborhoods and bother people in their homes to interrogate them about their voting habits, in places like Arizona and New Mexico.

Related is the creation of new state election "police" forces. In mid-March 2022, Florida, a state with some of the best election procedures in the nation, set aside $3.7 million for an Office of Election Crimes and Security. Florida does not have a major election crime problem. It doesn't have a minor election crime problem or even a microscopic election crime problem. Republican governor Ron DeSantis said so after the 2020 election, before "election integrity" became Pavlovian in GOP circles, calling Florida's procedures the "gold standard" and declaring the state passed its automatic post-2020 audits "with flying colors." In the two decades since the Florida 2000 debacle, the Sunshine State has become a model of election administration, making it easy to vote (early, in-person, or by mail), and in the rare cases of voter fraud, detecting it, investigating it, and prosecuting it. Florida's turnaround over the past twenty years is largely due to the professionals, of both parties, who run elections in its sixty-seven counties.

Those same election administrators in late 2021 begged politicians to "tone down the rhetoric and stand up for our democracy." Unified regardless of party, they went on to say:

> During and after the 2020 Presidential Election, the integrity of our democracy has been challenged by misinformation, disinformation, and malinformation that sows discord and undermines trust in America's electoral process. Many of us have been threatened by our fellow citizens who have been led astray by these deceptions. False claims of fraud do not strengthen our elections. Instead, they degrade confidence in institutions and discourage citizen participation in our democracy.

Florida took great strides to improve election administration after the 2000 Bush-Gore recount. It doesn't need a police force to hunt for imaginary election crimes or to enforce now punitive fines up to $50,000 for minor transgressions. Even worse, it appears the targets of this force's investigations aren't so much the handful of Floridians who seek to commit voter fraud—instead, it's those same election officials who managed the most successful election in Florida history. It was this election, it must be noted, where Republicans passing new laws in Tallahassee won by historic margins.

ELECTION OFFICIALS—PARTISAN OR PROFESSIONAL

In this regard, 2022 is producing unprecedented attention, campaign funds, and visibility for elections for two key, but historically lower-profile, statewide offices: secretary of state and attorney general. Responsibilities vary, but in most states, secretaries of state can oversee election procedures and certification of results. The attorney general is each state's chief law enforcement officer. It is not supposed to be part of their function, but as the 2020 election showed, attorneys general can exceed their state-based authority and try to band together to overturn a national election—and other states' certified election results—through judicial means. And in 2020, several attempted just that. Together, the positions of secretary of state and attorney general will loom large in 2024 if controversies arise over election procedures, election results, or election certification. In 2022, elections will be held in twenty-seven states for secretary of state, in thirty for attorney general. These races, it now appears clear, will draw unprecedented amounts of campaign cash and partisan pressure. They have already drawn divisions over election denialism and The Big Lie. One of the most immediate tests for democracy in 2022 is whether those who baselessly smear a free, fair, secure, and accurate election can catapult themselves into positions of overseeing and possibly overturning the next one. This is a test democracy cannot fail. It is one thing to advocate changes to existing election law as a candidate for these positions. It is quite another to accuse officials in your own state of violating the law by willfully producing a fraudulently certified election—which is exactly what Big Lie denialism alleges.

According to States United—a non-partisan group of former elected officials, law enforcement, election professionals, and ethics specialists—those who deny the results of the 2020 election are seeking statewide office in significant numbers in 2022. Here are the numbers: 36 states have races for governor and 53 election deniers are running in 25 states; 30 states have races for attorney general and 13 election deniers are running in 13 states; 27 states have races for secretary of state and 23 election deniers are running in 19 states.

States United defines an election denier as someone who: falsely claimed Trump won the 2020 election; publicly spread lies about the legitimacy of the 2020 election; called for a "forensic audit" of 2020 election results after they were certified, audited, or survived legal challenges; publicly promoted conspiracies about the 2020 election; or took actions in public or in court to undermine the integrity of the 2020 election.

Putting election deniers in charge of elections is like hiring a surgeon who does not believe in blood transfusions, anesthesia, or scalpels. Election deniers do not believe the way we cast and count ballots works. Election deniers would have voters believe that any election in which their party loses *must* be fraudulent. They cannot identify flaws, infirmities, or failures, and instead attempt to manufacture criticisms of a process they don't understand, and appear to have no desire to understand. They refuse to acknowledge that our election systems work. That is subversive and anti-democratic. It is a bright line.

And the money is already pouring in. Money, by itself, does not necessarily befoul politics, provided contributions are disclosed in timely and transparent ways. By the end of 2021, races for secretary of state had already attracted three times the amount of campaign donations as collected at a comparable time by candidates running in 2018. The amount collected by secretary of state candidates in late 2021 was eight times the amount collected by candidates in the same races at the same time in 2014. Record amounts are coming from out-of-state donors, for both Republican and Democratic candidates. This is not illegal, but it is worrisome in the sense that national partisan dynamics are now being visited upon races historically immune from them. National partisan pressures are the last thing secretaries of state need or want. Election administration is, as we have said, constitutionally delegated to the states. That means it is the proper role of residents of one state to pay attention to election procedures in their state, not fret and fund political figures overseeing elections in other states. Again, this is not illegal. But it is ill-advised in the sense that it diminishes federalism and union—that states function as separate entities but, during national elections, act in unison within our republic and under the rules of the Constitution. As we write this, election deniers are running for secretary of state in several battleground states. Elections in November for these and other secretary of state races will be a referendum on the potency of the Big Lie. Voters will have before them a stark choice: acceptance or denial, preservation of democracy or the harrowing of it.

Elections for attorney general in several states—some but not all battlegrounds in 2020—also command attention because these states saw all of the underhanded Trump efforts to overturn their election results. Attorney general approaches to election challenges matter enormously, especially when, as happened in 2020, a barrage of legal challenges appear before and after Election Day or, as in the unique case of Texas's attempt to overturn the national election, another state seeks Supreme Court nullification of another state's election results. How an attorney general approaches questions of state law, precedent, and the limits of federal intervention on election matters can be vital in pre- and post-election litigation, as it was in Pennsylvania, Michigan, Wisconsin, and Nevada in 2020.

These races have also attracted record amounts of campaign donations, with sizable involvement of out-of-state donors. In both cases, secretary of state and attorney general races may also be influenced by spending from super PACs, outside partisan groups that, in many cases, do not have to report their contributions in a timely or transparent way. This so-called "dark money" has been a force in national politics for nearly two decades but has, until very recently, ignored races for secretary of state and attorney general.

The aggregation of nationalized, largely unregulated campaign money in and around these races—where enormous institutional powers over election procedures and legal defenses are at play—is both unprecedented and worrisome. Do you really want election supervision in your state subject to the whims of anonymous big-money super PAC donors, be they liberal or conservative? Do you want the chief law enforcement officer in your state, your attorney general, to be similarly pressurized? It is happening. And it is happening as a direct result of Big Lie hysteria. These races would not have attracted the money, pressure, and visibility they did throughout 2021 and 2022 were it not for election denialism. The deniers raised money off their election slanders. Democrats in turn raised money to battle them in a general election. Ditto attorney general races. The arms race spawned by The Big Lie threatens to corrode and coarsen democracy for decades—unless it is decisively reversed in 2022 and 2024. Voters will decide and pillars of democracy wobble unnecessarily.

VOTES . . . WHO COUNTS AND HOW

Morgan County, Georgia, sits on the far outer ring of exurbs surrounding Atlanta's Fulton County. The county seat, Madison, named after the founding father and fourth U.S. president, James Madison, sits fifty-six miles due east of Atlanta. Madison is known statewide for dozens of antebellum homes. Its historic district is one of the largest in Georgia and is part of the National Register of Historic Places. Legend has it Union general William Tecumseh Sherman spared Madison during his destructive Civil War march to the sea because of its beauty, sophistication, and culture. (It probably had more to do with family ties to a pro-Union congressman who lived there.) Be that as it may, Madison remains a charming outpost, quiet and refined, its population just about 4,500 in 2020, almost evenly divided between white and Black residents. Morgan County's population is about 20,000 and its politics have been Republican and conservative since 1992 when Bill Clinton carried the entire state, the last Democrat to do so. Trump won Morgan County with 69 percent in 2016 and 70 percent in 2020, the biggest margins for a Republican ever. Morgan County is not contested turf. It is solidly, predictably Republican. It had no election issues in 2020.

And yet, Morgan County is illustrative of a new dynamic fed by The Big Lie. Under the new 2021 election law, county commissions could reconstitute county election boards as they saw fit. Majority-Republican county commissions, like the one in Morgan County, could take this opportunity to extend their partisan influence. Helen Butler, an African American woman with a booming voice and disarming demeanor, was removed under this new provision.

"I was on the Board of Election of Morgan County, and I was appointed in 2010 and I served until June of 2021, when the state legislature decided that they wanted to take over control of local boards of elections," Butler told us from her office in Atlanta where she is executive director of the Georgia Coalition for the People's Agenda. Butler is a proud Democrat and has never hidden this truth. Her office walls are covered with photos of civil rights leaders, among them Rev. Joseph Lowery, co-founder, with Martin Luther King Jr., of the Southern Christian Leadership Conference. Butler has a deep appreciation for the struggle to win the right to vote and is passionate about participating in its preservation and expansion.

She did this work for more than decade without strife or criticism, a strong Black woman helping to oversee elections in a biracial pro-Trump county. We asked her why she was removed from the Morgan County board of elections. "The general part was that our board was dysfunctional. I didn't know what dysfunctional meant because we've been operating since 2010. We've had Republican chairpersons, we've had Democratic or independent chairpersons appointed by the board of commissioners, and the rest were appointed by political parties. We executed our duties. We made sure registrations were accurate. We made sure that people got on the rolls. We hired poll workers. We determined which polling locations would be in place. We certified elections."

This is the work of election supervisors and election board members all over the country. It is time-consuming, meticulous, no-nonsense, nonpartisan, and unglamorous. "We never had an instance where we were brought before the state election board. So why were we dysfunctional only in 2021? I do not know. I have some suspicions as to why."

Butler's answer is one you will encounter in places across the country where sudden new pressures and whispered accusations shadow election specialists and election administrators. "To me this is a part of the process of taking over to augment The Big Lie that, you know, they wanted to find eleven thousand votes." That was a reference, of course, to Trump's gambit to badger Raffensperger to turn Georgia's election in his favor. "Well, you can find eleven thousand votes by having boards of elections, not certifying their results, and looking for other things to certify."

"Part of the takeover process is having people who are willing to say that the election was not done the way it was supposed to be done. If you reconstitute the board with a lot of members that are made up of one political party, and the political line is you have to change the outcome of the election to keep someone in power, then this is the way to do it." We were reminded of Trump's emphasis in early 2022 on being tougher when it comes to counting votes—an unmistakable bid to replace Americans like Butler with party-line automatons. "It comes down to the count, who counts the vote and when votes get counted," Butler said. "That is very critical to the process. And quite honestly, they've thrown a lot of good election officials under the bus in this crisis. It totally frightens me. They are really trying to kill democracy with a small *d*. That impacts this country. Not Georgia itself alone, but all fifty states."

This book is about election procedures, election rules, election workers, election professionals, and understood rules of the road for every voice in the democratic experience, whether it be a race for a relatively minor local office or president of the United States. One of the threats to democracy is mistrust or agitation around those rules of the road. Both have led to repeated threats of violence against poll workers across the country—even in states where the election outcome wasn't close, scrutinized, or fought over.

VIOLENCE STALKING OUR ELECTIONS

"You're all going to fucking die and it is what you deserve."

That is the call Staci McElyea, an employee in Nevada's secretary of state's office, received on January 7, 2021, at 8:07 a.m., the first of four abusive calls from the same enraged Trump supporter. "I hope you all go to jail for treason. I hope your children get molested." McElyea, a retired U.S. Marine, informed the authorities. The harassing phone caller was found and interviewed. No charges were filed. Making a generalized call with a threatening message to election workers may not be a federal crime or state crime because the First Amendment protects free speech that is general in nature. Many local and state police forces have no experience investigating these kinds of threats, and prosecutors are reluctant to wade into cases involving politics, free speech, and implied acts of violence.

This has left election workers across the country vulnerable, afraid, and questioning their longevity.

The Justice Department, in July 2021, established a task force to combat threats against election workers, creating a national hotline and web portal for tips and threats. In early 2022, however, arrests and prosecutions remained rare. In 2021, David Becker's nonprofit, the Center for Election Innovation & Research, created the Election Officials Legal Defense Network, partnering with top Republican election lawyer Ben Ginsberg, and top Democratic election lawyer Bob Bauer, to match election officials with pro bono legal representation if they're suffering harassment or threats. That such a nonprofit endeavor, simply to protect the lives and livelihoods of the civil servants who facilitate our democracy, would be needed in the United States of America as we near our 250th birthday is indictment enough of the current situation.

According to research conducted by Reuters, at least 102 threats were made to more than 40 election officials, workers, or their family. "Each was explicit enough," Reuters reported, "to put a reasonable person in fear of bodily harm or death, the typical legal threshold for prosecution. The messages often included highly personal, sometimes sexualized threats of violence or death, not only to the officials themselves but also to their family members and their children."

Some election workers were followed from work, trailed by car or truck as they tried to run errands or go home. Some affected election offices are installing security glass. Some officials now wear body armor, while others have taken firearms training. Every secretary of state in a 2020 battleground state received death threats. So have secretaries of state in Colorado, New Jersey, and Minnesota—states that weren't even close. Raffensperger's wife was threatened with sexual violence. Armed protestors came to the home of Michigan secretary of state Jocelyn Benson, menacing her and her family. In Wisconsin, state and local election officials have been threatened with violence and death, as well as arrest, merely for doing their jobs. Al Schmidt, city commissioner and head of election supervision in Philadelphia, had to move his family and obtain special police security for them and his parents. "Heads on spikes. Treasonous Schmidts," read one threat. No arrests were made. Pennsylvania's secretary of state at the time, Kathy Boockvar (she resigned in 2021), was told she would be killed in the middle of the night inside her home. She fled with her husband for a week, forced into hiding after she announced there would be no recount of the 2020 election results (a recount, you will remember, that Trump had a legal right to request, and chose not to). No arrests were made.

States have had to mobilize small units to offer near-constant security protection for election officials at the state and local level. Very little of this subsided in 2021, for the reasons outlined in the polling information at the beginning of this chapter. Doubts about the election, virtually every one of them unfounded and by now disproven, continue to fester, breeding resentment and alienation. All of this, of course, came to a nauseating crescendo in the Capitol riot. But it did not end there.

All through 2022 the phone inside the Bucks County Elections Office rang and rang until the answering machine recorded, day after day, death threats against Tom Freitag and his staff. We met Tom, director of the county board of elections, in the fall of 2020. He was in the middle of a renovation project worthy of HGTV. Because of a massive shift in voter preference to voting by mail, Bucks County, like every county in Pennsylvania, had to prepare for an onslaught of vote-by-mail ballots. That meant emptying one giant office in the county headquarters and installing machines to open, process, and count the ballots. Freitag, a quiet man in his mid-thirties, took up the task with purpose and apprehension. When we first met, his voice quavered a bit as he described the enormity of the job and the pressure he felt. He knew Bucks was a swing county in a swing state. He knew voters were nervous about voting during a pandemic, and he knew they would be hanging on the results of the election, as would the nation. We spoke through masks, as COVID protocols required, and small beads of sweat peeked through Freitag's slightly receding hairline.

We returned in late 2021 to see how he was doing. How the system worked. How the votes were counted. "We were all nervous going in," Freitag told us. "It was all brand new. New laws, brand-new technology we're using for the first time. Overall, I think it went really smoothly with what we were dealt. We were able to pull off all of this, but I mean, there were a lot of sleepless nights, a lot of long days working ten- to twelve-hour days, seven days a week for months on end. It was draining, but I think we accomplished a lot."

The election was long over, of course, but the pain of being villainized remained constant. Up through November 2021, Freitag and the employees he supervised received calls threatening violence.

We also received a lot of angry calls, emails, threats, just people that were dissatisfied with the outcome of the election and thought that there was some kind of fraud or something going on behind the scenes that was nefarious. At times it was directed towards me or just directed towards my staff. We received one email that said that we would all hang for treason. We had somebody that would call us every other day for months on end, telling us that we were all going to go to jail, that they knew what we did and it was time to come forward and let the authorities know what happened. And we would let them know that, I mean, there's nothing to report. Everything that was done here, we did everything legally and followed all of the protocols. It was a little disconcerting, you've worked this hard for a whole year for this one day, make sure everything goes as smooth as possible and then that's the thanks you get. It's difficult. I mean, you come to work every day trying to do the best job you can, always thinking of the voters, making sure that you're doing what you can for the county. It's upsetting. I mean, a lot of the calls might not even have been from voters here, but across the state, across the country. We had calls from Arizona. So it's just nationwide.

Freitag would rather avoid this conversation. We knew he was uncomfortable revisiting the threats and coping with abuse for what he believes in his heart was a genuine success for democracy. Like most of his colleagues in election offices all over the country, Freitag has no higher political ambitions. He doesn't want to be in the spotlight. He would give anything to be free of the harassment, second-guessing, and accusations of treason.

"There's been days where I wonder why I'm still doing this," Freitag said with a heavy, aching sigh. "It's just more stressful than it's ever been. I don't think I've gotten to the point where I want to quit just yet, but there's been days where I really don't want to come into work just because of the harassment that we sometimes get and just distrust for no good reason. I really don't even like to talk about what I do for a living when I'm out, like socializing, just because of some of the questions and accusations you get."

A Brennan Center survey of election officials in the summer of 2021 found that one in three fear job-related harassment and threats. More than two-thirds (78 percent) said social media contributed to threats of violence and made their job more difficult. Just over half (54 percent) said social media and the conspiracy theories trafficked there about the 2020 election made their job more difficult. Brennan followed this survey with a larger one in early 2022, conducting 596 online interviews from late January to early February. It noted a substantial increase in fear that political leaders will interfere in their work—up by nearly 66 percent from before the 2020 election. One in five election officials said they were either "very" or "somewhat unlikely" to continue their work through the 2024 election. They said attacks on the system from politicians, related stress from election denialism, and retirement plans were reasons they may quit before the next presidential election. In both surveys, anxieties among election officials ran the gamut: from external pressure to certify election results that did not match vote totals to being harassed in person or on social media to having their life threatened or their loved ones threatened. All these fears showed up in ways they never had before. Both surveys found that one in six reported already having been threatened on the job. The second survey revealed that fully half of these threats were never reported to law enforcement. Three-fourths of those who participated in the larger, second survey said they felt threats against local election officials had increased, and one-third said they knew personally of an election worker who quit because of the harassment. Stepping back a bit, you might be curious why these election officials took their jobs. Here are the answers: ensure verifiable election results (63 percent); serve my community (59 percent); being involved in democracy (56 percent); being involved in my neighborhood (48 percent); paid for doing a good deed (42 percent); my responsibility as a citizen (30 percent). If you believe these are the sentiments of election conspirators, we urge you to reexamine your own role in America's democratic experiment because you are doing more damage than you can imagine. As Dr. King wrote, "The one thing certain about bitterness is its blindness."

AUTHORITARIAN TOOLS

Election denialism, acceptance of violence (or the threat of violence), and tolerance of extremist groups threaten democracy. All are part of the Trumpist wing of the Republican Party. Majorities of Democrats and independents accept the 2020 election. Most Republicans do not. Most Republicans are silent on right-wing violence or threats of violence—note the attempts throughout 2021 to sanitize the Capitol riot and studied indifference to threats against election workers and officials. Extremist groups (white nationalists predominantly) continue to gravitate toward and find common cause with Republicans in Congress and at the state level. Violence committed in the name of The Big Lie can be traced to white nationalist, extremist, or anti-government militia groups.

We are all too familiar with Republican whataboutism surrounding violence and looting during nationwide protests following the murder of George Floyd in the summer of 2020. Initially, some protests were violent and accompanied by looting and property damage. At least nineteen people died. Damages easily exceeded $1 billion. For a time, neighborhoods in Seattle and Portland were, due to unrest, impassable or closed off. Other cities saw blocks of boarded up streets. Even so, with protests in more than 2,000 American cities, a report by the nonprofit Armed Conflict Location Event Data Project found that 93 percent were peaceful and non-destructive. The 2020 death toll was far smaller than race riots in the 1960s. The contemporary trip wire, specific deaths in specific places of African Americans at the hands of police officers—most if not all captured on cell phone video—was all too real. Again, as Dr. King wrote: "When there is rocklike intransigence or sophisticated manipulation that mocks the empty-handed petitioners, rage replaces reason." George Floyd protests were about rebalancing justice and securing life and liberty (protection from death over a $20 bill or through a no-knock-warrant shooting). Protests and violence around the 2020 election were about looting democracy and setting fire to the Constitution.

We have witnessed efforts to trample democracy by force. We may witness other efforts through controlling election procedures themselves. Both pose risks. We are on higher alert for the former than the latter, so shocking was the Capitol riot and so intense the desire to see marauders prosecuted. But democracies don't always die violently. Most die because rules are bent by authoritarians acting in defense of the rule of law. With the exception of some like Kim Jong-un in North Korea, many of the world's most powerful authoritarians—Putin in Russia, Orban in Hungary, Erdogan in Turkey—were elected. They have bludgeoned democracy via nominally constitutional methods, stretching and warping what the law means and how it will be applied.

Though we pray it's still unlikely, this could happen here if partisan election officials, bent on winning above all other considerations, use rules to invalidate or reject thousands or tens of thousands of ballots. Elections are rife with technicalities and small errors or omissions. Humans are imperfect and elections multiply imperfections—in using enough ink to fill in a space on a ballot, jotting your signature hurriedly so it may not match precisely with another for verification purposes, misspelling something on a ballot application, miscopying an address on an election form. Election officials and workers have long ironed out such mistakes by helping voters correct innocent mistakes or making sure they can properly submit a provisional ballot (which, if the voter is eligible, will be counted). This is where our modern democracy functions best, the intersection of rules and rational accommodation.

However, unforgiving application of rules, especially newly restrictive ones, could silence thousands of voices—millions if done at scale and cloaked in the deceptive language of consent. In late February, at the Conservative Political Action Conference (CPAC), Rep. Jody Hice, a candidate to be Georgia's secretary of state, said voter suppression "is when an illegal vote is cast and nullifies a legal vote." Hice voted against certifying electoral votes from Arizona and Pennsylvania after the Capitol riot. His formulation assumes "illegal" votes always nullify "legal" votes. How would he know? There were isolated cases in Nevada, Pennsylvania, and Florida of Trump voters breaking the law. Why couldn't an "illegal" vote reinforce a "legal" vote? Because in Hice's formulation, only opponents cast illegal votes. "We got to fight back," Hice told the crowd at CPAC, 90 percent of whom said fraud ushered Biden into the White House. "We are in serious trouble people trying to compromise that sacred trust at the ballot box." Said the man who tried to disenfranchise millions of voters in two states. "All of our states have election laws, but it is time that we start prosecuting people who violate our election laws."

Republicans even bare these fangs in the run-up to elections they are likely to win, just in case. While seeking the GOP nomination for governor in Virginia, Glenn Youngkin talked up the need for a forensic audit of Virginia's 2020 election. He said voter integrity was at the top of his agenda. Youngkin did not say Trump won in 2020, but he raised enough questions to pacify the Trump base. All of that talk vanished after Youngkin defeated Democrat Terry McAuliffe. Threats to democracy recede when Republicans win. That is authoritarianism in training. It means elections are not an emergency— subject to litigation, threats of violence, intimidation, and tumult—only when Republicans win. That is untenable.

"If we have strategic, bad faith actors out there we have seen that every level of the election process is vulnerable," Raskin told us. "It's vulnerable at the level of voter registration. It's vulnerable at the level of polling places and dropoff boxes. And everyone who is working in elections is theoretically vulnerable to violence and intimidation. That is already a reality. It does begin to feel like a constitutional crisis where there are repeated attacks taking place against the electoral system and voting rights and there is paralysis within the governmental system because one of the parties is obstructing any effort to interfere with its violations of people's rights. That's a pretty serious problem."

It's awful when eligible voters have barriers put in their path, intentionally or unintentionally. It's reprehensible when candidates and political leaders spread lies about election integrity so they can cast doubt about their defeat. It's dangerous when election deniers actually win office in a legitimate election, even as they planted seeds of doubt in case they lost. But perhaps an even greater risk is that election deniers, worried that voters are rejecting them, will subvert unfavorable election outcomes, using new laws and bastardized interpretations of federal and state constitutions to inject chaos and confusion into the post-election certification process. Even with efforts to suppress voters with whom they disagree, they still could lose and then employ an even more dangerous version of Trump's election denial playbook, one where violence becomes localized and aligned legislators overrule the will of the voters. There was a preview of this in 2020. In 2022 and 2024, voters might see sickly sequels.

8

WHERE DO WE GO FROM HERE?

AS we write this, war is raging in Ukraine. Free people, outnumbered and outgunned by a despotic regime, have taken to the streets and fields to fight and die for an abstraction.

They didn't die for food, clothing, fuel, or shelter. They didn't die for glory or money, new technology or more land. There is no shelf where you can buy liberty under law. They don't polish that up in a showroom. The ability to live with freedom under a constitution that guarantees essential liberties, to participate in regular elections that produce local, state, and federal laws is the essence of this mighty abstraction. It was worth dying for at this nation's founding. It has been worth dying for in countries different from ours in geography, culture, language, and history. Immediately upon Russia's criminal invasion of Ukraine came stories questioning the motivation of Russian troops—even the highly trained special forces. These questions were not raised about Ukrainian civilians who lined up for rifles and Molotov cocktails to do battle with tanks, artillery, cluster bombs, and other missiles.

The battle for Ukraine reminds all of us that freedom is precious, that there is a difference between real and concocted threats to freedom. It reminds us the process of upholding the law is and can be as important as the law itself. The barbarism and cruelty of the war in Ukraine shows us again that words, procedures, and laws can be mangled with murderous results. By the time this book is published, Ukraine may be free or still fighting for its life. What we know as we write in the spring of 2022 is that Russia misread what freedom, democracy, and the rule of law meant next door. Ukraine is not, as Vladimir Putin said, an invented country. It is real. And it fought for intangibles that free people make real. If Russia's war of choice turns into a war of occupation, history instructs it will be a nasty affair defined by local rebellion—snipers, mortars, improvised bombs—wielded in the name of freedom and sovereignty. Perhaps by the time this book is published, the U.S. and European nations will have sufficiently fortified Ukraine, will have noticeably harmed Russia's economy, and dissent within Russia—despite untold efforts at intimidation—will have risen to reverse Moscow's savagery. We cannot predict this history. We only know our beautiful abstraction has once again been exalted by human hearts called to defend it at all costs. Amid the blood, death, destruction, and scorched ruins of Ukraine, bravery in defense of an abstraction proved a potent foe to Russia and a stubborn reminder to America of a promise made to itself.

To properly understand where we go from here, we must appreciate what we have and rededicate ourselves to its preservation. Right now, America's experiment at self-governing is as good as it has ever been. We are not talking about results. We know people are dissatisfied on the left and the right. We are talking about the process to achieve self-governing, the difficult and foundational work of administering elections themselves. Our elections are more secure, more transparent, more verifiable, and more accessible than ever before. We are and have been perfecting our democracy, extending not only the right to vote to Americans previously excluded but seeing the fruits of the at Inclusion—a wider diversity of Americans than ever in positions of local, state, and national power and prestige. We are proving cynics wrong. A multi-racial democracy can survive and thrive. We are doing it every day. Are some Americans more comfortable than others? Of course. Every shift in power generates convulsions. We at times feel like very convulsed people. But are we genuinely as unhappy as we profess? Did not Ukraine remind us of the preciousness of our liberty, our freedom, of our daily acceptance of the rule of law and its beneficial predictability?

Campaigns are about voices clashing. Elections are how that clattering noise is temporarily recorded and ordered. The noise is neither silenced nor finalized. The noise continues in the contentious way a free people persistently questions authority and the application of power. Elections do not nullify rights and dissent. Elections protect rights and dissent by shielding both from authoritarianism and anarchy.

Ricky Hatch, the auditor and clerk of Weber County, Utah, has deep-seated anxiety about the 2022 midterm elections and what Republicans will conclude, should they win control of the House of Representatives or United States Senate or both. "I am concerned they will say, 'See, I told you so.' If they win big they will say 2020 was a total fluke and that they were able to stop the fraud. They will say 'We shined a light on these things.' They will claim that and that will extend the lack of trust in elections." If arguments like this arise after the 2022 midterms they will damage the nation by turning a shift in political winds—historically common in midterms after a change in party control of the presidency—into a phony indictment of the non-fraudulent 2020 election and an even phonier endorsement of wayward laws and reckless rhetoric. It will also deepen the sickening feeling among Democrats—widespread among lawmakers in Washington and party activists—that Republicans only retract the claws of election denialism when they prevail. This will deepen our national estrangement and fuel existing fires of discord.

Elections are the essential machinery of our experiment in self-governing. President Trump won in 2016. President Biden won in 2020. Scores of Democrats won races on ballots that produced Trump's victory. Even more Republicans won on ballots that produced Biden's victory. Those ballots were fairly counted in both races and applicable laws were applied in both elections. (In 2020, election rules altered for the pandemic were also adjudicated and fully understood by both sides before voting began.) Trump's election shocked Democrats and delighted insurgent Trump Republicans. Biden's election delighted Democrats and a good number of independents. Those passions are an outgrowth of an election. Both elections were pressurized by unexpected outside forces— malevolent foreign actors led by Russia in 2016, and the COVID-19 pandemic in 2020. Shabby partisans on both sides tried to use these external challenges to explain an unwelcome defeat.

Don't blame elections. Win them. That is our message to all who read this book. Your challenge is to win the argument, not undermine or destroy the single greatest method America has to distill those passionate arguments into a coherent governing structure. Blaming defeat on a supposedly faulty election has never been more odious, because our elections, up and until 2020, had never been more resilient and less vulnerable to naked partisan manipulation or abuse.

For this reason, though we are still optimists about American democracy, we recognize that when 70 percent of one of our two major political parties do not and will not accept any election, no matter how secure and verified, which results in their defeat, we are in crisis. If the losers of elections will not accept defeat, and if they work to undermine elections and voter confidence, we cannot sustain ourselves, either long term, or perhaps even in the immediate future. Our democracy is in triage, flatlining.

Triage is when the patient—in this case, the pluralistic democracy on which we rely—must first be saved and stabilized. It is not the best time to fix broad structural problems with massive legisla-tion, but rather to support the fundamentals that will sustain it and restore its resilience. When a patient is flatlining in the emergency room, we don't discuss her diet and exercise plan. We get the pad-dles and get her heart beating again. This is not to say we should abandon efforts at long-term reform and improvement, but rather that first we must recognize the fragile nature of our democracy and stabilize it. If we are to survive as a republic, several urgent inter-ventions are necessary.

REJECT ELECTION DENIALISM
AS AN ELECTION STRATEGY

Several Republican-majority legislatures have seized more control over election administration, in service to the Big Lie. Testimony leading to these new laws said this unprecedented oversight/meddling was necessary to increase integrity—even though the legislators writing the new rules were elected on the same ballots they alleged were somehow subject to fraud or unspecified irregu-larities, and even though many of the measures passed weakened election integrity in those states. In addition, as we write this, election deniers are running to become the chief election officials in their states. In several battleground and other key states, candi-dates (some of them under active investigation or indictment) are running in primaries on a platform of election denial—saying out loud that they will administer elections in such a way as to guar-antee the election of members of their own party. Even banana republic dictators are rarely so brazen. Whether these candidates will be successful and advance to the general election is an open question, but with the majority of their party openly rejecting secure elections and the idea of accepting the will of voters with whom they might disagree, there is reason for pessimism.

If you empower one political party, fueled by lies about "election integrity," to interpret the rules and administer elections, chaos will ensue. Obviously, legislatures can enact new laws. The 2020 election was valid and therefore legislators elected in that valid election are duly empowered to carry out legislative duties as they see fit. The laws are on the books. They must be monitored closely, as candidates, political parties, and lawyers surely will. How those laws are applied will tell a great deal about the motives behind them.

Similarly, candidates with whom we as voters might disagree, or who even espouse election denial conspiracies, can get elected legitimately by a majority of the voters. These candidates-elect might hold autocratic views that are anathema to a functioning democracy. But a democracy relies upon the consent of the governed, even when citizens are "wrong." Election denial or delegitimization of democracy by those that purport to defend it is no remedy to a slide toward autocracy, and could likely hasten it. The only way to defeat such toxic views legitimately, democratically, is by encouraging citizens to take a stand against attacks on our democracy. The irony here is that election deniers, on the Republican side, are likely the weaker candidates in the general election, and much less likely to appeal to swing and suburban voters. Republicans may see that supporting such weak general election candidates may harm their party's chances to take office, and choose true conservatives who represent their partisan values, but who tell the truth about the integrity of the 2020 election and stand for democracy.

But there is significant reason for alarm. A law drafted on a false premise that contains a built-in mechanism for partisan tampering must be viewed with suspicion. Those who spread lies about our elections could win narrow victories in November, enabling them to wreak powerful havoc on the integrity of future elections and the confidence of voters going into 2024. The key is vigilance and court intervention where necessary. Most importantly, we have a brief window in which we can attempt to strengthen the guardrails of democracy, significantly limiting the ability of those in power who might stray from democratic principles. Partisans who put themselves in charge of elections now may find different parties empowered later: fluidity in American politics is a feature, not a bug. Those who hunger to exert control over outcomes now may see those same powers used against them in the future, especially if they wielded them crudely and abusively. As Cicero wrote in the first century BCE, "Freedom is participation in power." We must respect the freedom of voters to participate in power by protecting their rights and access to the ballot box.

STRENGTHENING THE GUARDRAILS OF DEMOCRACY

As noted above, some state legislatures seek to inject more chaos and confusion into the election process. Legislative power grabs over the election process, weaponized partisan poll watchers, and the potential election of autocrats to key positions of power in election administration are a threat to the secure process of casting, counting, and certifying votes. These processes, which mostly take place after the polls have closed, must be transparent and secure, limiting the ability of those supporting election losers to cast doubt on the outcomes or attempt to seize power.

Article I, Section 4 of the U.S. Constitution—the "Elections Clause"—gives Congress broad power to regulate the conduct of federal elections:

> The Times, Places and Manner of holding Elections for Senators and Representatives, shall be prescribed in each State by the Legislature thereof; but the Congress may at any time by Law make or alter such Regulations.

While the states retain control of regulating most aspects of federal elections, Congress has wide latitude to regulate almost any aspect of these elections. Congress has used this power often in the past, with legislation including the Voting Rights Act, the National Voter Registration Act, the Help America Vote Act, the Military and Overseas Voter Empowerment Act, and many others. Its unsuccessful efforts over the past several years to pass bills such as the For the People Act, the Freedom to Vote Act, and the John Lewis Voting Rights Advancement Act were similarly intended to utilize this power under the Elections Clause. But these recent efforts were massive overhauls of federal election policy, requiring significant changes in many states, and were doomed to fail without bipartisan support.

Perhaps now, in triage, is not the best time to pass a 700–1,000-page omnibus bill that would change many aspects of election administration. While it is noble to attempt to perfect our system of elections, we are in crisis, and the urgent need is to shore up basic democratic principles and bind those who might otherwise seek to derail the will of the voters. Indeed, such a bill could be more likely to garner bipartisan support and could include several important protections.

Clarification and Strengthening of the Electoral Count Act of 1887

While the electoral vote counting process held, barely, in 2021, it did so largely due to the integrity and principles of several individuals, including Vice President Pence, rather than the clarity of this nearly 150-year-old law. It is clear from the text of the Constitution, the language of the Electoral Count Act itself, and the history of the peaceful transfer of power in this country that the joint session of Congress held to "count" the electoral votes is a ceremony, nothing more. We all know the results, and the states have transmitted their certified electoral votes pursuant to their state laws weeks before the joint session. At that point, the joint session is not an opportunity for a member of Congress to complain about or challenge laws in other states that were set well in advance, which governed the election of some of their congressional colleagues, or whine about an electoral outcome that took place two months earlier.

The joint session is intended to be more like a ceremony, where a presiding officer—in this case, the vice president—presides, reading the vote totals, and counting them ceremonially until a victor is confirmed. It is like the Academy Awards celebration (with the major difference that we don't know the winners of the Oscars beforehand). The Oscars host doesn't get to change the outcome of the winner of "Best Picture" just because he preferred a different movie. Similarly, the vice president, or any member of Congress, does not get to replace a candidate who lost as the winner just because they don't like what voters in another state decided.

The Electoral Count Act could be clarified to confirm the ceremonial nature of the joint session, and perhaps limit objections to where Congress has an appropriate constitutional role, including:

- Where a state failed to certify and/or transmit its electoral votes by the prescribed deadline
- Where there is a legitimate dispute, not yet resolved by the courts, over multiple duly certified slates of electors (similar to Hawaii's situation after the 1960 election)
- Faithless electors, who cast a different ballot than their pledge and inconsistent with state law

Similarly, the threshold for registering an official objection, debate, and upholding any objection could be raised to require true bipartisanship and prevent a party that holds bare majorities in both congressional chambers from installing a president of their own party in contravention of the will of the voters.

This appears to be an area where there is substantial agreement from key members of both parties, with ongoing serious discussions occurring during the spring of 2022. By the time you read this, it may well be that Congress has acted on this important reform, and perhaps even used it as a springboard toward other bipartisan agreement on foundational aspects of strengthening our democratic guardrails.

Limiting "Sore Loser" Lawsuits

As we saw in 2020, the losing candidate would not accept the clear will of the people, both before and after those results were confirmed, verified, and certified. Again and again, the loser complained about rules he knew were in place prior to Election Day, and in many cases did not challenge them until after his defeat. And he was aided in his efforts by lawmakers who were elected on the very same ballots he was delegitimizing.

But the courts held up admirably. Time after time, faced with frivolous lawsuits and concocted "evidence," courts rejected challenges to the election process and results, with many Trump-appointed judges rendering judgments supporting the results. Nevertheless, the losing candidate spread lies about the election procedures, and the judicial process, in the face of his unprecedented string of failures.

Despite the judiciary's success in 2020, we can do more to support its efforts, and ensure that only legitimate claims are brought before the courts, and that they are resolved comprehensively and quickly, before constitutional deadlines (such as the certification of electoral votes). Federal courts recognize a doctrine called *laches*, which requires litigants to bring a claim in a timely fashion, or to waive their right to relief. This makes sense—if someone thinks something is illegal or violates their rights, they should be required to let the courts know as soon as possible, and not wait around to see if their situation gets worse or better. In election terms, this is even more important. If a candidate doesn't like an election rule (say, mail voting, or philanthropic funding, or drop boxes), he or she shouldn't be able to wait around to see if they win or lose before bringing a claim. They should diligently seek to clarify the rules well in advance of the election. This serves not only the interests of the candidates, and democracy writ large, but even more importantly it serves the voters, who need to know what the rules are before they seek to cast their ballots.

Congress could enshrine this doctrine into law for federal elections, requiring any litigant, including federal candidates, to challenge any election rule or policy that they knew about, or should have known about, well before the election. Furthermore, Congress could bar any lawsuits brought after the close of polls regarding any procedure that existed prior to the end of voting. This could also bring clarity to the post-election narrative, undercutting efforts like so many we've seen to gripe about election procedures everybody knew about before voting even started.

Additionally, to bring further certainty to the post-election period, Congress could prescribe a single process for challenging any federal election after it has occurred, requiring challenges to be timely and brought well before certification, mandating a presumption of validity for election processes in place pre-election, shifting a high burden of proof for those challenging election outcomes, and expediting litigation and appeals to assure rapid resolution of any dispute. While legitimate issues with a post-election process should have their day in court (think Florida in the 2000 presidential election or Minnesota's U.S. Senate race in 2008), finality and certainty are important to the ongoing functioning of government, and frivolous claims should be disposed of as quickly and finally as possible.

Full Funding of Election Offices

Election offices are constantly suffering from underfunding. In the best of circumstances, they receive far less funding than they need. Election officials are notoriously underpaid, and election offices are often understaffed. And the last several years have been far from the best of circumstances. Election offices have had far more expenses than usual, as they must pay for pandemic-related expenses, more physical security than usual in the face of threats, legal expenses with increased litigation, and additional recounts and audits. This is all in addition to their usual needs to purchase new technology and retain and recruit skilled staff.

In the face of these challenges, state and federal budgeters have fallen short. In 2020, in the face of a global pandemic, Congress appropriated only $400 million for elections—less than $2 for each eligible voter. In 2022, the federal budget only offered $75 million to assist election offices, pennies per eligible voter. This has been a bipartisan problem and requires a bipartisan solution.

Congress could appropriate several billion dollars to assist election offices in the administration of federal elections. This would be a drop in the federal budgetary bucket, but an important and necessary level of support for offices dealing with more challenges, and more voters, than ever. Like past grants, made pursuant to the Help America Vote Act, the Election Assistance Commission is prepared and capable of issuing grants to the states under per-capita formulas it has used in the past. Unlike past grants, Congress could spread these out over ten years, with perhaps $1 billion granted out every year, to assist election offices in their planning for the next federal election. Further, Congress could require states match funds to some degree to receive the federal grants, to ensure that states don't pull funding from election offices and replace it with the new federal investment. In fact, as of this writing, the White House has proposed a federal budget that includes a request for more than $10 billion over ten years to support state and local election officials.

Such a federal commitment would allow for election offices to plan, knowing they have a stream of funds coming for the next decade, allowing for capital improvements (like advanced technology), hiring and retention of skilled workers, and additional expenses that come from increased need for security and transparency, and additional audits. With adequate federal and state funding, philanthropy would not need to step in, with the government fulfilling its role of supporting voters as they select their leaders.

Protection of Election Workers

Finally, and crucially, a basic federal bill should at least do the bare minimum to better protect election officials at every level from threats and harassment. The degree to which our public servants, from secretaries of state down to volunteer poll workers, are dealing with attacks is new, and requires a federal response.

We have celebrated election officials and poll workers in this book. That praise, from our perspective, can know no bounds. Election workers protect our democracy. They are the unarmed frontline forces who guarantee, as much as humanly possible, a sane and safe experience for you and all voters. They wake up early and stay late. They spend weeks, sometimes months, preparing. This was never truer than in 2020. Election workers make sure you know where to stand in line, where to cast your ballot, and how to cast your ballot if you are unsure about technology or the proper method to fill out your ballot. Think back to your trips to your local precinct. Picture in your mind the people sitting behind tables, checking in voters, organizing lines in and out of the precinct. Think of the person who hands out the "I voted" sticker. Can you see them? As we have said, they are your friends and neighbors.

We've met dozens of election workers—secretaries of state, state board of election officials, county registrars, local clerks, and polling place officials. They see themselves as participants in our experiment, activists not for a cause but for democracy itself. They stand guard while we stand in line. This requires attention to detail and a sense of purpose. America wants votes counted quickly. Poll workers and vote counters want votes counted accurately. Everyone who works more than one election knows how much the results matter, how the smallest error can create confusion or conflict. There is pressure in this work, pressure many of us may not realize, ignore, or take for granted. That baseline pressure turned ugly, menacing, and violent—needlessly so—after the 2020 election. We have chronicled the threats and the duration. While thousands of threats have occurred, and slightly fewer have been reported, only a few such threats have resulted in enforcement actions, with those engaging in threatening behavior held to account.

There are laws currently on the books that outlaw threats and interference with the election process. The Department of Justice has formed an Election Threats Task Force to deal with this issue, which as of this writing has brought two prosecutions against those engaging in threats against the professionals who administer elections. But two prosecutions in the face of thousands of cases of harassment isn't enough. And states aren't doing nearly enough to investigate and prosecute those engaged in violations of state law. Virtually no cases have been brought at the state level.

In the face of thousands of election threats and inadequate prosecution, and a lack of protection coming from the authorities, David Becker's nonprofit, the Center for Election Innovation & Research, created the Election Official Legal Defense Network (EOLDN). Partnering with two of the most prominent election lawyers in the country—Bob Bauer, former White House Counsel to President Obama, and Ben Ginsberg, former counsel to the George W. Bush and Mitt Romney campaigns and chief counsel to the Republican National Committee—EOLDN has been matching volunteer, pro bono lawyers to election officials all over the country, of both parties, who face harassment and need legal assistance. This effort has proved sadly necessary, as election officials from many states have sought protection and legal advice through EOLDN.

Our public servants shouldn't need to rely upon a nonprofit arranging basic legal advice and protection in the face of threats, harassment, and criminalization of their efforts. Election workers need preemptive protection that brings accountability for specific threats of violence on any election worker in any jurisdiction—by phone, text, social media posting, email, or snail mail. We need to think about threats, stalking, and doxing of election workers like we think about domestic terrorism. The goal is to create fear and then intimidate, as a means of pressuring election workers into doing something illegal, unethical, or that would undercut their sworn duty. Terrorism ripples, traumatizing the target and all those who make common cause. The 9/11 atrocities targeted the Twin Towers, the Pentagon, and, we suspect, the U.S. Capitol. But all Americans were victimized. Election-related terrorism has a similarly broad sweep: everyone is touched by attacks and by the threat of any attack. We understand the debate about democracy turns on access to voting and newly erected obstacles many on the left consider suppressive. We share some of these concerns. But we would humbly suggest protection of poll workers ought to take precedence over all other competing issues, chiefly because without poll workers the rest of the system—whatever its rules are from state to state—falls apart. Achieving satisfactory access to voting could prove meaningless if there are not enough poll workers to turn that guarantee of access into a reality. If citizens feel they are risking their lives by working polls or counting votes, they will do neither.

From our vantage point, protecting the vote means protecting the poll worker and vote counter. We caution that the most malevolent forces within the election denier movement see election workers and vote counters as juicy targets. In 2020, there was a concerted, organized, and funded effort to badger election workers. The goal of intimidation is always the same: to make someone do something they would not otherwise do. Election workers held firm, confident in the work they did and the validity of the results they produced. Their work stood up against fantasy affidavits alleging eyewitness accounts of fraud. Election workers—tens of thousands of proud, civically minded, patriotic Americans—deserve our gratitude and protection. Those who scorn and intimidate them should be relegated, by law and by custom, to the sidelines of democracy—shunned as democracy abusers.

ACCOUNTABILITY FOR CRIMINALS

Which brings us to what might be the most important thing we can do to restore faith and trust to American democracy: holding those who have wrecked that trust, in pursuit of their own wealth and power, accountable for their acts. Protection for election officials is a necessary step, but it is urgent that we prosecute those who seek to terrorize those civil servants, and perhaps even more crucially, those whose lies and grift led others to violent acts.

At the time of this writing, the process of accountability is ongoing. Over 800 indictments have been brought against those who stormed the Capitol on January 6. Over 250 convictions or guilty pleas have been obtained. Other investigations appear to be ongoing, as the foot soldiers in the war against American democracy are brought to feel the full weight of justice.

But the leaders of this effort remain at large. While those foot soldiers, and perhaps even some capos, are held to account, the consiglieres like Sidney Powell, Rudy Giuliani, John Eastman, Jeffrey Clark, and many others have largely avoided accountability, as they line their pockets with their ill-gotten grift. And, of course, the don himself, twice having dodged impeachment and thus still eligible to run for president, continues to direct the Big Grift from Mar-a-Lago, while threatening to amplify his unique brand of damage in a new campaign in 2024.

The House Select Committee on January 6 has done a remarkably comprehensive job to date, laying out the timeline and depth of the attempt by President Trump and his acolytes to abuse the machinery of the federal government to overturn a valid and verified election, and the will of the voters of the United States of

America. At this writing, they have not completed their investigation, nor has the Department of Justice publicly indicated that they are going after those higher up the criminal food chain. But the only way to deter autocratic conduct in the future is to make clear to those considering efforts to install another minority-preferred dictator that the price for such insurrection is high, that justice will find those who seek to overturn the will of the people in a democracy and hold them to account. Ultimately, this will be in the hands of the attorney general, the Department of Justice, and the courts.

Many of us know and may deeply revere the quotation "the arc of the moral universe is long, but it bends toward justice." It is often attributed to Dr. King because in writings and speeches he gave the sentiment resonance, and few in America experienced more personally the travails of waiting for justice's delayed arrival.

King's version condenses a longer, more nuanced meditation on justice and the lengthy, sometimes tortured, pursuit thereof. The sentiment came from Theodore Parker, a Unitarian minister and transcendentalist who opposed slavery. One of his sermons, "Of Justice and the Conscience" (first published in 1853), gave voice to what King would later so memorably and meaningfully distill.

> Look at the facts of the world. You see a continual and progressive triumph of the right. I do not pretend to understand the moral universe, the arc is a long one, my eye reaches but little ways. I cannot calculate the curve and complete the figure by the experience of sight; I can divine it by conscience. But from what I see I am sure it bends toward justice. Things refuse to be mismanaged long. Jefferson trembled when he thought of slavery and remembered that God is just. Ere long all America will tremble.

Throughout the early twentieth century, preachers and rabbis used variations of Parker's sermon, shortening it along the way. King first used his version "the arc of the moral universe is long, but it bends toward justice" in an article in 1958.

Parker's original sentiment was that the moral universe is beyond the full comprehension of any person but that which is right comes from it and flows through it in unpredictable ways, its timing immutable. King made it sound inevitable whereas Parker said that seemed to be the case, but conditioned that upon recognition of injustice, recognition of sin, or mismanagement. The key was to see that which is wrong and seek redress.

The case against the 2020 election is flat wrong. It is worse than wrong because it threatens democracy, the rule of law, and the durability of justice. We believe many who cling to grievances about the 2020 election know, deep down, they are wrong. They know lies are masquerading as truths. They rationalize both as tools in a larger enterprise—defeating Democrats, reversing socialism, wokeness, radicalism, and the like. But in their marrow they know, they must feel, the gnawing contradictions at the heart of assailing democracy to protect it. They know the ends do not justify the means. But they feel pushed and prodded by forces they feel incapable of slowing or stopping, so they let the tide carry them in what they tell themselves are unknowable directions.

We know the direction. Defaming democracy can only lead to its destruction. If a case can be made about votes being cast illegally and a candidate—any candidate from any party—winning fraudulently, we would be the first to raise awareness and denounce the result. We would do so in defense of democracy: democracy denied for one is democracy denied for all. But that is not what happened in 2020. Regrettably, those who yell and scream otherwise—many of whom do so for profit or political prominence—know this better than almost everyone, because they have to keep inventing ways to propagate increasingly absurd allegations. The engines of The Big Lie know the truth. They always have.

We have only scorn for purveyors of The Big Lie. We have deep sympathy for those in its corrupt thrall. The last book King wrote was *Where Do We Go from Here: Chaos or Community?*. In it, King describes the civil rights movement at a crossroads, cleaved by division over tactics: nonviolent civil disobedience or "Black power" resistance that accepted some manner of violence. At one point, King reminded readers of the sympathy he felt for white Americans swept up in racist teachings and mores they were seemingly powerless to stop or shed. He quoted a letter James Baldwin wrote to a nephew on the hundredth anniversary of the Emancipation Proclamation. We do not compare racism with election denialism. But there are sentiments in Baldwin's letter to his nephew that we invite you to inspect and evaluate.

> The really terrible thing, old buddy, is that *you* must accept *them*. And I mean that very seriously. You must accept them and accept them with love. For these innocent people have no other hope. They are, in effect, still trapped in a history which they do not understand; and until they understand it, they cannot be released from it.

Baldwin goes on to write that "people find it very difficult to act on what they know. To act is to be committed and to be committed is to be in danger." The letter, as quoted by King, concludes as follows: "These men are your brothers—your lost, younger brothers . . . we, with love, shall force our brothers to see themselves as they are, to cease fleeing from reality and begin to change it."

The context was racism, segregation, and the violence required to extend both. Our context is to believe what is clear: that our elections are as good—meaning verifiable, accurate, secure—as they have ever been. We need not change that reality. We need to embrace it. We need to see ourselves as we are, participants in a grand experiment of self-government, forbearance, equality, and freedom. All are strengthened through reliable elections. All are weakened by wicked, unsubstantiated slander. To our lost brothers and sisters, we say there is hope—hope in a democratic process that remains the envy of the world, the bulwark of justice, and the bequest of the visionaries who conceived of original American audacity. This is the answer to *Where Do We Go from Here?*

EPILOGUE

If we are not careful, we will find it is easier to kill American democracy than it is to sustain it. We are, as we have warned, on a springboard to civil war. The most corrosive issue is how we run, and trust, elections. Slowly at first but with increased speed and viciousness, we have come to a place of uncertainty about how we cast and count ballots.

This is as absurd as it is destructive, particularly given how far we've come and how much more secure our elections are today than ever before. American elections in the nineteenth and early twentieth century were, in the common argot of "rigged," veritable carnivals of manipulation and graft. Our elections now are without question the most ethical, transparent, verifiable, and secure in American history. It isn't even close. This includes the 2020 election. Don't take our word for it. Take the word of Republicans elected to Congress and state legislatures in the supposedly "contested" states of Arizona, Georgia, Michigan, Nevada, Pennsylvania, and Wisconsin. They hold office based on results from the same ballots, same counting process, same verification regime, and same certification process. They know their elections were legit, but still spread cowardly lies about President Biden and others elected on those same ballots.

Not wanting Joe Biden to be president is not the same thing as him not being legitimately elected president. The same applied to Trump after 2016. This is the hard part of democracy, tolerating an outcome you might legitimately fear is damaging for the country's future. Guess what? This is not a new hardship. Generations of Americans have accepted it as the shared burden of a unique, world-changing experiment.

It is not constructive to gnaw on the gristle of "fraud," "rigging," or "suppression" in the 2020 election, or elections of the recent past. America doesn't promise perfect elections any more than it promises perfect trials. It promises a process, a system of rules known on all sides and administered by humans doing the best they can under varied, sometimes difficult, circumstances. That said, it's remarkable how well our elections are run now, and how much professionalism has been brought to bear to support our democracy.

We, as citizens, are the building blocks of democracy and justice. It is one thing to say our elections can be improved. It is quite another to say they are mechanisms of intentional, felonious fraud. In the past five years, doubts such as these have begun to become corrosive—elections are valid when our side wins, questionable or invalid when it doesn't. Former president Trump is responsible for most, but not all, of this toxic mindset. Republicans and Democrats can and will play "whataboutism" all day. It ran rampant in 2022. At this perilous stage of our nation, it no longer matters who started what. It doesn't matter who is most to blame. It must stop. Self-righteousness must give way to self-reflection. Vengeance will be our destructive undoing. We inch closer to it by the day.

Raskin remains deeply critical of Trump and expressions of political dissent that turned hideously violent on January 6.

"What happened on January 6th was the unleashing of brutal violence that injured, hospitalized, and wounded more than one hundred and fifty of our officers who ended up with broken jaws and necks and arms and legs and traumatic brains injuries and post-traumatic stress syndrome," Raskin said. "That is the highest level of incivility and hostility you can imagine."

Even so, Raskin offered cautionary words for fellow Democrats, many in his progressive wing.

"That doesn't mean my side is in any way perfect. You know, the major problem is the kind of puritanical intolerance that comes under the name of political correctness. Most Americans don't have the opportunity to go to college much less go to a great liberal arts college and come out with the most advanced understanding of the most cutting-edge issues that most of the country has never been able to talk about or explore. And we can feel judged and belittled because we are not part of that neo-puritan squad."

Raskin schools young Democratic activists in what he calls the other form of PC politics, the politics of courage. He asks them to canvass in conservative areas and meet people who disagree with them.

"The right has very shrewdly honed in on people's sense that they are being judged and typecast simply because they don't have the most up-to-date language," Raskin said. "I don't think most working-class white people in America are reactionary. A lot of the political correctness has gone so far off the deep end that it makes you wonder about what kind political judgement is there. Politics is a game of addition not subtraction, it's not about asserting your moral superiority over everybody else."

Raskin said condescension from the left pales compared to dangers posed by the Trumpian right.

"I'm not equating in any way this flaw on our side, which could become a political Achilles' heel if we don't address it, with an authoritarian assault on the constitutional structure itself. We have an entire political party that operates like an authoritarian religious cult. They are a rule or ruin party right now. On our side we have to get over that puritanical inheritance and go out and organize America to stand up strong for democracy."

Cheney told us she too has found reason for hope among young Americans shocked into consciousness by January 6.

"The most moving experiences that I've had have been with young people all over the country," Cheney said. "And I mean college age and a little bit older and some high school age. Just young people who watched what happened and it has put things into stark relief. You know. Wait a minute. We can't take the peaceful transfer of power for granted. What's our responsibility? What is our obligation? It gives me hope that there is an understanding of sort of moving away from partisanship, realizing you might have substantive policy differences, but that you kind of work together to make sure that the Constitution and this system survives."

We had one civil war. We must never have another. That war came on slowly. It took decades for resentment to build and positions to harden. The war was in large part over an evil at the heart of the American experiment. It could not be compromised away. Slavery had to die and, in the end, it had to die via the implacable instruments of bullet and bayonet. This is not that. Not remotely.

We speak casually of a coming civil war now. Over what? Communism? Fascism? Only if we destroy the system that has been a bulwark against both since their inception. Only if we destroy the system that led many nations in the world—yes, in fits and starts—to develop their own versions of popular sovereignty. We have worked to amend and improve our birthright. We have bequeathed the power of this idea to a receptive world, to the benefit of millions. To speak of civil war is to desecrate our heritage and demean what much of the world doggedly admires.

This is Major Garrett speaking here. I have traveled the world with four presidents. Trust me, America is admired—not for our perfection, our military might, our economic clout, or even our founding documents. We are admired because we strive: strive to better ourselves, strive to make our actions align with the rhetoric of our founding, strive to dilute the cynicism that has run through humanity since antiquity. It's not that we are not cynical, flawed, or without baseless boasting. But in my travels, I have talked to prime ministers, government ministers, diplomats, soldiers, painters, seamstresses, journalists, laborers, cooks, and cabbies (of course!). In one language or another it always comes back to the same thing: grudging respect for our striving.

And this is David Becker speaking. I have observed elections around the world, where democracy was new and struggling, and in remote counties in this country, where democracy was supposedly present but stagnant. I've watched as autocrats like Egypt's Hosni Mubarak sought, in the last gasps of autocracy, to hold power by subjugating his people at "voting" sites. And I've been a voting rights attorney with the United States Department of Justice observing and protecting the election of Selma, Alabama's first African American mayor in that majority-Black city's history, over thirty-five years after Bloody Sunday, in the shadow of the Edmund Pettus bridge. We have come so far, and still have so far to go, but we are still a beacon to the world, and can be a beacon to ourselves.

In this world there will always be power. There will always be armies. There will always be propaganda, murder, greed, mayhem—all at a national and transnational scale of a state or a terrorist group. But there isn't always striving for betterment. We are a striving nation. Our own internal progress—halting, bloody, and contested though it has been—proves the premise. We set about this glorious experiment as an act of striving. We measure ourselves against our founding principles, our audaciously soaring rhetoric.

And yes, people of color assess that progress through their own prism of our history—not the almost entirely white and male power structure handed down over the decades. Men and women of color have their say about this nation's future in ways more politically, economically, and culturally potent than ever before. This is genuine progress. It is not always easy. It carries with it the friction of our nation's original sin. But we work through it. We strive to work through it. Nations silently sit in awe that we even try. We try. That is, until we stop trying.

Talk of civil war is the language of fatalism, of retreat, of quitting. Further, it is a headlong rush toward madness, born of an addiction to grievances based on falsehoods (on the right and left). Our challenge, one we have been worthy of in the past, is to stop confusing patriotism with sedition, glory with vanity, and courage with cowardice.

ACKNOWLEDGMENTS

First, my thanks to America. That sounds corny but is not. I believe in America's past, present, and future. I wouldn't have joined with David to write this book if I didn't. I believe in our nation's ability to be better, dream bigger, and achieve more—no matter the difficulty, friction, and bouts of disappointment or disillusionment. If democracy within a constitutional republic was easy, everyone would do it. They don't. That we do and did it first, no matter how imperfectly in its origins, matters more than almost any political initiative in human history.

Thank you to my mother, Kay Garrett. Though she passed away in 2014, Kay was, during her professional career, a corporate executive and, when the time called for it, a poll worker. She worked the polls every election without fail. In 2020 my eldest daughter, Mary Ellen Garrett, served as a poll worker in part to honor her grandmother's legacy. Thank you to all poll workers across our country. Thank you to my coauthor David Becker. Without you, this book would have been impossible. We were thrown together by the tumult of the 2020 election and have become colleagues and dear friends amid the fire of election denialism and manifest threats to democracy.

Thank you to Kevin Bohn, an irreplaceable researcher, reader, thinker, reporter, and voice of reason.

Thank you to Keith Wallman, Jane Glaser, and the entire team at Diversion Books. Thank you to my agents, Ann Tanenbaum and Kate Ellsworth at Tanenbaum International.

Thank you to CBS colleagues who provided valuable research, feedback, and perspective: Arden Farhi, Serafin Gomez, Robert Legare, Adam Brewster, Sara Cook, Eleanor Watson, Jamie Benson, and Jake Rosen. Thank you to CBS News and ViacomCBS senior management.

Thank you to my dear friend and expert proofreader Steve Chaggaris.

My most profound thanks are reserved for my brilliant and beautiful wife, Lara, whose support, encouragement, and love sustained, energized, and motivated me throughout.

Major Garrett
Washington, D.C.

This book is first and foremost dedicated to the hundreds of thousands of men and women—our family, friends, and neighbors—who work tirelessly to administer elections in our country, from secretaries of state to volunteer poll workers. These citizens give voice to voters in our democracy, often without any thanks or credit, and work tirelessly to ensure the will of the voters governs, regardless of whether they personally agree with the outcome. They have suffered unprecedented attacks and threats since the 2020 election, but we see them, and thank them, for their immeasurable service to our republic.

This book would not have been possible without the leadership, passion, kindness, and unmatched work ethic of my coauthor Major Garrett. We haven't known each other long, but our shared love for American democracy and the citizens who make it happen led to this collaboration, and I'm fortunate to call him friend and colleague.

I echo Major's thanks to Kevin Bohn, without whom this book would still be a set of unorganized thoughts in our heads. His guidance and research were invaluable. Likewise, many thanks to the entire team at Diversion Books, who marshalled us through this process.

I am very grateful to the entire team at CBS News, who has welcomed me into their fold during a tumultuous time in our history, and taught me everything I know about dedicated, balanced, tireless journalism.

I am immeasurably grateful, every day, to the staff and board of the Center for Election Innovation & Research, who do more to preserve American democracy on a daily basis than anyone else. Thanks to Jacob Kipp, Sally Steffen, Kristin Sullivan, Kathren Coleman, Kyle Upchurch, Jennifer Charette, Kyle Yoder, Jennifer Lovell, and Christian Kearney for all they do.

And finally, my endless love and gratitude goes to my wife Jamie and son Jacob. Your support for all that I do means everything to me. You revitalize me every day, and remind me why I do what I do.

David Becker

Montgomery County, MD

SOURCES

In addition to the sources listed here, Major Garrett interviewed the following individuals during 2021. Direct quotations and paraphrased content from these individuals not listed in this Sources section come directly from those interviews:

Doris Kearns Godwin, historian and best-selling author; Barry Richard, attorney for George Bush in *Bush v. Gore* litigation; Kathy Bernier, Republican member of Wisconsin State; Helen Butler, former member of the Morgan County, Georgia, board of elections; Tom Freitag, director of the Bucks County, Pennsylvania, board of elections; Bob Harvie, chair of the Bucks County, Pennsylvania, board of elections and as of January 2022, chairman of the board of the Bucks County Commissioners; Brad Raffensperger, Georgia secretary of state; Mick Mulvaney, Former White House Chief of Staff; Rep. Liz Cheney (R-Wyoming); Rep. Jamie Raskin (D-Maryland); and Ricky Hatch, the Weber County, Utah, Clerk Auditor.

1

"Already in progress": Interview with Margaret Atwood, "People Confuse Personal Relations with Legal Structures," Gender Forum, https://web .archive.org/web/20160427013239/http://www.genderforum.org /fileadmin/archiv/genderforum/queer/interview_atwood.html.

Historically high rates: Alexa Ura. "Vote-by-Mail Rejections Are Testing Integrity of Texas Republicans' Voting Law," *Texas Tribune*, January 24, 2022, https://www.texastribune.org/2022/01/24 /texas-vote by mail rejections/.

Fifteen times higher: Nick Corasaniti, "Mail Ballot Rejections Surge in Texas, with Signs of a Race Gap," *New York Times*, March 18, 2022, https://www.nytimes.com/2022/03/18/us/politics/texas-primary -ballot-rejections.html.

"Gonna have to question": Grace Panetta. "'Everything's Up for Grabs': The 2022 Midterms Could See Open Warfare Over Election Results in an Increasingly Polarized Congress," *Business Insider*, January 18, 2022, https://www.businessinsider.com/midterms -could-see-ugly-disputes-over-congressional-elections-2022-1.

"Of this election": President Joe Biden news conference, January 19, 2022, https://www.whitehouse.gov/briefing-room /speeches-remarks/2022/01/19/remarks-by-president-biden-in-press -conference-6/.

"won a race.": Nicholas Stephanopoulos, "The New Pro-Majoritarian Powers," 109 California Law Review 2357, March 12, 2021.

"It is now.": Herb Jackson, "Will Democrats Go to War on Voting Rights?" *Roll Call*, June 14, 2021.

"after the Civil War.": Nicholas Stephanopoulos, "The New Pro-Majoritarian Powers," 109 California Law Review 2357, March 12, 2021.

"Choice to seat or oust is a nonjusticiable political question": Nicholas Stephanopoulos, "The New Pro-Majoritarian Powers," *California Law Review* 109 (2021), p. 2366, https://papers.ssrn.com/sol3/papers .cfm?abstract_id=3803349.

"If there ever was a need for it to do so, it is now": Herb Jackson, "Will Democrats Go to War on Voting Rights?" Roll Call, June 14, 2021, https:// rollcall.com/2021/06/14/will-democrats-go-to-war-on-voting-rights/.

"Given the history and law of the Judging Elections Clause": Nicholas Stephanopoulos, "The New Pro-Majoritarian Powers."

"Abide by the Constitution": "Texas GOP Chair Allen West Suggests 'Law-Abiding States' Should 'Form a Union' After Supreme Court Rejects Lawsuit on Election Results," CBS 21 (Dallas-Fort Worth), December 11, 2020, https://dfw.cbslocal.com/2020/12/11/texas-gop -chair-allen-west-suggests-law-abiding-states-form-union-supreme -court-rejects-lawsuit-election-results/.

<h1 style="text-align:center">2</h1>

As Black Lives Matter: John Kruzel, "Russia's Social Media Efforts in 2016 Were Not Just False but Inflammatory," PolitiFact, December

21, 2017. https://www.politifact.com/article/2017/dec/21/russia-social
-media-2016-false-inflammatory/.

Illinois board of elections: Lynn Sweet, "Mueller Report Confirms
Russians Compromised Illinois State Board of Elections," *Chicago Sun-Times*, April 18, 2019, https://chicago.suntimes.com/news
/2019/4/18/18619441/mueller-report-confirms-russians-compromised
-illinois-state-board-of-elections.

Online voter registration system: Ellen Nakashima, "Russian Hackers Targeted Arizona Election System," *Washington Post*, August 29, 2016, https://
www.washingtonpost.com/world/national-security/fbi-is-investigating
-foreign-hacks-of-state-election-systems/2016/08/29/6e758ff4-6e00
-11e6-8365-b19e428a975e_story.html.

Election being "rigged": Jeremy Diamond, "Trump: 'I'm Afraid the Election's Going to Be Rigged,'" CNN, August 2, 2016, https://www.cnn
.com/2016/08/01/politics/donald-trump-election-2016-rigged/index
.html.

Democratic National Committee: Ellen Nakashima and Shane Harris,
"How the Russians Hacked the DNC and Passed Its Emails to WikiLeaks,"
Washington Post, July 13, 2018, https://www.washingtonpost.com
/world/national-security/how-the-russians-hacked-the-dnc-and
-passed-its-emails-to-wikileaks/2018/07/13/af19a828-86c3-11e8-8553
-a3ce89036c78_story.html.

"Rigging" only seemed to increase: Zachary Roth, "Donald Trump's
'Rigged Election' Claims Raise Historical Alarms," NBC News,
October 17, 2016, https://www.nbcnews.com/politics/2016-election
/donald-trump-s-rigged-election-claims-raise-historical-alarms-n667831.

Investigation into Clinton's emails: Lisa Lerer and Kathleen Hennessey,
"FBI's October Surprise Complicates Race for Hillary Clinton," Associated Press, October 28, 2016, https://cbs2iowa.com/news/election
/fbis-october-surprise-complicates-race-for-hillary-clinton-10-29-2016.

Jill Stein requested (and paid for): Daniel Strauss, "Jill Stein Gets Her
Recount Bill," Politico, November 29, 2016, https://www.politico.com
/story/2016/11/jill-stein-recount-231939.

To make the call: Marc Caputo and Kyle Cheney, "How Trump Won
Florida," Politico, November 8, 2016, https://www.politico.com
/story/2016/11/florida-results-not-in-2016-231004.

Won the presidency: Gregory Krieg, "The Day That Changed Everything:
Election 2016, As It Happened," CNN, November 8, 2017, https://www

.cnn.com/2017/11/08/politics/inside-election-day-2016-as-it-happened /index.html.

Audited and recounted: David Savage, "Pennsylvania's Aging Voting Machines Could Be 'Nightmare Scenario' in the Event of a Disputed Election," *Los Angeles Times*, October 20, 2016, https://www.latimes .com/politics/la-na-pol-pennsylvania-voting-paperless-20161020-snap -story.html.

Victories for Trump: Steve Eder, "Stein Ends Recount Bid, but Says It Revealed Flaws in Voting System," *New York Times*, December 13, 2016, https://www.nytimes.com/2016/12/13/us/stein-ends-recount-bid-but -says-it-revealed-flaws-in-voting-system.html.

Had mysteriously disappeared: Bob Woodward and Robert Costa, "Jan. 6 White House Logs Given to House Show 7-Hour Gap in Trump Calls," *Washington Post*, March 29, 2022, https://www.washingtonpost.com /politics/2022/03/29/trump-white-house-logs/.

3

With President Trump: Monmouth University Poll, January 27, 2022, https://www.monmouth.edu/polling-institute/reports/monmouthpoll _us_012722/.

Methods and mechanisms: Lila Hassan and Dan Glaun, "COVID-19 and the Most Litigated Presidential Election in Recent U.S. History: How the Lawsuits Break Down," PBS *Frontline*, October 28, 2020, https://www.pbs.org/wgbh/frontline/article/covid -19-most-litigated-presidential-election-in-recent-us-history/.

Including Bernard Kerik: Andrew Feinberg, "Trump Allies Planned Harassment and Intimidation Campaign Against Election Officials and 'Weak' House Members, Documents Show," *The Independent*, January 3, 2022, https://www.independent.co.uk/news/world/americas/us-politics /donald-trump-documents-election-harassment-b1985982.html.

Unfold throughout 2021: Letter from January 6th Committee, January 20, 2022, https://january6th.house.gov/sites/democrats.january6th.house .gov/files/2022-1-20.BGT%20Letter%20to%20Ivanka%20Trump%20 -%20Cover%20Letter%20and%20Enclosures_Redacted%202.pdf.

"Heart of the federal republic.": Text from Rep. Chip Roy to Mark Meadows, Jan. 1, 2021, in possession of Jan. 6 Select Committee.

Electoral vote slates: Evan Perez and Tiffany Sneed, "Exclusive: Federal Prosecutors Looking at 2020 Fake Elector Certifications, Deputy

Attorney General Tells CNN," CNN, January 26, 2022, https://www
.cnn.com/2022/01/25/politics/fake-trump-electoral-certificates
-justice-department/index.html.

Drafted for President Trump: Betsy Woodruff Swan, "Read the Never-
Issued Trump Order That Would Have Seized Voting Machines," Politico, January 21, 2022, https://www.politico.com/news/2022/01/21
/read-the-never-issued-trump-order-that-would-have-seized-voting
-machines-527572.

For President Biden.: "Former Trump lawyer, amid clash with Jan. 6 committee,
pushing to decertify 2020 election," Will Steakin and Katherine Faulders
and Laura Romero, ABC News, April 11, 2022. https://abcnews.go.com
/Politics/trump-lawyer-amid-clash-jan-committee-pushing-decertify
/story?id=83965757

"Overturned the election": John Wagner, Felicia Sonmez, and Josh Dawsey,
"Trump Suggests Pence Should Have 'Overturned' the Election on Jan.
6," *Washington Post*, January 31, 2022, https://www.washingtonpost
.com/politics/2022/01/31/trump-pence-overturned-election/.

Of the January 6 rioters: Stefan Becket, Melissa Quinn, and Rob Legare, "Oath
Keepers Founder, 10 Others Charged with Seditious Conspiracy for January 6 Attack," CBS News, January 14, 2022, https://www.cbsnews.com
/news/oath-keepers-stewart-rhodes-seditious-conspiracy-january-6/.

Biden's statewide victory: "Special Grand Jury Requested in Fulton
County Investigation into Donald Trump," WXIA, January 20, 2022,
https://www.11alive.com/article/news/politics/fulton-county-trump
-investigation-fani-willis-special-grand-jury/85-7157b07a-bda2-41bc
-81d4-0c9a759bb602.

"Elections are corrupt": Alana Wise, "Georgia District Attorney Calls for FBI
Security Help After Trump's Rally Comments," NPR, January 31, 2022,
https://www.npr.org/2022/01/31/1077093027/georgia-district-attorney
-calls-for-fbi-security-help-after-trumps-rally-comment.

Her and her employees: Alana Wise, "Georgia District Attorney Calls for
FBI Security Help After Trump's Rally Comments."

Violated the state constitution: Nick Corasaniti, "Pennsylvania Court
Says State's Mail Voting Law Is Unconstitutional," *New York Times*,
January 28, 2022, https://www.nytimes.com/2022/01/28/us/politics
/pennsylvania-mail-voting-law-unconstitutional.html.

Democrats were more split: For full voting record, see https://legiscan
.com/PA/rollcall/SB421/id/895746.

Invaded the U.S. Capitol: Melissa Quinn, "Supreme Court Rejects Trump's Bid to Shield January 6 Records, Bringing End to Legal Battle," CBS News, February 22, 2022, https://www.cbsnews.com/news /trump-supreme-court-january-6-committee-documents/.

"They are breaking": Domenick Mastrangelo, "Cheney Hits Gingrich for Saying Jan. 6 Panel Members May Be Jailed," *The Hill*, January 24, 2022, https://thehill.com/homenews/house/591007-cheney-hits -gingrich-for-saying-jan-6-panel-members-may-be-jailed.

"Really lost it": Gerrard Kaonga, "Zoe Lofgren Says 'I Think Newt Has Really Lost It,' as Jan. 6 Remarks Spark Outrage," *Newsweek*, January 24, 2022, https://www.newsweek.com/zoe-lofgren-newt-gingrich -january-6-committee-jail-jim-acosta-1672121.

"It's an experiment": President Biden/Justice Stephen Breyer event, January 27, 2022, https://www.whitehouse.gov/briefing-room /speeches-remarks/2022/01/27/remarks-by-president-biden-on-the -retirement-of-supreme-court-justice-stephen-breyer/.

"Treated so unfairly": "Trump Says He Would Pardon Jan. 6 Rioters if He Runs and Wins," Reuters, January 29, 2022, https://www.reuters.com/world/us /trump-says-he-would-pardon-jan-6-rioters-if-he-runs-wins-2022-01-30/.

In the Capitol riot: Clare Hymes, Robert Legare, and Eleanor Watson, "A Year After January 6 Capitol Riot, Hundreds Face Charges but Questions Remain," CBS News. January 5, 2022, https://www.cbsnews.com /news/january-6-capitol-riot-year-later-hundreds-face-charges-questions -remain/.

"Lawless, treasonous traitors": Reid J. Epstein, "Texas Man Charged with Threatening to Kill Georgia Election Officials," *New York Times*, January 21, 2022, https://www.nytimes.com/2022/01/21/us/politics/georgia -election-worker-threats-charges.html.

Ferreting out fraud: Michael Wines, "Republicans Want New Tool in Elusive Search for Voter Fraud: Election Police," *New York Times*, January 20, 2022, https://www.nytimes.com/2022/01/20/us/voting-rights-election -police.html.

"Or Jefferson Davis": President Biden remarks, January 11, 2022, https:// www.whitehouse.gov/briefing-room/speeches-remarks/2022/01/11 /remarks-by-president-biden-on-protecting-the-right-to-vote/.

"Literal traitors": Sen. Mitch McConnell remarks, January 11, 2022, https://www.republicanleader.senate.gov/newsroom/remarks /profoundly-unpresidential.

Which he plainly did: President Biden news conference, January 19, 2022, https://www.whitehouse.gov/briefing-room/speeches-remarks/2022/01/19/remarks-by-president-biden-in-press-conference-6/ (page 38)

Its electoral vote scheme: Text to Mark Meadows handed over to January 6 Committee, Jacqueline Alemany, Tom Hamburger, Josh Dawsey, and Tyler Remmel, "Texting Through an Insurrection," *Washington Post*, February 16, 2022, https://www.washingtonpost.com/politics/interactive/2022/texting-insurrection/.

4

Around 95 percent of the voters in our nation voted with them in 2020: Scott Pelley, "Fired Director of U.S. Cyber Agency Chris Krebs Explains Why President Trump's Claims of Election Interference Are False," *60 Minutes*, CBS News, https://www.cbsnews.com/news/election-results-security-chris-krebs-60-minutes-2020-11-29/.

Paper ballots: "Paper ballots give you the ability to audit, to go back and check the tape and make sure that you got the count right. And that's really one of the keys to success for a secure 2020 election. 95% of the ballots cast in the 2020 election had a paper record associated with it. Compared to 2016, about 82%." Since the rates are going up that would mean it would be the largest in history." Scott Pelley, "Fired Director of U.S. Cyber Agency Chris Krebs Explains Why President Trump's Claims of Election Interference Are False."

Six feet away: "Philadelphia Court Decision: Poll Watchers Now Allowed Within 6 Feet of Ballot Counting at Pennsylvania Convention Center," CBS 3 (Philadelphia), November 5, 2002, https://philadelphia.cbslocal.com/2020/11/05/philadelphia-court-decision-poll-watchers-now-allowed-within-6-feet-of-ballot-counting-at-pennsylvania-convention-center/.

Hundreds upon hundreds of cases of harassment: Kenneth Polite, head of Justice Department's criminal division, interview with *Washington Post*, January 21, 2022, https://www.washingtonpost.com/national-security/georgia-election-threat-arrest/2022/01/21/cf5f8ca8-7880-11ec-83e1-eaef0fe4b8c9_story.html. "Kenneth Polite Jr., head of the Justice Department's criminal division, said the election threats task force has received more than 850 referrals of potentially harassing and offensive statements."

Had been filed: Matt Zapotosky, "Texas Man Charged with Threatening Election, Government Officials in Georgia," *Washington Post*, January 21, 2022, https://www.washingtonpost.com/national

-security/georgia-election-threat-arrest/2022/01/21/cf5f8ca8-7880
-11ec-83e1-eaef0fe4b8c9_story.html; Justice Dept. press release, January 27, 2022, https://www.justice.gov/opa/pr/man-charged-threatening
-nevada-state-election-worker.

"Illegal aliens": Louis Jacobson, "Donald Trump's Pants on Fire Claim That
Millions of Illegal Votes Cost Him Popular Vote Victory," PolitiFact,
November 28, 2016, https://www.politifact.com/factchecks/2016/nov/28
/donald-trump/donald-trumps-pants-fire-claim-millions-illegal-vo/.

2016 to 2020: Ford Fessenden, Lazaro Gamio, and Rich Harris, "Trump
Found More Than 10 Million New Voters. They Were Not Enough," *New
York Times*, November 17, 2020, https://www.nytimes.com/2020/11/17
/us/trump-found-more-than-10-million-new-voters-they-were-not
-enough.html.

Potential financial crimes.: "Hunter Biden Paid Tax Bill, but Broad Federal
Investigation Continues," Katie Benner and Kenneth P. Vogel and Michael
S. Schmidt, *New York Times*, March 16, 2022. https://www.nytimes
.com/2022/03/16/us/politics/hunter-biden-tax-bill-investigation.html

"We own you": C-Span camera, January 6, 2021, 1:37:41 into video:
"We own it. We own you," https://www.c-span.org/video/?507745-1
/protesters-breach-us-capitol-security.

"Our country back!": "Inside the U.S. Capitol," ITV News, January 6,
2021, 2:19 into the clip, https://youtu.be/UBp42536IhE?t=135.

On democracy: Dan Balz, Scott Clement, and Emily Guskin, "Republicans and Democrats Divided over Jan. 6 Insurrection and Trump's
Culpability, Post-UMD Poll Finds," *Washington Post*, January 1, 2022,
https://www.washingtonpost.com/politics/2022/01/01/post-poll
-january-6/; Meryl Kornfield and Mariano Alfaro, "1 in 3 Americans Say
Violence Against Government Can Be Justified, Citing Fears of Political Schism, Pandemic," *Washington Post*, January 1, 2022, https://www
.washingtonpost.com/politics/2022/01/01/1-3-americans-say
-violence-against-government-can-be-justified-citing-fears-political
-schism-pandemic/.

"Political discourse": Josh Dawsey and Felicia Sonmez, "'Legitimate Political Discourse': Three Words About Jan. 6 Spark Rift Among Republicans," *Washington Post*, February 8, 2022, https://www.washingtonpost.
com/politics/2022/02/08/gop-legitimate-political-discourse/.

An inside job: Glenn Kessler, "How Trump Supporter Ray Epps Became
Entangled in a Trump-touted Conspiracy Theory," *Washington Post*,

January 19, 2022, https://www.washingtonpost.com/politics/2022/01/19/how-trump-supporter-ray-epps-became-entangled-trump-touted-conspiracy-theory/.

In early 2022: Jeremy W. Peters, "Trump Rally Underscores G.O.P. Tension Over How to Win in 2022," *New York Times*, January 15, 2022, https://www.nytimes.com/2022/01/15/us/politics/trump-rally-republicans.html.

Forty-seventh president: Andy Roberts, "Donald Trump Says He's the '45th and 47th' US President on the Golf Course," GolfMagic, January 26, 2022, https://www.golfmagic.com/golf-news/donald-trump-says-hes-45th-and-47th-us-president-golf-course.

Voters used them: Former CISA director Chris Krebs interview, *60 Minutes*, CBS News, November 29, 2020, https://www.cbsnews.com/news/election-results-security-chris-krebs-60-minutes-2020-11-29/.

Million cast: Election Atlas, https://uselectionatlas.org/RESULTS/stats.php?year=1960&f=0&off=0&elect=0; county victory percentages under election statistics tab.

The reversal: Andrew Chamings, "Here's How California Has Voted in the Past 15 Presidential Elections," SFGate, November 2, 2020, https://www.sfgate.com/bayarea/article/who-did-California-vote-for-president-15694779.php.

To Kennedy: Herb Jackson, "What Happens When a State Can't Decide on Its Electors," Roll Call, October 26, 2020, https://rollcall.com/2020/10/26/we-the-people-what-happens-when-a-state-cant-decide-on-its-electors/; Tom Hamburger, "For Lesson on Deadline, Look to Hawaii in 1960," *Wall Street Journal*, December 11, 2000, https://www.wsj.com/articles/SB976490410560832829. The best details are in Roll Call; The *Wall Street Journal* has some of the key dates used in the book.

Al Gore: Lyle Denniston, "Supreme Court, in 5-4 Vote, Halts Recount, Stinging Gore," *Baltimore Sun*, December 10, 2000, https://www.baltimoresun.com/bal-00election31-story.html.

Televised drama: Samantha Levine, "Hanging Chads: As the Florida Recount Implodes, the Supreme Court Decides Bush v. Gore," *US News & World Report*, January 17, 2008, https://www.usnews.com/news/articles/2008/01/17/the-legacy-of-hanging-chads.

Of a recount: "Bush v. Gore," *Encyclopedia Britannica*, https://www.britannica.com/event/Bush-v-Gore.

7,211 votes: Federal Election Commission report, June 2001, p. 12, https://www.fec.gov/resources/cms-content/documents/federalelections00.pdf; The American Presidency Project, University of California Santa Barbara, https://www.presidency.ucsb.edu/statistics/elections/2000.

Procedures in Ohio: John Schwartz, "Glitch Found in Ohio Counting," *New York Times*, November 6, 2004, https://www.nytimes.com/2004/11/06/politics/campaign/glitch-found-in-ohio-counting.html.

Electoral votes: CNN, January 6, 2005, https://www.cnn.com/2005/ALLPOLITICS/01/06/electoral.vote/; Kyle Cheney, "House Democrats Fail to Muster Support to Challenge Trump's Electoral College Win," Politico, January 6, 2017, https://www.politico.com/story/2017/01/no-trump-electoral-college-challenge-233294.

ERIC: Electronic Registration Information Center, https://ericstates.org/.

Corporate value: Yun Li, CNBC, March 9, 2020, https://www.cnbc.com/2020/03/08/dow-futures-drop-700-points-as-all-out-oil-price-war-adds-to-coronavirus-stress.html; William Watts, MarketWatch, December 31, 2020, https://www.marketwatch.com/story/oil-prices-on-track-fall-of-more-than-20-for-2020-due-to-coronavirus-pandemic-1160941902, for the year WTI, the US benchmark fell 20.5% in 2020; Chevron: closed Friday March 6 at 95.32 and closed March 9 at 80.67, –15% change, https://chevroncorp.gcs-web.com/stock-information/historical-price-lookup?8c7bdd83-a726-4a84-b969-494be2477e47%5BCVX%5D%5Bdate_month%5D=03&8c7bdd83-a726-4a84-b969-494be2477e47%5BCVX%5D%5Bdate_day%5D=9&8c7bdd83-a726-4a84-b969-494be2477e47%5BCVX%5D%5Bdate_year%5D=2020&url=; ExxonMobil: closed Friday March 6 at 47.69 and closed March 9 at 41.86, –12% change, https://ir.exxonmobil.com/historical-price-lookup?8c7bdd83-a726-4a84-b969-494be2477e47%5BXOM%5D%5Bdate_month%5D=03&8c7bdd83-a726-4a84-b969-494be2477e47%5BXOM%5D%5Bdate_day%5D=6&8c7bdd83-a726-4a84-b969-494be2477e47%5BXOM%5D%5Bdate_year%5D=2020&url=.

Of 601,219: Michigan secretary of state. 2020, https://mielections.us/election/results/2020PPR_CENR.html; 2016, https://mielections.us/election/results/2016PPR_CENR.html; 2008: Voter Election Project, https://docs.google.com/spreadsheets/d/1-OsNYFiXNTL6kM_0LZCTm8QtuLJ4-sdI2E28Y3o2tdc/edit#gid=0.

Virus transmission: Shia Kapos, "Biden Cancels Fundraisers, Rally in Chicago Days Before Illinois Primary," Politico, March 11,

2020, https://www.politico.com/news/2020/03/11/biden-cancels
-fundraisers-rally-chicago-coronavirus-126383.

"And supporters": Tal Axelrod, "Biden Campaign Announces Public Health
Panel to Advise on Coronavirus," *The Hill*, March 11, 2020, https://thehill
.com/homenews/campaign/487093-biden-campaign-announces
-public-health-panel-to-advise-on-coronavirus.

Virus transmission: "Gatherings Should Be Limited to 10 People,
Trump Says," *New York Times*, March 16, 2020, https://www.nytimes
.com/2020/03/16/world/live-coronavirus-news-updates.html.

Briefing room: President Trump Coronavirus Remarks, White House
Transcript, March 16, 2020, https://trumpwhitehouse.archives.gov
/briefings-statements/remarks-president-trump-vice-president-pence
-members-coronavirus-task-force-press-briefing-3/.

"Until further notice": Shia Kapos, "Biden Cancels Fundraisers, Rally in
Chicago Days Before Illinois Primary."

Shut down: Rebecca Morin, "Closed Locations, a Lack of Poll Workers: How Coronavirus Is Affecting Tuesday's Election," *USA Today*,
March 16, 2020, https://www.usatoday.com/story/news/politics
/elections/2020/03/16/march-17-primary-what-arizona-illinois-florida
-ohio-doing-amid-coronavirus/5047458002/.

(March 8, 12, 16): Yun Li, "Plunging Stocks Triggered a Key Market 'Circuit Breaker'—Here's What That Means," CNBC, March 16, 2020,
https://www.cnbc.com/2020/03/15/the-sp-500-futures-hit-limit-down
-at-5-percent.html.

Global oil prices fell 10 percent: Pippa Stevens, "Oil Drops Nearly 10%,
Breaking Below $29 as Demand Evaporates," CNBC, March 16, 2020,
https://www.cnbc.com/2020/03/16/oil-drops-more-than-6percent
-breaking-below-30.html.

Increase liquidity: Jeff Cox, "Fed Says It Will Offer an Additional $500
Billion in Overnight Repo Funding Markets," CNBC, March 16, 2020,
https://www.cnbc.com/2020/03/16/fed-says-it-will-offer-an-additional
-500-billion-in-overnight-repo-funding-markets.html.

Than most: Of about 4.06 million registered voters in Arizona, about 3.04
million are on the early voting list, or about 75 percent. In the 2012 general election, 61 percent of Arizona voters cast an early ballot according
to the secretary of state's office. By 2018, that number grew to 79 percent.
Christopher Conover, Arizona Public Media, https://www.azcentral
.com/restricted/?return=https%3A%2F%2Fwww.azcentral

.com%2Fstory%2Fnews%2Fpolitics%2Farizona%2F2020%2F09
%2F14%2Fvoting-by-mail-arizona-tradition-unlike-much-of-us-story
-how-happened%2F5707050002%2F.

Ballots were cast: Arizona secretary of state, 2020 results, https://results
.arizona.vote/#/featured/28/0; 2016 results: https://apps.azsos.gov
/election/2016/PPE/canvass2016ppe.pdf.

As April 13: Tucker Higgins, "US Supreme Court Sides with GOP in Wisconsin: Absentee Ballots Must Be Sent by Tuesday," CNBC, April 6, 2020,
https://www.cnbc.com/2020/04/06/wisconsin-supreme-court-halts
-absentee-ballot-deadline-extension.html.

Over 180: Alison Dirr and Mary Spicuzza, "What We Know So Far
About Why Milwaukee Only Had 5 Voting Sites for Tuesday's Election
While Madison Had 66," *Milwaukee Journal Sentinel*, April 9, 2020,
https://www.jsonline.com/story/news/politics/elections/2020/04/09
/wisconsin-election-milwaukee-had-5-voting-sites-while-madison
-had-66/2970587001/.

Voters participated: Richard Pildes and Charles Stewart III, "The Wisconsin Primary Had Extraordinarily High Voter Turnout," *Washington Post*,
April 15, 2020, https://www.washingtonpost.com/politics/2020/04/15
/wisconsin-primary-had-extraordinarily-high-voter-turnout/.

Legal dogfights: Wisconsin Elections Commission, p. 9, https://elections
.wi.gov/sites/elections/files/County%20by%20County%20Report
%20by%20Congressional%20District_President.pdf.

Super-spreader event: Richard Pildes and Charles Stewart III, "The Wisconsin Primary Had Extraordinarily High Voter Turnout."

Mail-in voting: Bridget Bowman, "Pennsylvania Moves Primaries to
June 2 Amid Coronavirus Pandemic," Roll Call, March 27, 2020,
https://rollcall.com/2020/03/27/pennsylvania-moves-primaries-to-june
-2-amid-coronavirus-pandemic/.

Mail-in ballots: Jan Murphy, "Pa. Gov. Tom Wolf Signs Historic Election Reform
Bill into Law," *PennLive/Patriot-News*, October 31 2019, https://www
.pennlive.com/news/2019/10/pa-gov-tom-wolf-signs-historic-election
-reform-bill-into-law.html.

1,681,427 votes: United States Election Project, 2020 turnout: https://
docs.google.com/spreadsheets/d/1kygorcjoehboZkdmV0kKf
-xSiBC6N57uhwfegMIYqoY/edit#gid=0; 2016 turnout: https://
docs.google.com/spreadsheets/d/1_2zR7LlDVUpVs1WM5S
_bzeuooOvlVPvJVsEj4MXCOa4/edit#gid=0.

Officially canceled: Ben Nadler, "Georgia Primaries Postponed Again Due to the Coronavirus," *Fortune*, April 9, 2020, https://fortune. com/2020/04/09/georgia-primary-date-coronavirus-voting-elections -covid-19/. Of the 200,000 mail-in votes originally cast in March counting, the *Atlanta Journal-Constitution* says they did count. We say they did not, https://www.ajc.com/news/state--regional -govt--politics/what-you-need-know-vote-mail-georgia-primary /rHPajaaBthzZpGXharCeJM/.

Four years earlier: Georgia secretary of state, 2020 turnout: https://results. enr.clarityelections.com/GA/103613/web.247524/#/summary; 2016 turnout: https://results.enr.clarityelections.com/GA/58980/163369 /en/summary.html.

Have been fleeced: Maggie Gile, "Former Overstock CEO Patrick Byrne Donated $2M to Conduct Arizona Election Audit," *Newsweek*, July 30, 2021, https://www.newsweek.com/former-overstock-ceo-patrick-byrne -donated-2m-conduct-arizona-election-audit-1614718.

American history: National turnout, United States Election Project, http:// www.electproject.org/2020g.

Voting Eligible Population (VEP): 1994 VEP turnout, United States Election Project, https://docs.google.com/spreadsheets /d/1or-N33CpOZYQ1UfZo0h8yGPSyz0Db-xjmZOXg3VJi-Q /edit#gid=1670431880.

Turnout of 41 percent: 2010 VEP turnout, United States Election Project, http://www.electproject.org/2010g.

Registered 37 percent: 2014 VEP turnout, United States Election Project, http://www.electproject.org/2014g.

Of the House: 2018 VEP turnout, United States Election Project, http:// www.electproject.org/2018g.

The presidential question: 2020 Undervote, http://www.electproject.org /2020g. The chart shows 159,738,337 voted overall but only 158,407,854 voted for the president, making a difference of 1,330,483.

The presidential contest: Arizona Result, CNN, https://www.cnn.com /election/2020/results/state/arizona/president; United States Election Project, Undervote, http://www.electproject.org/2020g.

The presidential contest: Georgia Result, CNN, https://www.cnn.com /election/2020/results/state/georgia/president; United States Election Project, Undervote, http://www.electproject.org/2020g.

More outreach: Pennsylvania, Nevada, Michigan, Wisconsin, CNN, Results, https://www.cnn.com/election/2020/results/president; United States Election Project, Undervotes, http://www.electproject.org/2020g.

Not close: 2020 General election popular vote, WLS/AP, https://abc7chicago .com/2020-election-results-live-map/7710705/ (AP numbers).

Biden margin, 20,862: Arizona, Georgia, Wisconsin results, CNN, https:// www.cnn.com/election/2020/results/president.

270 to 268: Nebraska 2nd District Results, Nebraska secretary of state, https://electionresults.nebraska.gov/resultsSW.aspx?text=Race&type =PC&map=CTY.

Requested recounts: "A Survey and Analysis of Statewide Election Recounts, 2000–2019," FairVote, November 4, 2020. file:///C:/Users/Owner /Downloads/A%20Survey%20and%20Analysis%20of%20Statewide %20Election%20Recounts,%202000%E2%80%932019%20.pdf. There were 31 recounts among 5,778 general elections, of which 16 were deemed consequential (p. 2); 3 elections were reversed (p. 5); 20 states have automatic recount laws; 43 allow for requested recounts (p. 6); chart 4 (p. 15). Note: FairElection says 16 states have automatic recount laws and 42 allow for requested ones as well as D.C.

Florida 537 margin: "On This Day Bush v Gore Settles 2000 Presidential Race," Constitution Center, https://constitutioncenter.org/blog /on-this-day-bush-v-gore-anniversary.

Than 120,000 votes: Rich Exner, "Bush Wins by Less Than 120,000 Votes in Ohio: 2004 Ohio presidential election results," Cleveland.com, June 15, 2016, https://www.cleveland.com/datacentral/2016/06/2004_ohio _presidential_electio.html.

Than 78,000 votes: "Trump lost popular vote by nearly 3 million votes: Presidential Election Results," *New York Times*, https://www.nytimes .com/elections/2016/results/president.

Won Michigan, Pennsylvania, and Wisconsin by less than 78,000 votes: Michigan results: 12,704 difference, *New York Times*, https:// www.nytimes.com/elections/2016/results/michigan; Pennsylvania results: 44,292 difference, *New York Times*, https://www.nytimes.com /elections/2016/results/pennsylvania; Wisconsin results: 22,748 difference, *New York Times*, https://www.nytimes.com/elections/2016 /results/wisconsin.

2020 election widest popular vote of these four elections: 2020 popular vote margin: 7,060,140, AP/ WLS, https://abc7chicago

.com/2020-election-results-live-map/7710705/; 2016 popular vote margin: 2,868,519, *New York Times*, https://www.nytimes.com/elections /2016/results/president); 2004 popular vote margin: 3,012,497, CNN, https://www.cnn.com/ELECTION/2004/pages/results/president/; 2000 popular vote margin: 547,179, American Presidency Project, University of California Santa Barbara, https://www.presidency.ucsb.edu /statistics/elections/2000.

Compared to 2016: Joey Garrison, "Trump Baselessly Claims Voter Fraud in Cities, but Suburbs Actually Lost Him the Election," *USA Today*, November 13, 2020, https://www.usatoday.com/in-depth/news/politics /elections/2020/11/13/donald-trump-lost-election-suburbs-not-cities -despite-claims/6263149002/. Joe Biden fared about the same in Philadelphia, Detroit, and Milwaukee as Democratic nominee Hillary Clinton did in 2016. Trump actually won more votes in Philadelphia and Detroit in 2020 than he did in 2016. Growth was modest in Milwaukee, where Biden beat Trump by just 3,000 more votes than Clinton did in 2016.

Compared to 2016: Reid Wilson, "Trump's Gains in Rural America Offset by Biden's Urban Dominance," *The Hill*, September 14, 2021, https:// thehill.com/homenews/state-watch/571792-trumps-2020-gains-in-rural -america-offset-by-bidens-urban-dominance.

A middle suburb: Richard Florida, Marie Patino, and Rachael Dottle, "How Suburbs Swung the Election," Bloomberg CityLab, November 17, 2020, https://www.bloomberg.com/graphics/2020-suburban -density-election/.

Delaware and Bucks: Pennsylvania: Jonathan Lai and Andrew Seidman, "The Philadelphia Suburbs Were the Key to Joe Biden's Pennsylvania Victory. Here Are the Numbers," *Philadelphia Inquirer*, November 30, 2020.

Macomb and Ottawa counties: Michigan/Wisconsin: Domenico Montanaro and Connie Hanzang Jin, "How Joe Biden Defeated President Trump in 2020 Election," NPR, November 18, 2020, https://www.npr .org/2020/11/18/935730100/how-biden-won-ramping-up-the-base-and -expanding-margins-in-the-suburbs.

In-person voting: 2020 total early voting, United States Election Project, https://electproject.github.io/Early-Vote-2020G/index.html; 2016 total early voting, United States Election Project, http://www.electproject .org/early_2016. CNN says: In 2016, around 58.3 million pre-election ballots were cast, including ballots in the three vote-by-mail states that

year, according to a CNN analysis, https://www.cnn.com/2020/10/25
/politics/pre-election-voting-surpasses-2016-early-ballots/index.html.

Early in-person: In 2020, 43 percent of voters cast ballots by mail and
another 26 percent voted in person before Election Day. In 2016, 21
percent mailed in their ballots and 19 percent voted in person prior to
Election Day. Zachary Scherer, "Majority of Voters Used Nontraditional
Methods to Cast Ballots in 2020," US Census Bureau report, April 29,
2021, https://www.census.gov/library/stories/2021/04/what-methods
-did-people-use-to-vote-in-2020-election.html.

Younger than sixty-five: A larger share of voters age sixty-five and over
voted nontraditionally than younger voters. Zachary Scherer, "Majority
of Voters Used Nontraditional Methods to Cast Ballots in 2020," US
Census Bureau report, April 29, 2021; https://www.census.gov/library
/stories/2021/04/what-methods-did-people-use-to-vote-in-2020
-election.html.

5

None of the books actually agree on what happened: One book, by
Patrick Byrne, contends "industrial scale vote flipping" stole the election from Trump. Another book, by Peter Navarro, says, flatly, that no
vote flipping happened at all, but that the real culprit was "ballot box
stuffing." Another book, by Mollie Hemingway, dismisses both of those
so-called explanations while contending the election wasn't stolen so
much as it was "rigged" by hostile media coverage, social media censorship, and Democrats who bent the rules.

"Licking their chops": "So I say to whatever Republican loyalists . . . licking their chops," Patrick Byrne, *The Deep Rig*, chapter 5.

"The steal": *The Deep Rig*, chapter 5.

As was his right: Shane Goldmacher and Rachel Shorey, "Trump's Sleight
of Hand: Shouting Fraud, Pocketing Donors' Cash for Future," *New
York Times*, February 1, 2021, https://www.nytimes.com/2021/02/01/us
/politics/trump-cash.html.

The race blank: Josh Salman, Matt Wynn, and Dinah Voyles Pulver, "Tens of
Thousands Left the President Option Blank, Though 'Undervotes' Were
Down from 2016," *USA Today*, November 11, 2020, https://www.usatoday
.com/story/news/investigations/2020/11/11/thousands-who-voted-didnt
-choose-president-competitive-states/6244098002/.

Trump campaign had an absolute legal right to full, statewide recounts in the states of Michigan, Pennsylvania, and Wisconsin: Molly Olmstead, "How a Recount Would Work in Each of the Swing States," *Slate*, November 5, 2020, https://slate.com/news-and-politics/2020/11/election-recount-rules-georgia-wisconsin-nevada-michigan-arizona-pennsylvania.html.

Wisconsin reference: Victoria Saha, WAOW, November 5, 2020, https://www.waow.com/news/politics/comparing-wisconsin-in-the-2016-and-2020-presidential-election/article_37a57490-ec19-5648-ad9e-68b80facc626.html.

Pennsylvania reference: CNN, https://www.cnn.com/election/2020/results/state/pennsylvania.

Michigan reference: CNN, https://www.cnn.com/election/2020/results/state/michigan.

Verified and certified: Mike Lindell comments, Ron Filipkowski tweet, March 5, 2022, https://twitter.com/ronfilipkowski/status/1500232296091246595?s=12.

Or inadvertently: Linda Qiu, "Donald Trump's Baseless Claims About the Election Being 'Rigged,'" PolitiFact, August 15, 2016, https://www.politifact.com/factchecks/2016/aug/15/donald-trump/donald-trumps-baseless-claims-about-election-being/.

For his claim: "Inaccurate, Costly and Inefficient Evidence That America's Voter Registration System Needs an Upgrade," Pew Center on the States, https://www.pewtrusts.org/~/media/legacy/uploadedfiles/pcs_assets/2012/pewupgradingvoterregistrationpdf.pdf.

Widespread voter fraud: Eric Lipton and Ian Urbina, "In 5-Year Effort, Scant Evidence of Voter Fraud," *New York Times*, April 15, 2007, https://www.nytimes.com/2007/04/12/washington/12fraud.html.

Trump's administration: Michael Tackett and Michael Wines, "Trump Disbands Voter Fraud Commission," *New York Times*, January 3, 2018, https://www.nytimes.com/2018/01/03/us/politics/trump-voter-fraud-commission.html.

Arizona and Utah: Wendy Weiser, Eliza Sweren-Becker, Dominique Emery, and Anne Glatz, "Mail Voting: What Has Changed in 2020," Brennan Center, September 17, 2020, https://www.brennancenter.org/our-work/research-reports/mail-voting-what-has-changed-2020. "Generally, thirty-four states and the District of Columbia allow all registered voters to vote by absentee ballot in any election."

By mail (one in four voters voted by mail in 2016): Drew Desilver, "Most Mail and Provisional Ballots Got Counted in Past U.S. Elections—But Many Did Not," Pew Research Center, November 10, 2020, https://www.pewresearch.org/fact-tank/2020/11/10/most-mail-and-provisional-ballots-got-counted-in-past-u-s-elections-but-many-did-not/. "In the 2016 general election, voters submitted nearly 33.5 million mail ballots." Hannah Hartig, Bradley Jones, and Vianney Gomez, "As States Move to Expand the Practice, Relatively Few Americans Have Voted by Mail," Pew Research Center, June 24, 2020. The report shows 20.9 percent in 2016.

Trump in 2016: For these facts Trump certainly didn't raise concerns about overwhelmingly high mail ballot returns in states he won in 2016, such as Arizona (73 percent mail ballots), Iowa (41 percent), Montana (64 percent), or Utah (69 percent). Ballotpedia, https://ballotpedia.org/Analysis_of_absentee/mail-in_voting,_2016-2018.

Of the thirty-five electoral jurisdictions that allowed widespread mail voting heading into the 2020 election, twenty of them had cast their electoral votes for President Trump in 2016: For a map showing mail voting rules in 2020, see https://www.nytimes.com/interactive/2020/08/11/us/politics/vote-by-mail-us-states.html; Also see https://www.ncsl.org/research/elections-and-campaigns/vopp-table-18-states-with-all-mail-elections.aspx.

A mail ballot: In Florida, Georgia, Wisconsin, and Ohio you must request a ballot; Colorado, Oregon, and Utah check lists. "How States Verify Voted Absentee/Mail Ballots," National Conference of State Legislatures, March 15, 2022, https://www.ncsl.org/research/elections-and-campaigns/vopp-table-14-how-states-verify-voted-absentee.aspx.

Georgia Bureau of Investigation: Daniel Funke, "No Evidence of Fraud in Georgia Election Results," *USA Today*, June 1, 2021, https://www.usatoday.com/story/news/factcheck/2021/06/01/fact-check-georgia-audit-hasnt-found-30-000-fake-ballots/5253184001/.

In those jurisdictions: Louis Jacobson, "No, President Trump, 'Ballot Dumps' in Key States Were Not a Magical Surprise," PolitiFact, November 4, 2020, https://www.politifact.com/factchecks/2020/nov/04/donald-trump/no-president-trump-ballot-dumps-key-states-were-no/.

Before Election Day: Michigan, Pennsylvania, and Wisconsin can't start pre-processing before Election Day. "When Absentee/Mail Ballot Processing and Counting Can Begin," National Conference of State Legislatures, March, 15, 2022, https://www.ncsl.org/research

/elections-and-campaigns/vopp-table-16-when-absentee-mail-ballot
-processing-and-counting-can-begin.aspx. Ten states and Washington,
D.C., permit election officials to begin processing absentee/mail ballots on Election Day, but prior to the closing of the polls: Alabama,
District of Columbia, Michigan, Mississippi, New Hampshire, Pennsylvania, South Carolina, South Dakota, West Virginia, Wisconsin, and
Wyoming.

Overcome the problem: Miles Parks, "In Swing States, Officials Struggle to Process Ballots Early Due to Strict Local Laws," NPR, October
14, 2020, https://www.npr.org/2020/10/14/922202497/in-swing-states
-laws-add-pressure-prevent-officials-from-processing-ballots-earl.

Counting of ballots: Li Cohen, "6 Conspiracy Theories About the Election
Debunked," CBS News, January 15, 2021, https://www.cbsnews.com
/news/presidential-election-2020-conspiracy-theories-debunked/.

Watching the counting: Davey Alba, "There's a Simple Reason Workers
Covered Windows at Detroit Vote-Counting Site," *New York Times*,
November 5, 2020, https://www.nytimes.com/2020/11/05/technology
/michigan-election-ballot-counting.html.

Trump to Biden: Camille Caldera, "Fact Check: Dominion Voting
Machines Didn't Delete Votes from Trump, Switch Them to Biden,"
USA Today, November 14, 2020, https://www.usatoday.com/story/news
/factcheck/2020/11/14/fact-check-dominion-voting-machines-didnt
-delete-switch-votes/6282157002/.

Infrastructure Security Agency: Joseph Marks, "DHS Planning Largest Ever Operation to Secure U.S. Against Election Hacking," *Washington Post*, October 30, 2020, https://www.washingtonpost.com
/nation/2020/10/30/dhs-is-planning-largest-ever-operation-secure-us
-election-against-hacking/.

Was accurate: "Looking Back on the 2020 Election, the Most Secure
in US History," Center for Election Innovation and Research, https:
//electioninnovation.org/research/one-year-since-january-6/.

Georgia, North Carolina, and Pennsylvania enacted auditable ballots:
Joseph Marks, "More States Now Have Paper Trails to Verify Votes
Were Correctly Counted," *Washington Post*, November 5, 2020, https://
www.washingtonpost.com/politics/2020/11/05/cybersecurity-202-more
-states-now-have-paper-trails-verify-votes-were-correctly-counted/.

South Carolina, Virginia handed out paper ballots: National Conference of State Legislatures, https://www.ncsl.org/research/elections

-and-campaigns/voting-system-paper-trail-requirements.aspx. Nine states (Delaware, Massachusetts, Missouri, Nebraska, North Dakota, Oklahoma, South Carolina, Virginia, and Wyoming) use paper ballots or machines with a paper trail statewide even though there is no statutory requirement.

Nearly 95 percent of all ballots were auditable: Center for Election Innovation and Research, https://electioninnovation.org/research /nov-2021-election-integrity-survey/. Almost 95 percent of all ballots were cast on auditable paper, up from less than 80 percent in 2016.

Ballots were paper: For a list of states using paper ballots, see https:// www.ncsl.org/research/elections-and-campaigns/voting-system-paper -trail-requirements.aspx.

Accurate results: "Election Audits Across the United States," Election Assistance Commission, https://www.eac.gov/sites/default/files/bestpractices /Election_Audits_Across_the_United_States.pdf.

On November 19: Jane Timm, "Rudy Giuliani Baselessly Alleges Centralized Voter Fraud at Free-Wheeling News Conference," NBC News, November 19, 2020, https://www.nbcnews.com/politics/donald-trump /rudy-giuliani-baselessly-alleges-centralized-voter-fraud-free-wheeling -news-n1248273.

In that state: John Schwartz, "The 2004 Campaign: TECHNOLOGY; Executive Calls Vote-Machine Letter an Error," *New York Times*, May 16, 2004, https://www.nytimes.com/2004/05/12/us/the-2004-campaign -technology-executive-calls-vote-machine-letter-an-error.html.

Session of Congress: "Democrats Challenge Ohio Electoral Votes," CNN, January 6, 2005, https://www.cnn.com/2005/ALLPOLITICS/01/06 /electoral.vote.1718/.

Transparent elections: For more on lawsuits in Georgia, North Carolina, and Pennsylvania over paper ballots being dismissed, see Voting Rights Litigation Tracker 2020, Brennan Center for Justice, https:// www.brennancenter.org/our-work/court-cases/voting-rights-litigation -tracker-2020; for Georgia, see Coalition for *Good Governance v. Raffensperger*, No. 1:20-cv-1677 (N.D. Ga.).

"Case wide open": Peter Navarro, *In Trump Time: My Journal of America's Plague Year* (All Season's Press), p. 236.

"Earned it": Peter Navarro, *In Trump Time*, p. 155.

By the plaintiffs: Draft, December 16, 2020, Trump executive order, obtained by Politico, https://www.politico.com/f/?id=0000017e -7db3-d1fc-ad7f-fff3fd720000.

Under state law: Alan Feuer, "Trump Campaign Knew Lawyers' Voting Machine Claims Were Baseless, Memo Shows," *New York Times*, September 21, 2021, https://www.nytimes.com/2021/09/21/us/politics/trump -dominion-voting.html.

The campaign requested a recount of only two Democratic-leaning counties in Wisconsin—Dane and Milwaukee: Hailey Fuchs, "Recounts in 2 Wisconsin Counties Reinforces Biden's Victory," *New York Times*, November 29, 2020, https://www.nytimes.com/2020/11/29 /us/politics/recount-in-two-wisconsin-counties-reinforces-bidens -victory.html.

On counties not using Dominion: "Setting the Right Straight: Facts and Rumors," Dominion Voting Statement, March 18, 2022, https://www .dominionvoting.com/strs-wisconsin/. "Dominion does not operate in the districts in which the Trump legal team requested a recount, including Milwaukee and Dane counties."

Also confirmed Trump's loss there: David Wickert, Patricia Murphy, and Mark Niesse, "Georgia Recount Confirms Biden Win, but Trump Still Battling," *Atlanta Journal-Constitution*, December 7, 2020, https://www.ajc.com/politics/election /georgia-recount-confirms-biden-win-again-but-trump-still-battling /OZGAOQCMKVFG7G43L5PSF3BNHM/.

The pandemic: U.S. Election Assistance Commission statement, https:// www.eac.gov/payments-and-grants/2020-cares-act-grants.

Auditable paper ballot: Jonathan Lai, "Every Pa. County Will Have New Voting Machines—with Paper Trails—in 2020," *Philadelpha Inquirer*, January 1, 2020, https://www.inquirer.com/politics/pennsylvania/pa -new-voting-machines-for-2020-with-paper-trails-20200101.html.

Election officials: Tom Scheck, Geoff HIng, Sabby Robinson, and Gracie Stockton, "How Private Money from Facebook Saved the 2020 Election," *All Things Considered*, NPR, https://www.npr.org/2020/12/08/943242106 /how-private-money-from-facebooks-ceo-saved-the-2020-election.

Their resources: Kenneth Vogel, "Short of Money to Run Elections, Local Authorities Turn to Private Money to Run Elections," *New York Times*, December 8, 2020, https://www.npr.org/2020/12/08/943242106 /how-private-money-from-facebooks-ceo-saved-the-2020-election.

Losing them all: Joseph Marks, "The Cybersecurity 202: Courts Rule Election Money from Facebook Founder Will Stay Despite Conservative Attempts to Reverse It," *Washington Post*, October 27, 2020, https://www.washingtonpost.com/politics/2020/10/27/cybersecurity -202-courts-rule-election-money-facebook-founder-will-stay-despite -conservative-attempts-reverse-it/.

Assisted elections: Center for Election Innovation and Research 2020 Voter Education Grant Program, https://electioninnovation.org /research/ceir-2020-voter-education-grant-program/.

Ballot harvesting: National Conference of State Legislatures, "Voting Outside the Polling Place" report, Table 10: Ballot Collection Laws, January 6, 2022, https://www.ncsl.org/research/elections-and-campaigns/vopp-table -10-who-can-collect-and-return-an-absentee-ballot-other-than-the-voter .aspx.

Alleged video evidence: Ali Swenson, "FACT FOCUS: Gaping holes in the claim of 2K ballot 'mules,'" AP News, May 3, 2022, https:// apnews.com/article/2022-midterm-elections-covid-technology-health -arizona-e1b49d2311bf900f44fa5c6dac406762.

Cell phone location data: Ali Swenson, "FACT FOCUS: Gaping holes in the claim of 2K ballot 'mules,'" AP News, May 3, 2022, https://apnews .com/article/2022-midterm-elections-covid-technology-health-arizona -e1b49d2311bf900f44fa5c6dac406762.

"Ballot trafficking mules.": Jen Fifield, VoteBeatUS reporter, tweet, May 3, 2022, https://twitter.com/ https://twitter.com/JenAFifield/status /1521629135604379648?s=20&t=F9fRWCYMwMK66q-4HLSkBw.

"Were illegal ballots": Philip Bump, "The dishonest pivot at the heart of the new voter-fraud conspiracy," *Washington Post*, April 29, 2022, https://www.washingtonpost.com/politics/2022/04/29/dishonest -pivot-heart-new-voter-fraud-conspiracy/.

Jimmy Carter in 1980: Brendan Cole, "Joe Biden's Popular Vote Share Is Third Largest by Presidential Challenger in Electoral History," *Newsweek*, November 14, 2020. https://www.newsweek.com/joe-biden -donald-trump-popular-vote-1547483.

"for their relevant conduct.": Motion by Robert Palmer's attorneys, Dec. 13, 2021, https://ecf.dcd.uscourts.gov/docl/04518943543.

"most sincere apologies.": Robert Palmer letter sent to U.S. District Court Judge Tanya Chutkan, filed Dec. 13, 2021, https://ecf.dcd.uscourts.gov /docl/04518943545.

"invited us there.": Boyd Camper told the court, Aug, 5, 2021.

"official in the country.": James Bonet attorney in court, March 9, 2022.

"everyone enraged.": Zachary Wilson statement to the court, Jan. 27, 2022, https://twitter.com/MacFarlaneNews/status/1486742840763953169.

"a big mistake.": Leonard Gruppo letter to US District Court Judge Beryl Howell, filed Oct. 19, 2021, https://ecf.dcd.uscourts.gov/docl /04518836186.

"that day back.": Leonard Gruppo letter to US District Court Judge Beryl Howell, filed Oct. 19, 2021, https://ecf.dcd.uscourts.gov/docl /04518836186.

"to do so.": Leonard Gruppo letter to US District Court Judge Beryl Howell, filed Oct. 19, 2021, https://ecf.dcd.uscourts.gov/docl/04518836186.

"from this court.": Leonard Gruppo letter to US District Court Beryl Howell, filed Oct. 19, 2021, https://ecf.dcd.uscourts.gov/docl/04518836186.

"The election results.": Dustin Thompson defense attorney Samuel Shamansky, "Ohio man who argued he was "directed" by Trump to join the Jan. 6 Capitol riot convicted on all counts," Rob Leagare, CBS News, April 14, 2022. https://www.cbsnews.com/news/dustin -thompson-trump-january-6-guilty/?intcid=CNM-00-10abd1h.

"Care about power.": Dustin Thompson testimony, "US Capitol rioter who said he believed he was following Trump's orders found guilty on all charges," Holmes Lybrand and Hannah Rabinowitz, CNN, April 14, 2022. https://www.cnn.com/2022/04/14/politics/dustin-thompson -january-6-trump/index.html

6

Georgia, Michigan, Nevada, Pennsylvania, Wisconsin paper ballots: See https://ballotpedia.org/Voting_methods_and_equipment_by_state.

Arizona, Georgia, Michigan, Nevada, Pennsylvania, Wisconsin less than 10,000 vote margin; North Carolina more than 75,000 vote margin: See https://www.nytimes.com/interactive/2020/11/03/us/elections /results-president.html.

Menacing mob: Rich Schapiro, Anna Schecter, and Chelsea Damberg, "Officer Who Shot Ashli Babbitt During Capitol Riot Breaks Silence: 'I Saved Countless Lives,'" NBC News, August 26, 2021, https://www .nbcnews.com/news/us-news/officer-who-shot-ashli-babbitt-during -capitol-riot-breaks silence n1277736

"Will repeat itself.": U.S. District Judge David Carter ruling, page 44, March 28, 2022, https://s3.documentcloud.org/documents/21561085/eastman-ruling.pdf.

Go to SCOTUS: Jeremy Herb and Ryan Nobles, "'Need to End This Call': January 6 Committee Reveals New Text Messages to Meadows on House floor," CNN, December 14, 2021, https://www.cnn.com/2021/12/14/politics/january-6-committee-text-messages/index.html.

"2nd term now.": Donald Trump, Jr. text to Mark Meadows, "CNN Exclusive: 'We control them all': Donald Trump Jr. texted Meadows ideas for overturning 2020 election before it was called," Ryan Nobles and Annie Grayer and Zachary Cohen, CNN, April 8, 2022, https://www.cnn.com/2022/04/08/politics/donald-trump-jr-meadows-text/index.html.

"Them do it": Judge Amit Mehta ruling, February 18, 2022, p. 4, https://storage.courtlistener.com/recap/gov.uscourts.dcd.227536/gov.uscourts.dcd.227536.66.0_6.pdf.

"An honest election": Rep. Mo Brooks tweet, November 6, 2020, https://twitter.com/repmobrooks/status/1324501794328875009.

Media was ignoring: Catherine Sanz, "Eric Trump, Donald Trump Jr. Amplified Claims of Election Fraud, Analysis Shows," ABC News, November 18, 2020, https://abcnews.go.com/Politics/eric-trump-donald-trump-jr-amplified-claims-election/story?id=74261329.

December 20 dress rehearsal: See https://www.instagram.com/sandibachom/p/CYDTwGusR4s/?utm_medium=twitter.

Accused of going "woke.": "Trump accuses Mo Brook of going 'woke' as he pulls endorsement," WSFA, March 23, 2022, https://www.wsfa.com/2022/03/23/mo-brooks-responds-loss-trump-endorsement/.

Brooks body armor: Rep. Mo Brooks confirms he wore body armor during Jan. 6 speech, WAFF, July 29, 2021, https://www.waff.com/2021/07/29/rep-mo-brooks-confirms-he-wore-body-armor-during-january-6-speech/.

"and kicking ass.": Rep. Mo Brooks, Politico, Jan. 6, 2021, https://www.politico.com/video/2021/02/08/mo-brooks-today-is-the-day-american-patriots-start-taking-down-names-and-kicking-ass-122615.

"what President Trump asks. Period.": "Rep. Mo Brooks says Trump asked him 'to rescind the 2020 election,' remove Biden and call special election," Dan Mangan, CNBC, March 23, 2022, https://www.cnbc.com/2022/03/23/mo-brooks-says-trump-asked-him-to-rescind-election-remove-biden.html.

In late March 2022: "Virginia Thomas urged White House chief to pursue unrelenting efforts to overturn the 2020 election, texts show," *Washington Post*, Bob Woodward and Robert Costa, March 24, 2022, https://www.washingtonpost.com/politics/2022/03/24/virginia -thomas-mark-meadows-texts/.

"Heist of our history.": "Virginia Thomas urged White House chief to pursue unrelenting efforts to overturn the 2020 election, texts show," *Washington Post*, Bob Woodward and Robert Costa, March 24, 2022, https://www.washingtonpost.com/politics/2022/03/24/virginia -thomas-mark-meadows-texts/.

"tribunals for sedition.": "Virginia Thomas urged White House chief to pursue unrelenting efforts to overturn the 2020 election, texts show," *Washington Post*, Bob Woodward and Robert Costa, March 24, 2022, https://www.washingtonpost.com/politics/2022/03/24/virginia -thomas-mark-meadows-texts/.

"knowingly or not.": "Ginni Thomas' texts make Clarence Thomas' non-recusal look worse," *Washington Post*, Aaron Blake, March 25, 2022, https://www.washingtonpost.com/politics/2022/03/25/thomas -texts-recusal-worse/.

Trump wanted Pence to "overturn" the election: "Trump says he wanted Pence to overturn the 2020 election and falsely claims it was vice president's 'right'", CNN, Sarah Fortinsky, Jan. 30, 2022, https://www.cnn .com/2022/01/30/politics/trump-pence-2020-election/index.html.

"That accompanied them": Judge Amit Mehta ruling, p. 8.

Therefore protected: Harper Neidig, "Judge Questions Trump's Claim of 'Absolute Immunity' in January 6 Lawsuits," *The Hill*, January 10, 2022, https://thehill.com/regulation/court-battles/589058-judge-questions -trumps-claim-of-absolute-immunity-in-jan-6-lawsuits.

"required acts": Judge Amit Mehta ruling, p. 70.

"without precedent": Judge Amit Mehta ruling, p. 40.

Praising the Capitol riot at a rally in Arizona: Live updates, *Arizona Republic*, January 14, 2022, https://www.azcentral.com/story /news/politics/arizona/2022/01/14/trump-rally-arizona-live-updates -florence/6529316001/.

Rally in Texas: Jill Colvin, "Trump Dangles Prospects of Pardons for January 6 Defendants at Texas Rally," AP/KXAN, January 30, 2022, https://www. kxan.com/news/texas/trump-dangles-prospect-of-pardons-for-jan-6 -defendants-during-texas-rally/.

"Than the candidate": Tweet, January 15, 2022, https://twitter.com /ronfilipkowski/status/1482355548565745670?lang=en (page 123).

"Than in 2024": Meredith McGraw, "Pence Rebukes Trump: 'I Had No Right to Overturn the Election,'" Politico, February 4, 2022, https:// www.politico.com/news/2022/02/04/pence-2020-election-january -6-00005846 .

"Forward that day": Jake Thomas, "Mike Pence Trolled by Stanford Students Shouting, 'We Are the Woke Left!,'" Newsweek, February 18, 2022, https://www.newsweek.com/mike-pence-trolled-stanford-students -shouting-we-are-woke-left-1680471.

"stone-cold coward": Aila Slisco, "Steve Bannon Calls Mike Pence 'Stone-Cold Coward' for Rebuking Trump," Newsweek, February 4, 2022, https://www.newsweek.com/steve-bannon-calls-mike-pence-stone-cold -coward-rebuking-trump-1676517.

"Political discourse": Jonathan Weisman and Reid Epstein, "GOP Declares January 6 'Legitimate Political Discourse,'" February 4, 2022, https:// www.nytimes.com/2022/02/04/us/politics/republicans-jan-6-cheney -censure.html.

"Administration to another": Sahil Kapur, "McConnell Calls January 6 a 'Violent Insurrection,' Breaking with RNC," NBC News, February 8, 2022, https://www.nbcnews.com/politics/congress/mcconnell -calls-jan-6-violent-insurrection-breaking-rnc-rcna15404. Note on the first part of the quote, "we were all here," NBC, NPR, and USA Today quote him as saying: "We all were here."

"reflects the view of most Republican voters": Steve Peoples, "Republican Rift Exposes Choice: With Trump or Against Him," AP/ABC News, February 10, 2022, https://abcnews.go.com/Politics/wireStory /republican-rift-exposes-choice-trump-82790752.

"Have to choose": David Cohen, "Every Republican Has to Answer About January 6, Kinzinger says," Politico, February 13, 2022, https:// www.politico.com/news/2022/02/13/kinzinger-jan6-republicans -courage-00008464.

Run in 2024: Dan Balz, "Do Republicans Love Trump as They Once Did," Washington Post, January 29, 2022, https://www.washingtonpost.com /politics/2022/01/29/sundaytake-trump-polls/.

"Comes right at last": Rep. Jamie Raskin, "Read Rep. Jamie Raskin's Closing Argument in Impeachment Trial of Donald Trump," ABC News, February 13, 2021, https://abcnews.go.com/Politics

/read-democrat-jamie-raskins-closing-argument-impeachment-trial
/story?id=75878802.

Over 10,000 votes: Alexa Corse, "Arizona GOP's Election Audit Confirms Biden Win in State," *Wall Street Journal*, September 24, 2021, https://www .wsj.com/articles/arizona-gops-election-audit-confirms-biden-win-in -draft-report-11632467822?tesla=y&mod=article_inline.

pro-Biden voters: Jeremy Stahl, "Arizona's Republican-Run Election Audit Is Now Looking for Bamboo-Laced 'China Ballots,'" *Slate*, May 5, 2021, https://slate.com/news-and-politics/2021/05/arizona-republican -audit-bamboo-ballots-china.html.

Voter evaluation: Derek Gilliam, "Cyber Ninjas, Firm That Led Arizona Ballot Review, Is Closed, CEO Confirms," *Sarasota Herald-Tribune*, January 7, 2022, https://www.azcentral.com/story/news /politics/elections/2022/01/07/cyber-ninjas-firm-led-arizona-ballot -review-closed/8634921002/.

"A lot of proof": Patrick Reilly, "Trump Repeats Claims That 2020 Election Was Stolen at First Rally of New Year," *New York Post*, January 16, 2022, https://nypost.com/2022/01/16/ex-president-donald-trump -claims-2020-election-was-stolen-at-first-rally-in-arizona/.

Investigating January 6: Justice Department release, November 12, 2021, https://www.justice.gov/opa/pr/stephen-k-bannon-indicted -contempt-congress.

Criminal contempt: Mariana Alfano and Jacqueline Alemany, "House Votes to Hold Meadows in Contempt for Refusing to Comply with January 6 Committee Subpoena," *Washington Post*, December 15, 2021, https://www.washingtonpost.com/politics/jan-6-house-committee -meadows-trump/2021/12/14/ae2d10a8-5ce9-11ec-ae5b-5002292337c7 _story.html.

Reference to Conservative Partnership Institute: Jonathan Allen, "Trump Gave $1M to Meadows Nonprofit Weeks After January 6 Panel's Creation," CNBC, February 1, 2022, https://www.cnbc .com/2022/02/01/trump-gave-1m-to-meadows-nonprofit-weeks-after -jan-6-panels-creation.html.

"Tip of the spear": "House Votes to Hold Mark Meadows in Contempt of Congress," CNN, December 15, 2021.

"electors pursuant to state law.": Sen. Mike Lee text to Meadows, Jan. 3, 2021. 'READ: Mark Meadows' texts with Chip Roy and Mike Lee,"

CNN, April 15, 2022. https://www.cnn.com/2022/04/15/politics /read-mark-meadows-texts-mike-lee-chip-roy/index.html

state legislative determination.": Sen. Mike Lee text to Meadows, Jan. 3, 2021. 'READ: Mark Meadows' texts with Chip Roy and Mike Lee," CNN, April 15, 2022. https://www.cnn.com/2022/04/15/politics/read-mark -meadows-texts-mike-lee-chip-roy/index.html

Mostly intoxicated reference: Carol Leonning and Philip Rucker, "'I Alone Can Fix It' Book Excerpt: Inside Trump's Election Day and the Birth of the 'Big Lie,'" *Washington Post*, July 15, 2021, https://www .washingtonpost.com/politics/2021/07/13/book-excerpt-i-alone-can-fix -it/. "Some people thought Giuliani may have been drinking too much."

"No reasonable person": Katelyn Polantz, "Sidney Powell Argues in New Court Filing That No Reasonable Person Would Believe Her Election Fraud Claims," CNN, March 22, 2021, https://www.cnn .com/2021/03/22/politics/sidney-powell-dominion-lawsuit-election -fraud/index.html.

"Itself zany": Peter Navarro, *In Trump Time*, p. 237.

Powell and Giuliani: Joseph Clark, "Cyber Expert Says Team Can't Prove Mike Lindell's China Election Hack Claims," *Washington Times*, August 11, 2021, https://www.washingtontimes.com/news/2021/aug/11 /mike-lindells-lead-cyber-expert-says-they-cant-pro/.

A dark curtain: Cheryl Teh, "MyPillow CEO Mike Lindell Fled the Stage at His Cyber Symposium at the Same Time News Broke That Dominion's Billion-Dollar Defamation Lawsuit Against Him Would Proceed," *Business Insider*, August 12, 2021, https://www.businessinsider.com /mike-lindell-ran-off-stage-cyber-symposium-dominions-lawsuit -proceed-2021-8.

"It's everywhere": Josh Marcus, "MyPillow CEO Says He Has Evidence to put 300 Million in Jail for Election Fraud," Yahoo, January 12, 2022, https://sports.yahoo.com/mypillow-ceo-mike-lindell-says-213226118 .html.

Evidence of fraud: Nicholas Wu and Kyle Cheney, "Bernard Kerik Provides Batch of Documents to January 6 Select Committee," Politico, December 31, 2021, https://www.politico.com/news/2021/12/31 /kerik-documents-jan-6-committee-526297.

Elect Biden: Alan Feuer, "A Retired Colonel's Unlikely Role in Pushing Baseless Election Claims," *New York Times*, December 21, 2021, https:// www.nytimes.com/2021/12/21/us/politics/phil-waldron-jan-6.html.

"Those six states": Patrick Byrne, *The Deep Rig*, chapter 6.

Was rigged: Alan Feuer, "A Retired Colonel's Unlikely Role in Pushing Baseless Election Claims."

Electoral votes: Catie Edmondson and Maggie Haberman, "Federal Judge Dismisses Election Lawsuit Against Pence," *New York Times*, January 1, 2021, https://www.nytimes.com/2021/01/01/us/politics/mike-pence -louie-gohmert-lawsuit.html.

Biden the presidency: Josh Dawsey, Jacqueline Alemany, Jon Swaine, and Emma Brown, "During January 6 Riot, Trump Attorney Told Pence Team the Vice President's Inaction Caused Attack on Capitol," *Washington Post*, October 29, 2021, https://www.washingtonpost.com /investigations/eastman-pence-email-riot-trump/2021/10/29/59373016 -38c1-11ec-91dc-551d44733e2d_story.html.

Facilitated them: Evan Perez and Tiffany Sneed, "Federal Prosecutors Looking at 2020 Fake Elector Certifications, Deputy Attorney General Tells CNN," CNN, January 25, 2022, https://www.cnn.com/2022/01/25 /politics/fake-trump-electoral-certificates-justice-department/index .html; Miles Parks, "Prosecutors in Multiple States Are Investigating False Electoral College Submissions," NPR, January 25, 2022, https://www .npr.org/2022/01/25/1075304670/prosecutors-in-multiple-states-are -investigating-false-electoral-college-submiss.

"To the American people": Peter Navarro, *In Trump Time*, p. 263.

Eastman memos: Two-page version obtained by CNN, https://cdn.cnn .com/cnn/2021/images/09/20/eastman.memo.pdf; six-page ver- sion obtained by CNN: http://cdn.cnn.com/cnn/2021/images/09/21 /privileged.and.confidential.--.jan.3.memo.on.jan.6.scenario.pdf; one-page version obtained by CNN, https://www.documentcloud.org /documents/21066248-eastman-memo.

"Election officials": Eastman memo, p. 1.

"Likely unconstitutional": Eastman memo, p. 3.

"Queensbury rules": Eastman memo, p. 5.

"Of the Senate": Eastman memo, p. 1.

Authentic certificates: For images of fake elector slate images, see American Oversight, March 7, 2021, https://www.americanoversight.org/american -oversight-obtains-seven-phony-certificates-of-pro-trump-electors.

"Is 454": Eastman memo, p. 2.

"There as well": Eastman memo, p. 2.

"That in mind": Eastman memo, p. 2.

"No more, no less": "January was a tragedy. So would be busting the filibuster." Former vice president Mike Pence op-ed, *Washington Post*, January 14, 2022, https://www.washingtonpost.com/opinions/2022/01/14 /mike-pence-filibuster-nationalize-elections/.

Electoral votes: Josh Dawsey, Jacqueline Alemany, Jon Swaine, and Emma Brown. "During January 6 Riot, Trump Attorney Told Pence Team the Vice President's Inaction Caused Attack on Capitol."

On January 6: Ellis Kim and Rebecca Kaplan. "Pence's Former Chief Counsels Speaks to January 6 Committee," CBS News, https:// www.cbsnews.com/news/mike-pence-greg-jacob-chief-counsel -january-6-committee-interview/.

"Bullshit legal strategy": Lexi Lonas, "Trump Lawyer Blamed Pence for Causing Capitol Attack," *The Hill*, October 10, 2021, https://thehill.com /blogs/blog-briefing-room/news/579265-trump-lawyer-blamed-pence -for-causing-jan-6-attack-as-it.

"Themselves what happened": Josh Dawsey, Jacqueline Alemany, Jon Swaine, and Emma Brown. "During January 6 Riot, Trump Attorney Told Pence Team the Vice President's Inaction Caused Attack on Capitol."

"Not legally viable": John McCormack, "John Eastman Says Election Memo Doesn't Reflect His Views," *National Review*, October 22, 2021, https://www.nationalreview.com/2021/10/john-eastman-vs -the-eastman-memo/.

"Answer to this question": Jacqueline Alemany, Emma Brown, Tom Hamburger, and Jon Swaine, "Ahead of January 6, Willard Hotel in Downtown D.C. Was a Trump Team 'Command Center' for Effort to Deny Biden the Presidency," *Washington Post*, October 23, 2021, https:// www.washingtonpost.com/investigations/willard-trump-eastman -giuliani-bannon/2021/10/23/c45bd2d4-3281-11ec-9241-aad8e48f01ff _story.html.

Memos suggested: For a list of House delegations, see ProPublica, https:// projects.propublica.org/represent/states.

January 6 proceedings (more than 100 House Republicans and 11 U.S. senators sought delay): John Eastman, interview with Daily Beast, "We spent a lot of time lining up over 100 congressmen, including some senators." Jose Pagliery, "Trump Adviser Peter Navarro Lays Out How He and Steve Bannon Planned to Overturn Biden's Electoral Win," Daily Beast,

December 27, 2021, https://www.thedailybeast.com/trump-advisor
-peter-navarro-lays-out-how-he-and-steve-bannon-planned-to-overturn
-bidens-electoral-win.

The election results: Katherine Faulders and Alexander Mallin, "DOJ Officials Rejected Colleague's Request to Intervene in Georgia's Certification: Emails," ABC News, August 3, 2021, https://abcnews.go.com/US
/doj-officials-rejected-colleagues-request-intervene-georgias-election
/story?id=79243198.

"Grow on this": John Eastman Memo Released in Report by Senate Judiciary Committee, "Subverting Justice," p. 25, https://www.judiciary
.senate.gov/imo/media/doc/Interim%20Staff%20Report%20FINAL
.pdf.

"State of Georgia": draft John Eastman letter to Georgia officials released
in report by Senate Judiciary Committee, "Subverting Justice," p. 25.

"On January 6": John Eastman memo released in report by Senate Judiciary Committee, "Subverting Justice," p. 189.

"Individual state": Bill Barr DOJ memo to U.S. attorneys, November 9,
2020, p. 1, https://s3.documentcloud.org/documents/20403380/barr
electionmemo110920.pdf.

"Vice President Pence": John Eastman memo released in report by Senate
Judiciary Committee, "Subverting Justice," p. 188.

"Conducts its elections": Supreme Court order, December 11, 2020,
https://www.supremecourt.gov/orders/courtorders/121120zr_p860.pdf.

"On the nonsense": Sen. Ben Sasse statement, December 11, 2020, https://
www.sasse.senate.gov/public/index.cfm/2020/12/sasse-statement
-on-supreme-court-s-election-decision.

"Of the United States": Brief to U.S. Supreme Court by Pennsylvania,
December 10, 2020, p. 26, https://www.supremecourt.gov/DocketPDF/2
2/22O155/163367/20201210142206254_Pennsylvania%20Opp%20to
%20Bill%20of%20Complaint%20v.FINAL.pdf.

"Remotely like this": Aaron Blake, "A Key Witness Emerges in Probe of
Trump's DOJ Election Scheme," *Washington Post*, August 4, 2021, https://
www.washingtonpost.com/politics/2021/08/04/key-witness-emerges
-probe-trump-doj-election-scheme/?utm_source=facebook&utm
_medium=news_tab&utm_content=algorithm.

"Over a century": Michael email released in report by Senate Judiciary
Committee, "Subverting Justice," p. 27.

"Multiple calls/texts": Olson email released in report by Senate Judiciary Committee, "Subverting Justice," p. 27.

"Of the U.S. Constitution": Draft of Trump lawsuit released in report by Senate Judiciary Committee, "Subverting Justice," p. 27.

"Court-appointed special master": Draft of Trump lawsuit released in report by Senate Judiciary Committee, "Subverting Justice," p. 256.

Refiling the Texas suit: Senate Judiciary Committee, "Subverting Justice," p. 30. Timeline from Senate Judiciary Committee report "Subverting Justice."

"See you in D.C." (January 1 tweet): Timeline from Senate Judiciary Committee report "Subverting Justice," pp. 57–58.

Staff and lawyers (January 3): Timeline from Senate Judiciary Committee report "Subverting Justice," p. 58.

More about call: Amy Gardner, "'I Just Want to Find 11,780 Votes': In Extraordinary Hour-Long Call, Trump Pressures Georgia Secretary of State to Recalculate the Vote in His Favor," *Washington Post*, January 3, 2021, https://www.washingtonpost.com/politics/trump-raffensperger -call-georgia-vote/2021/01/03/d45acb92-4dc4-11eb-bda4-615aaefd0555 _story.html.

"Any means necessary": Senate Judiciary Committee, "Subverting Justice," p. 8.

"There was not": Draft of Trump lawsuit released in report by Senate Judiciary Committee, "Subverting Justice," p. 256.

"at the National Archives.": Draft of Trump lawsuit released in report by Senate Judiciary Committee, page 203, Interim Staff Report FINAL. pdf (senate.gov).

"Of presidential power": Stewart Rhodes indictment, p. 2, Department of Justice, January 12, 2022, https://www.justice .gov/opa/press-release/file/1462481/download?utm_medium=email &utm_source=govdelivery.

"'Lexington.' It's coming.": Stewart Rhodes indictment, page 22, Department of Justice, January 12, 2022, https://www.justice.gov/opa/press-release /file/1462481/download?utm_medium=email&utm_source=govdelivery.

"Associated with militias": Stewart Rhodes indictment, p. 3.

Rhodes has pleaded not guilty to the charges: Robert Legare, "Oath Keeper Leader Stewart Rhodes Pleads Not Guilty to January 6 Charges,"

CBS News, January 25, 2022, https://www.cbsnews.com/news /oath-keepers-stewart-rhodes-not-guilty-plea-january-6/.

"Transfer of presidential power": Stewart Rhodes indictment, p. 3.

Timeline with various remarks: Stewart Rhodes indictment, p. 8.

Firearms attachments: Stewart Rhodes indictment, p. 19.

"Worst case scenarios": Stewart Rhodes indictment, p. 19.

"Had enough": Stewart Rhodes indictment, p. 19.

7

"Developed world.": Chip Bergh, "The Biggest Threat to Our Democracy Isn't Hackers or Fake News. It's Apathy," Yahoo/Fortune, 2018, September 23, 2018, https://www.yahoo.com/news/biggest-threat-democracy -isn-apos-003512700.html.

"Democracy suffer": David Becker, "A New Approach to Reversing the Downward Spiral of Low Voter Turnout," *Stanford Social Innovation Review*, February 11, 2016, https://ssir.org/articles/entry/a_new _approach_to_reversing_the_downward_spiral_of_low_turnout.

Statewide offices: Harry Enten, "2021 Shows Republicans Shouldn't Fear High Voter Turnout," CNN, November 10, 2021, https://www.cnn .com/2021/11/07/politics/turnout-republicans-analysis/index.html.

Roughly a century: Ballotpedia chart, https://ballotpedia.org /Voter_turnout_in_United_States_elections.

In the White House: Shawn Johnson, "Assembly Speaker Rejects Decertification Call In," Wisconsin Public Radio, March 16, 2022, https://www.wpr .org/assembly-speaker-rejects-election-decertification-call-wisconsin.

Ill-informed and illogical: Shawn Johnson, "Gabelman Report Calls for Decertifying 2020 Election. The Legislature's Nonpartisan Lawyers Say That's Not Possible," Wisconsin Public Radio, March 1, 2022, https://www .wpr.org/gableman-report-calls-decertifying-2020-election-legislatures -nonpartisan-lawyers-say-thats-not.

And South Dakota: Scott Bauer, "Wisconsin Election Probe Leader Traveled to Arizona," AP, August 12, 2021, https://apnews.com/article /joe-biden-elections-wisconsin-arizona-d7e52b6c5f806e606a.

And "suspicion only": Jennifer Agiesta, "A Growing Number of Americans Don't Think Today's Elections Reflect the Will of the People," CNN, February 11, 2022, https://www.cnn.com/2022/02/10/politics /cnn-poll-democracy/index.html.

Access to voting: "Voting Laws Roundup: December 2021," Brennan Center for Justice, December 12, 2021, https://www.brennancenter.org/our-work/research-reports/voting-laws-roundup-december-2021.

Local election officials: Alison Chang and Emma Bowman, "Georgia Secretary of State Says New Voting Law 'Restores Confidence,'" April 9, 2021, https://www.npr.org/2021/04/09/985474722/georgia-secretary-of-state-says-new-voting-law-restores-confidence.

Not yet law: Benjamin Swasey, "After Georgia Here Are 4 States to Watch Next on Voting Legislation," NPR, April 13, 2021, https://www.npr.org/2021/04/13/977234354/after-georgia-here-are-4-states-to-watch-next-on-voting-legislation.

Eligible voters: Amy Gardner, "Texas Counties Reject Unprecedented Numbers of Mail Ballots Ahead of March 1 Primary Under Restrictive New Law," *Washington Post*, February 11, 2022, https://www.washingtonpost.com/politics/2022/02/11/texas-voting-law-ballots-rejected-poll-watchers/.

Confirm the counts: Christina Cassy and Holly Ramer, "Some in GOP Want Ballots to Be Counted by Hand, Not Machines," AP, March 12, 2022, https://apnews.com/article/2022-midterm-elections-new-hampshire-nevada-donald-trump-elections-3f6785364fd52655cbd034f0708c6f0f.

Voter access: Paul Webber and Acacia Coronado, "Texas Flagged 27,000 Mail Ballots for Rejection in Primary," AP, March 9, 2022, https://apnews.com/article/2022-midterm-elections-elections-austin-texas-voting-f28a41bf6482c25299c99a8ea52734be.

Of 11.8 percent: Release from Texas secretary of state, April 6, 2022.

Of a percent: "Texas officials rejected one out of eight mail ballots cast in primary," Adam Brewster, CBS News, April 6, 2022, https://www.cbsnews.com/news/texas-election-officials-rejected-one-out-of-eight-mail-ballots-cast-in-primary/.

March 1, 2022 primary: Amy Gardner, "A Texas County Didn't Count 10,000 ballots. Now the Parties Are at War Over Who's to Blame," *Washington Post*, March 10, 2022, https://www.washingtonpost.com/politics/2022/03/11/harris-county-primary-uncounted-votes-lawsuit/.

Some of the following: "Showdown 2022: The State of State Election Law—and the Fights Ahead," Voting Rights Lab, February 16, 2022, https://votingrightslab.org/showdown-2022-the-state-of-state-election-law-and-the-fights-ahead/.

Of the Republican Party: Megan O'Matz, "Billionaire-Backed Group Enlists Trump-Supporting Citizens to Hunt for Voter Fraud Using Discredited Techniques," ProPublica, March 7, 2022, https://www.propublica.org/article/voter-ref-foundation.

Corrected and updated: Election Registration Information Center, https://ericstates.org/statistics/.

Crimes and Security: Lawrence Mower, "Florida Legislature Sends Voting Rights Bill to Gov. Ron DeSantis' Desk," *Tampa Bay Times*, March 9, 2022, https://www.tampabay.com/news/florida-politics/2022/03/09/florida-legislature-sends-voting-bill-to-gov-ron-desantis-desk/.

For Attorney General: Ballotpedia, https://ballotpedia.org/Secretary_of_State_elections,_2022; https://ballotpedia.org/Attorney_General_elections,_2022.

Time for 2014: "Money Pours into Secretary of State Races," Brennan Center for Justice, February 15, 2022, https://www.brennancenter.org/our-work/analysis-opinion/money-pours-secretary-state-races. A new monthly series of Brennan Center reports confirms that the stakes have been raised in races to oversee state elections. My colleague Ian Vandewalker found that across key battleground states, "contributions are three times higher than they were at this point in the 2018 cycle and eight times higher than 2014. The numbers are particularly high in Arizona, Georgia, and Michigan."

The Big Lie: "Replacing the Refs," States United Action, https://statesuniteddemocracy.org/resources/replacingtherefs/. See also https://www.washingtonpost.com/magazine/2022/02/28/secretary-of-state/.

Their election results: James Barragan and Kate McGee, "Texas Attorney General Ken Paxton Head to Runoff with George P. Bush," *Texas Tribune*, March 1, 2022, https://www.texastribune.org/2022/03/01/texas-attorney-general-election-ken-paxton/.

Running in 19 states.: "Replacing the Refs," States United, April 4, 2022. https://statesuniteddemocracy.org/resources/replacingtherefs/

For a Republican ever: Morgan County, GA: 2020 election results: https://results.enr.clarityelections.com/GA/Morgan/105474/web.264614/#/summary?v=270614%2F; 2016 results: Summary-11-8-2016 (morganga.org).

For perspective on the question of how much Blacks have been replaced: James Oliphant and Nathan Layne, "Georgia Republicans Purge Black Democrats from County Election Boards,"

Reuters, December 9, 2021, https://www.reuters.com/world/us/georgia
-republicans-purge-black-democrats-county-election-boards-2021
-12-09/.

"What you deserve": Linda Szo and Jason Eps, "U.S. Election Workers
Get Little Help from Law Enforcement as Terror Threats Mount," Reuters, December 8, 2021, https://www.reuters.com/investigates/special
-report/usa-election-threats-law-enforcement?utm_source=twitter
&utm_medium=Social.

Remained rare: DOJ press release, July 29, 2021, https://www.justice.
gov/opa/blog/justice-department-launches-task-force-combat-threats
-against-election-workers-0.

"And their children": Linda Szo and Jason Eps, "U.S. Election Workers Get
Little Help from Law Enforcement as Terror Threats Mount."

Received death threats: Isaac Dovere and Jeremy Herb, "'It's Absolutely
Getting Worse': Secretaries of State Targeted by Trump Election Lies Live
in Fear of Their Safety and Are Desperate for Protection," CNN, October 26, 2021, https://www.cnn.com/2021/10/26/politics/secretaries
-of-state-personal-threats-trump-election-lies/index.html.

Doing their jobs: Matt Smith, "Election Officials Still Face Violent Threats
in Wake of 2020 Election, Ask FBI to Do More," WISN, November
11, 2021, https://www.wisn.com/article/election-officials-face-violent
-threats-in-wake-of-2020-election/38223928#.

Read one threat: "Election Officials Under Attack," Brennan Center for Justice
/Bipartisan Policy Center, June 16, 2021, https://www.brennancenter
.org/sites/default/files/2021-06/BCJ-129%20ElectionOfficials
_v7.pdf https://www.wisn.com/article/election-officials-face-violent
-threats-in-wake-of-2020-election/38223928#.

Inside her home: Linda Szo and Jason Eps, "U.S. Election Workers Get
Little Help from Law Enforcement as Terror Threats Mount."

Harassment and threats: Brennan Center for Justice/Bipartisan Policy
Center, June 16, 2021, https://www.brennancenter.org/sites/default
/files/2021-06/BCJ-129%20ElectionOfficials_v7.pdf; https://www.wisn
.com/article/election-officials-face-violent-threats-in-wake-of-2020
-election/38223928#.

January into February: Local Election Officials Survey, Brennan Center,
March 10, 2022.

"Is its blindness": Martin Luther King, https://www.goodreads.com/quotes /8689421-i-should-have-been-reminded-that-disappointment-produces -despair-and.

"Nullifies a legal vote": Rep. Jody Hice, remarks at Conservative Political Action Conference, February 27, 2022.

2020 election: Zach Monterallo, "Youngkin Continues to Call for Audit of Election Machines in Virginia," Politico, October 5, 2021, https://www.politico.com/news/2021/10/05/youngkin-virginia -governor-election-audit-machines-515166.

8

Arizona, Colorado, Georgia, Michigan, Nevada, and elsewhere: Jennifer Medina, Nick Corsianti, and Reid Epstein, "Campaigning to Oversee Elections While Denying the Last One," *New York Times*, January 30, 2022, https://www.nytimes.com/2022/01/30/us/politics/election -deniers-secretary-of-state.html.

Active indictment of Tina Peters: Maggie Astor, "Colorado County Clerk Indicted in Voting Security Breach Investigation," *New York Times*, March 9, 2022, https://www.nytimes.com/2022/03/09/us/politics /tina-peters-colorado-election.html.

"Freedom is participation in power": https://www.goodreads.com /quotes/106593-freedom-is-participation-in-power.

"Or alter such regulations . . .": U.S. Constitution, https://constitution .congress.gov/browse/article-1/section-4/#:~:text=The%20Times %2C%20Places%2and%20Manner,the%20Places%20of %20chusing%20Senators.

Their right to relief: Legal Information Institute, Cornell University Law School, https://www.law.cornell.edu/wex/laches.

Each eligible voter: U.S. Election Assistance Administration, https://www .eac.gov/payments-and-grants/2020-cares-act-grants.

Per eligible voter: Kate Lobosco and Tami Luhby, "What's in the Government Spending Law," CNN, March 15, 2022, https://www.cnn .com/2022/03/09/politics/government-omnibus-spending-bill-2022 /index.html.

legal assistance: Election Official Legal Defense Network, https://eoldn .org/.

On January 6: "At least 800 People Have Been Charged in the Capitol Insurrection So Far," Yahoo, March 17, 2022, https://news.yahoo.com/most-arrests-capitol-riots-misdemeanor-225235647.html.

Have been obtained: Zoe Tillman, "Over 200 People Have Pleaded Guilty in the January 6 Insurrection," BuzzFeed News, January 26, 2022, https://www.buzzfeednews.com/article/zoetillman/200-people-guilty-plea-jan-6-insurrection.

"Toward justice": Dr. Martin Luther King, March 31, 1968, https://www.si.edu/spotlight/mlk?page=4&iframe=true.

"America will tremble": Theodore Parker, *Ten Sermons of Religion* (1852), p. 6, http://www.fusw.org/uploads/1/3/0/4/13041662/of-justice-and-the-conscience.pdf (page 198).

"Chaos or Community?": Dr. Martin Luther King, *Where Do We Go From Here: Chaos or Community?* (Beacon Press, 1968).

"Cannot be released from it": James Baldwin, *Progressive Magazine*, https://progressive.org/magazine/letter-nephew/.

INDEX

ABOUT THE AUTHORS

MAJOR GARRETT is the chief Washington correspondent for CBS News and the host and creator of *The Takeout* and *The Debrief* podcasts. For more than thirty years, his award-winning reporting and writing has tackled the nation's biggest political issues and campaigns. Garrett is the author of four books: *Mr. Trump's Wild Ride*, *The Enduring Revolution*, *The 15 Biggest Lies in Politics*, and *Common Cents* with former Rep. Tim Penny (D-Minnesota).

DAVID BECKER is the executive director and founder of the nonpartisan nonprofit Center for Election Innovation & Research, which works with election officials of both parties to ensure accessible, secure elections. He is one of the foremost election experts in the nation, having worked in elections for a quarter century and litigated major cases as a trial attorney in the Voting Section of the United States Department of Justice under both presidents Bill Clinton and George W. Bush.